General Amin

General Amin

DAVID MARTIN

Faber and Faber
London

First published in 1974
by Faber and Faber Limited
3 Queen Square, London WC1
Reprinted 1974 and 1975
Printed in Great Britain by
Butler & Tanner Limited, Frome and London

ISBN: 0 571 10585 8

CONTENTS

LIST OF ILLUSTRATIONS

The author and publisher gratefully acknowledge
the following illustration sources

The Sunday Telegraph (1)

The Camera Press (2, 3, 4, 13 and 15)

Camerapix, Nairobi (5, 11 and Jacket)

The Associated Press (10 and 12)

Maps

---•◆◆◆•---

Preface

A near hysterical phone call on New Year's Day 1972 opened my eyes fully for the first time to the reality of Idi Amin's Uganda. The caller said several hundred soldiers and civilians had been transferred to a prison on Uganda's border with Tanzania under the pretext that they were to be court-martialled. But he insisted they were to be murdered and it would be claimed Tanzanian troops had attacked the prison and were responsible for their deaths.

I was highly sceptical. I had heard stories of massacres and murders throughout 1971. But they were mainly from exiled supporters—as was my caller—of the deposed President, Dr. Milton Obote. He insisted the story was true, and, in guarded terms quoting him, I put out a story which appeared in a London newspaper the next morning. For the sake of my conscience I am glad I did. A month later at a ramshackle refugee camp in north-west Tanzania I was to interview nineteen of the twenty-three survivors of what became known as the Mutukula Massacre. In all, 555 people were murdered in that grim prison.

Just how many people have been slaughtered in Uganda since Amin seized power in a *coup d'état* on 25 January 1971 will probably never be known. One of Amin's own Ministers, who fled early in 1973, in a memorandum secretly distributed to a number of African leaders put the death toll in the first twenty-four months at 80,000–90,000—and he stressed that this figure might be conservative.

Yet to many people Amin remains a funny figure. Largely that is because he fits their prejudices about the black man. He is illiterate, unpredictable, an incompetent ruler and a killer.

Even so he has been underestimated. While people laugh at his latest idiosyncrasy or mourn the latest tragedy they rarely stop to examine the ruthless man who was so erroneously referred to initially as a 'gentle giant'. He never was the model soldier his former British officers in the 'good old days' of the King's African Rifles would have us now believe. The slaughter in Uganda began the moment he seized power and has continued ever since. What was once a proud nation has been brought to its knees. The economy is in ruins. In the wake of his expulsion of 40,000 Asians, prices have spiralled and chronic shortages set in. The army has tripled to over 20,000 men who rampage at will through the country. And above all Amin has degraded Uganda, Africa and humanity.

Given the veil of fear which cloaks Uganda today this has been a difficult book to write. It is not intended to be a historical or academic work. Rather it is a piece of reportage—an interim report. When Amin has gone it will be possible to ascertain in much greater detail all of the forces that motivated him and the damage he did.

Many people have helped me in gathering material for this book. I dare not publicly thank all of them. Some are still living in Uganda and would be killed if their names were mentioned. Others are in exile and their relatives would be killed. But one friend I must mention is Mary O'Shea. Without her encouragement, research and fortitude, I doubt this book would have been completed.

1 The Rise of Amin

Among the first recorded words of Major-General Idi Amin Dada after he seized power in Uganda on 25 January 1971, were: 'I am not a politician but a professional soldier. I am therefore a man of few words and I have been very brief throughout my professional career.' Since then he has not stopped talking.

In his first three years in power Amin has become one of the anti-heroes of the seventies. The spirit of his once proud country has almost been broken and the economy wrecked. He has done more to confirm the prejudices of the white racialist about the black man than any African in the past turbulent decade. In Amin, South Africa has a black ally that her enormous resources spent on propaganda could never have achieved. Breathing a mixture of brotherhood and brimstone his outrageous utterances and actions have shocked and amused a world which in its civilised inertia has turned a bland face to his savagery and Uganda's suffering.

'Hitler was right about the Jews, because the Israelis are not working in the interests of the people of the world, and that is why they burned the Israelis alive with gas in the soil of Germany,' he sounded off in a cable in September 1972 to United Nations' Secretary-General, Kurt Waldheim.

West German Chancellor, Willy Brandt, angrily denounced that statement as 'an expression of mental derangement'. But it takes more than that to deter Amin. When fighting flared up again in the Middle East in October 1973, Amin's postscript to this remark was: 'People all over the world now agree with me that the Israelis are criminals.' Hitler had been 'right to burn six million Jews during the Second World War'.

'I want to assure you that I love you very much, and if you had been a woman, I would have considered marrying you, although your head is full of grey hairs, but as you are a man that possibility does not arise,' he told neighbouring President Julius Nyerere in a telegram in August 1972 just before the Tanzanian backed over 1,000 supporters of deposed President, Dr. Milton Obote, in an invasion aimed at ousting the General.

Another infamous remark came in August 1973 in a speech when the colour-conscious General said: 'Some Asians in Uganda have been painting themselves black with shoe-polish. Asians are our brothers and sisters. If anyone is found painting himself with black polish, disciplinary action will be taken against him.'

And to students at Kampala's Conference centre: 'I am told that venereal disease is very high with you. You had better go to hospital and make yourselves very clean, or you will infect the whole population.'

An unending stream of idiocies have punctuated his first three years in power. A 'get-well-soon from Watergate' telegram outraged President Richard Nixon. While he was ejecting 40,000 Asians and seizing British assets he frequently solemnly declared that Britain 'is my best friend'. The incongruity of wearing Israeli paratrooper wings on his uniform in a picture on the new Ugandan currency after breaking relations with Jerusalem was lost on the General. And when his Finance Minister pleaded with him in 1972 to check military spending because the country was teetering on the brink of bankruptcy, Cabinet colleagues at the meeting say he angrily ordered: 'Print more money.'

In the wake of his break with Israel he became the most vocal proponent of the Arab cause. Frequently he offered to lead Arab armies to liquidate Israel, woke Jordan's King Hussein, his Cabinet and military commanders in the middle of the night in 1972 to voice his master plan to conquer Israel, and during the 1973 war, flew around Arab capitals offering advice and bullying a wounded Israeli soldier in a hospital bed in Damascus. Long forgotten was his comment on 5 February 1971: 'The Minister of War of the United Arab Republic is my best friend and the Minister of Defence of Israel is also my best friend.' By 10 June 1972 he had changed his tune to: 'African and Arab leaders must sit down together and consider what to do to destroy the Zionists in the Middle East.'

At an Organisation of African Unity meeting he startled his African colleagues by demonstrating how to suffocate people with a handkerchief, and at the OAU summit in Addis Ababa he reduced the African presidents to speechless laughter when he explained he had in fact been Ugandan President since 1966 and that the fracas in January 1971 was simply his predecessor, Obote, trying to stage a counter-*coup*.

It is possible to go on *ad infinitum* with examples illustrating Amin the 'funny' man. I recall late in 1973 asking a London taxi driver why he was so amused by Amin. 'Well, he's a typical nig nog, isn't he?' was the frank reply. But didn't he care about all the murders in Uganda? 'Well all these blacks are the same, aren't they?' the cabbie answered. To him Amin was a fun figure and a very typical black man.

Millions of words have been devoted to reporting Amin's unending speeches and bluster. Journalists hungrily focus on him at international gatherings ignoring the more substantial speakers, for 'Big Daddy', as the press dubbed him early on, is good copy. His name crops up as an answer in the *Daily Telegraph* crossword —the simplified version. A calypso was written about him after he seized power, and a London radio personality amused his listeners in an interview with Amin by first asking him if it was true he ate people and concluding by persuading the General to sing and accompany himself on an accordion.

'A latter-day Hitler or a simple soldier out of depth in international politics?' asked the *Sunday Times* Magazine in an article devoted to Amin. Glaring balefully from the cover was the General: a hulking 240 lb behemoth with eyes puckered in apparent concentration. 'To most of the British officers under whom Idi Amin served in the King's African Rifles he was "a splendid chap, though a bit short on the grey matter". But more than one of them noted a native shrewdness which, despite his inability to speak more than basic English, marked him out from an early date.'

The 'splendid chap' tag given to him by the British colonial officers masked the reality of his rule for eighteen months. Even today few people have any conception of what has occurred in

Uganda during his first three years in power. Little effort has been made to delve into his background, and the sparse accounts that have appeared have generally been wrong. In addition it is neither true, nor adequate, to write him off as mad as many have done, nor to suggest glibly that he is suffering from mental disease of physical origin, thereby ducking one of the more rigorous rules of libel.

Amin was born in Koboko county, the smallest in Uganda's West Nile District, which is the rough boundary of the 50,000-strong Kakwa tribe. His father was a Kakwa, who had spent much of his life in the southern Sudan and his mother was from the neighbouring and ethnically related Lugbara tribe. His parents separated at his birth with his father continuing to scratch a subsistence living on his small holding near Arua.

Both of his parents' West Nile tribes are frequently described as Sudanic-Nubian, and like his parents Amin became a Muslim. The Nubians originally came from the northern parts of the Sudan from the Nubian Desert bounded by the Nile to the west and Red Sea to the east. They were brought south into Uganda as mercenaries in the armies of Captain Lugard, Emin Pasha and Sir Samuel Baker, bringing with them the Muslim religion. Today Muslims in northern Uganda such as the Alur, Kakwa, Lugbara and Mahdi are referred to as Nubians although in anthropological terms this is not strictly correct.

However, Nubians is the all-embracing description used in Uganda, and long before the 1971 *coup*, among their fellow countrymen, they enjoyed an unenviable reputation of having one of the world's highest homicide rates. The Nubians were renowned for their sadistic brutality, lack of formal education, for poisoning enemies and for their refusal to integrate, even in the urban centres. In the Kenya capital, Nairobi, for instance, there is a substantial Nubian colony which Amin has used as a spy network against exiles living there since he came to power.

Amin's mother, with her newly born son, after separating from her husband moved to one of the Nubian colonies in Uganda at Lugazi twenty-six miles from the Lake Victoria town of Jinja. An office had been set up at Arua to recruit labourers from West

Nile to work in the sugar plantations near Lugazi which was owned by the Mehtas one of the two Ugandan-Asian millionaire families, and although contracts were generally only for six months, a substantial number of labourers stayed on to form the Nubian colony. Almost forty years later Amin was to expel both of the millionaires with some 40,000 other Asians.

Amin joined the King's African Rifles in 1946 as an assistant cook, although since coming to power he has claimed he fought in Burma in the Second World War and has awarded himself a series of medals. His service record shows that he was in trouble early on. But he was the type of material the British officers liked in the ranks—physically large at six feet four inches and un-educated. The theory was that material of this type responded better to orders and were braver in battle. He endeared himself to his commanders by becoming the Ugandan heavyweight boxing champion—a title he held for nine years—and by taking up rugby, where even if his skills were limited, his weight as a second-row forward was a valuable contribution.

The full extent of his mother's influence on his life is unclear, but his upbringing was certainly far from traditional. His mother was what used to be described as a camp follower, and she finally moved to Buikwe, about twelve miles from Jinja. African soldiers serving at Jinja remember that she had been living with a man about her age until 1954 when she moved into the Jinja barracks to live with Corporal Yafesi Yasin, a clerk in 'D' Company of the 4th King's African Rifles.

The Corporal was in his early twenties and about half her age, and his friends laughed at him for living with such an old woman. Amin's mother had practised witchcraft since moving to the area—and possibly before—and this was her only means of liveli-hood until she moved into the camp. One of the soldiers serving there recalls a woman nicknamed 'Pepsi Cola' who they all be-lieved was mad. She was brought to Amin's mother, and in a darkened room with flashing lights and ringing small bells she sought to drive the evil spirits from the woman.

It seems the treatment failed, for 'Pepsi Cola' continued to be regarded as being as mad as ever. But the cynicism as to the magic powers of Amin's mother were soon to be shaken. Corporal Yasin tired of the woman and ordered her to leave the camp, and she went back to Buikwe. A few days later the Corporal reported one morning that he was feeling sick. The orderly sergeant sent him to the doctor, but before he could be examined, he died. Whether a post-mortem was carried out was not known, but the belief in the ranks at Jinja was that he had been poisoned or bewitched.

The practice of witchcraft, although generally proscribed, is common enough throughout Africa today. The powers of the witchdoctors are enormous, and it is not unusual to find highly educated Africans visiting them to ensure promotions to better posts. But Amin, characteristically, has taken his belief in occult powers to a ridiculous extent.

Just before he seized power, a Zambian seer, Dr. Ngombe Francis, who qualified as a doctor of medicine from Madagascar University, claims he predicted the overthrow of the Uganda President, Dr. Obote. Since the *coup* the wealthy Zambian has been Amin's personal soothsayer and prophet. A Ghanaian mystic claimed he could raise people from the dead, so he was flown to Uganda and Amin subsequently claimed he talked with a man who had been resurrected. God, the General said, had told him in a dream to launch his economic war and expel the country's Asians. When a journalist sarcastically asked him if he had such dreams often Amin blandly replied: 'Only when necessary.'

Amin saw nothing of his father through this period, and before joining the army sold *mandazi*, a common sweet biscuit made from wheat flour and sugar. His first real contact with his father came in 1958 when an uncle took him to see his father at his house one and a half miles from Arua Airport. Nine years seem to have elapsed before the next meeting in 1967 when Amin, by then Army Commander, asked his father to Kampala where he stayed for a month. After that, contact was more frequent. His mother died in 1970, not long after the murder of the Army Deputy Commander whose death led directly to Amin seizing power.

Amin's mixed background has given him a smattering of five

languages. He speaks some Kakwa and some Luganda having been raised in the part of Uganda where those vernacular are spoken. From the army he learned Swahili which is the language of command, as well as limited English, which is laboured when he is reading a prepared text, and somewhat better during his impromptu harangues. The only language which he speaks reasonably well is a type of broken Arabic referred to as Nubian which is used by the West Nile Muslim colony in Buganda.

Since coming to power, and for several months before that, Amin has made much of his Islamic beliefs. The Nubian-Islamic impact was felt most in West Nile but at the time of the *coup* less than 6 per cent of Ugandans were Muslims. Amin's devotion to Islam has been particularly manifest publicly since he broke relations with Israel early in 1972, but it is clear his beliefs are tailored to his political needs. The background of his four wives is revealing. The first, Sarah, also known as 'Mama Maliam', only converted to Islam in 1968 aften ten years of marriage. The second, Kay, is the daughter of a Protestant clergyman and still a Christian. The third, Norah, is also a Protestant, and her parents are Balokoli, which is the Uganda equivalent of Puritans. His fourth wife, Medina, whom Amin claims was 'given' to him in 1971, was the only one who was a Muslim at marriage. To marry three Christians in succession and to make so little effort to convert them to Islam hardly smacks of a devout Muslim.

A more interesting side of his nature is provided by his service record in colonial times. Africans who served with him in this period in the King's African Rifles recount that he was frequently in trouble.

One story holds that after Amin had become a sergeant he was caught in bed with a colleague's wife and pursued naked down Nakuru Street. A British officer, quoted in the *Sunday Telegraph*, recalled: 'In 1955 there was only one blot on his copybook. His records showed that he had had venereal disease which made him ineligible for a good conduct stripe.'

But other stories are far less humorous. As a corporal fighting the Mau Mau in Kenya in the 1950s he established a sadistic record. In Uganda the north-eastern Karamajong tribe, who traditionally go about naked, were notable cattle rustlers who periodically had to be disarmed. Naturally they were reluctant to surrender their spears and shields, and another British officer who served with Amin at the time has boasted that Amin was remarkably successful in persuading them. He claimed that Amin made them stand with their penes on a table and then threatened to cut the organs off with a machete unless they told him where their spears and shields were hidden.

If these incidents were not an indicator to Amin's true nature then certainly the Turkana murders in north-west Kenya were early in 1962. Like the Karamajong the Turkana are semi-nomadic herdsmen with a penchant for cattle rustling. But unlike the Karamajong, the Turkana use guns on their forays, and periodically, during the dry season, when there are only limited water-holes in the area, joint police–army sweeps were launched to disarm them. One of these operations was made late in 1961 and into 1962 and the force included 'C' Company of the 4th King's African Rifles in which Amin was a lieutenant and a platoon commander.

That Amin's platoon carried out a series of murders has been disputed as Obote propaganda, but I have obtained irrefutable evidence that a number of killings did take place. The story goes that platoons of 'C' Company carried out a series of raids on Turkana villages to seize arms, and only Amin's platoon returned empty-handed. Angered by this apparent failure Amin took his platoon out again that night and they returned from a Turkana village with guns they had seized. A few days later complaints were received from the Turkana, and a number of bodies were exhumed from shallow graves at the village. They showed clear signs of having been tortured and beaten before death.

The then Commissioner of the Kenya Police, Sir Richard Catling recalled: 'I remember the incident well. A number of Turkana had been ill-treated and some were killed.' He said that the 4th King's African Rifles had been responsible adding that he had had some difficulty in insisting that the investigation of the murders should be carried out by the police and not by the army.

Sir Walter Coutts, the last British Governor of Uganda, re-members being telephoned early in 1962 by the Deputy Governor of Kenya, Sir Eric Griffith-Jones. 'He rang me and said some pretty fearful things had been going on in Turkana and it looks as though there is some evidence apparently that one of your Ugandan army people has so brutally beaten up a complete Turkana village, including killing them, that I think I shall have to take criminal proceedings against him.' The officer mentioned by Sir Eric was Idi Amin.

The Governor said he pointed out to Sir Eric that it was only six months before Uganda independence and that it would be politically highly disastrous to bring one of the only two black officers in the Ugandan army to trial for murder on the eve of independence. 'I told him, "Why can't you let me have him back and deal with him here?"' Sir Walter recalled. 'Eric felt he should proceed according to law. But I was quite convinced it would be politically wrong. We got Amin back.'

Sir Walter says he consulted the former Commander of the 4th King's African Rifles, Colonel Bill Cheyne, as to whether Amin should be court-martialled. The Colonel's view was that there should be a court-martial, but they decided that Obote, who was then Prime Minister, should be consulted.

Obote had never met Amin at this point, although he must have been aware that he was one of the only two African officers in the army. He subsequently wrote:

'I had been Prime Minister for only a few months when the Governor, Sir Walter Coutts, asked me to go to State House. There he told me the story of the murder of the Turkana by one Lt. Idi Amin. Sir Walter told me about the inquiries made by the KAR G.O.C. HQ in Nairobi about these kill-ings and the case against Amin. Sir Walter was Commander-in-Chief of the 4th KAR. The G.O.C., as I understood it, found Amin guilty and sent the file to the C-in-C to confirm sentence, which was dismissal. Sir Walter sought my opinion whether he should confirm the sentence or not.

I regret to say that part of Uganda's present suffering,

sickness and inhumanity can be traced to the opinion I gave
to Sir Walter. Even now I cannot explain why I came to give
that opinion for it does not fall into the various decisions
involving the loss of human life which I made subsequently
or made before that opinion was given. I advised that Amin
be warned—severe reprimand! After I had given my advice
Sir Walter told me that an officer like Lt. Idi Amin was not
fit to remain in the KAR; the case against him should have
had the sentence of at least imprisonment and that I was
wrong to advise that Amin should not be dismissed. Then
Sir Walter added: "I warn you this officer could cause you
trouble in the future." I remember that warning word for
word except for the word *could*, about which I have some
doubt whether Sir Walter said would or could.'

Obote remembers that in 1966 Sir Walter visited Uganda
during the Congo gold and ivory scandal and repeated his prophetic warning.

'In 1966, Sir Walter, in the presence of Sam Odaka, re-
minded me about the warning he had sounded some four
years back. We were in the PM's office in Entebbe and it
was after the Ocheng allegations in the National Assembly.'

Thus the political wind of change saved Amin on the eve of
Ugandan independence. Sir Walter's recollection of exactly what
action was taken against Amin is hazy, but he believes that the
matter was dealt with by an army court at Jinja where he thinks
Amin was fined. However, the main point is that at independence
on 9 October 1962, Obote was well aware of the nature of Amin,
as were the British when they so happily greeted his seizure of
power in 1971.

At independence the Ugandan army consisted of only about
1,200 men with almost fifty British officers and senior non-
commissioned officers. Gradual and rational expansion of the
army marked the next two years until January 1964, when troops
in Kenya, Tanzania and Uganda mutinied in a chain-reaction
against pay and the predominance of white officers, in the wake

of the successful Zanzibar revolution which overthrew the Sultan and Arab minority Government.

The Cabinet decided to send the Defence Minister, Felix Onama, to Jinja with three other Ministers to see the mutineers. At the barracks he signed an order increasing pay which had been agreed in November for army, police and prisons and partially announced by the British commander of the army on the eve of the mutiny. This announcement unwittingly led directly to the mutiny, for only the officer scales, which had been worked out first, were given and other ranks rebelled. The Cabinet, while the four Ministers were still on their way to Jinja, decided to call in British troops, and several hundred soldiers were discharged and sent home. The order Onama had signed was honoured, leaving the erroneous impression that the mutiny had paid dividends.

The responses of the three East African leaders to their mutinies varied greatly. President Jomo Kenyatta has had British troops stationed in Kenya more or less permanently ever since. Theoretically they are a territorial group, but in practice they are a behind-the-scenes deterrent. President Julius Nyerere swiftly removed the British troops who had quelled his mutiny and replaced them with a Nigerian regiment, sent the whole Tanzanian army home and then set about recruiting a new one from members of the ruling Tanganyika African National Union (TANU) party youth wing. West Germany, Canada and China, in that order, undertook training. The officer corps was Africanised and, most important, a political education programme, which has met with considerable success, was established.

The importance of Nyerere's approach in politically educating his army, who had to be party members, to integrate them into society, cannot be over-emphasised. British policy in East Africa and elsewhere was to keep the army totally apolitical and separate from the growth of nationalism. The desirability of such a policy, even in established democracies, is questionable enough. But in the newly-independent states of Africa it has proved a fatal mistake.

In Uganda a balance of sorts existed between the northern

Nilotic, Nilo-Hamitic and Sudanic tribes who make up a little over 34 per cent of the population and the southern Bantu people. The former dominated the military while the latter were more prominent in the central administration and rural cash economic activities such as working on plantations as well as growing cotton and coffee. Poor soil in parts of Teso, Lango and East Acholi, with families needing to supplement subsistence incomes, was a further magnet for army service. The British height qualification of five feet eight inches, dropped after independence, tended to discriminate against some of the generally shorter Bantu people. By the time of the *coup* the army establishment had increased to nearly 9,000 men with the Acholi making up about a third of this. Lango was the country's third largest cotton producing area with the result that Obote's tribesmen were less inclined to military service, and their small contingent in the army contributed to the lack of resistance to the *coup*.

Obote's Uganda People's Congress (UPC) party had achieved independence through a marriage of convenience with the conservative and reactionary Baganda party, the Kabaka Yekka, meaning 'King Only'. It was a frail affair under which Obote became the first Prime Minister of independent Uganda, and the Kabaka, King Freddie or Mutesa II, the first President. In 1964, by which time Obote's UPC had achieved an absolute Parliamentary majority, the alliance collapsed and Obote was increasingly forced to keep a wary eye on the Baganda. Here began the series of events which allowed Amin to bulldoze his way to power.

The army establishment began to increase more rapidly and the Baganda began to formulate plans to oust Obote. The major confrontation came in February 1966 with Obote suspending the 1962 constitution and becoming President on 15 April when the new constitution came into being. Troops commanded by Amin stormed the Kabaka's place at Mengo forcing him to flee into exile in Britain where he eventually died. Amin had had his first real taste of the power of the gun in an independent African state and the attack on Mengo further alienated Obote and the Baganda. In writing he insisted on minimal force and Amin on maximum. Either way Baganda determination to remove Obote grew, and he in turn was increasingly forced to rely on the security forces.

The 1966 crisis with Buganda staved off another political crisis for Amin. Daudi Ocheng, a northern Member of Parliament closely associated with the Kabaka, had produced Amin's bank account in Parliament, insisting Amin had embezzled some £17,000 from the Congo nationalists at that point fighting Moise Tshombe. A motion was carried in the House during Obote's absence on a northern tour to suspend Amin pending an inquiry. This was subsequently found to be unconstitutional, but it led directly to the crisis with Buganda. Ocheng had alleged that Obote, Amin and others had embezzled the proceeds from gold and ivory from the Congo nationalists. However a subsequent judicial inquiry exonerated Obote and the others, although a question mark was left against Amin's name.

In the space of nineteen days Amin, from facing the possibility of suspension as demanded by Parliament, had been promoted to Army Chief of Staff, with Brigadier Opolot, who because of his Baganda links was regarded as unreliable and who was to be detained eight months later, being promoted sideways to Chief of the Defence forces.

What happened to Opolot in 1966 is an important factor in understanding why Amin seized power in 1971. Late in 1970 Obote appointed an Army and an Air Force Chief of Staff, promoting Amin sideways and loosening his absolute control over the armed forces. Whether Obote was intending to dispose of Amin or not is irrelevant, for the General must certainly have recalled the Opolot lesson, and rumours were rife in Uganda at that time that the sands of time were rapidly running out for Amin.

The intervening years between 1966 and 1971 were to provide Amin with a base—largely through dissent—which at the time of the Mengo attack he had lacked. In the wake of the Kabaka's flight to Britain, Uganda's notoriously ill-disciplined troops went on the rampage through Buganda. Obote's official figure of dead was forty-seven, but the Baganda to this day insist that at least 700 people died.

Outside Buganda Obote was at the height of his power. The army had backed him in his confrontation with the Kabaka, and Amin had been duly rewarded. The soldiers had received more money and sophisticated equipment, but Obote's alliance with the army was as uneasy and unstable as his alliance had been with the Kabaka Yekka. Obote had been the only possible civilian leader with a national base at independence, and through the district commissioners and a reasonably well-organised political party he exercised effective control with his continuing theme of national unity.

In December 1969 came the final incident which set in motion the series of events resulting finally in the *coup*. A group of Baganda tried to assassinate Obote as he left a UPC conference after introducing his 'move to the left' policy. He was shot in the mouth but not badly injured. Amin disappeared for several hours, and within a few days there was an angry meeting of senior officers where he was accused of desertion. The group who made these charges was headed by the second-in-command of the army, Brigadier Pierino Okoya, who was murdered a few days later. Once more the army went on the rampage in Kampala, and 1970 saw a year of increasing tension in Uganda with Obote's popularity waning in a number of influential areas.

There was discontent within the army, particularly among the Acholi, over promotion delays. Police morale had slipped to its lowest level and it is indicative of the degree of violence in Uganda at this time that in 1970 there were 2,400 murders (against 983 in neighbouring Tanzania in the same period with a third more people), only a small percentage of which were solved. The business sector was deeply worried by Obote's 'move to the left', and the stated intention to nationalise many firms exacerbated these fears. The cost of living had risen considerably and the General Service Department headed by Obote's cousin, Akena Adoko, instilled fear into many people.

These factors in isolation, while ingredients of a *coup*, would not have been enough to allow a successful one. The critical point in 1970 was that Obote was moving closer towards the Sudan military leader in Khartoum, General Jaafar Nimeri, who was regarded as a progressive African leader intent on settling the fifteen-year-old war in the south of his country which had accounted for the loss of an estimated 500,000 lives. Israel, influential in Uganda, had long been attacking the soft underbelly of the Arab world by materially backing the Anyanya African guerrillas fighting for independence in southern Sudan in what was generally erroneously seen as a war between Christian southern Africans and Muslim northern Arabs. Late in 1970 Obote refused to allow Israeli planes flying arms to the guerrillas to refuel in Uganda. But what Obote did not realise at this point was the degree to which his army commander was involved with the Anyanya.

There are indications that, immediately after the reshuffle of the Ugandan army hierarchy, Amin began recruiting Anyanya guerrillas to back him in a bid to topple Obote. By the time of the *coup* 500 had been recruited, and within a few months after it, some 1,500 were in the Ugandan army. Today they are thought to number over 3,000. The full extent of Amin's involvement in the southern Sudan emerged during August 1970. A West German mercenary and former French Foreign Legionnaire, Rolf Steiner, who had fought in Biafra and was now with the Anyanya, came out of the Sudan to make contact with a Ugandan army unit. He was arrested by Ugandan police and his diaries showed that on at least two occasions, Amin, with an Israeli military officer, had been in the southern Sudan with the Anyanya. The security committee of the Cabinet decided that Steiner should be deported, and Obote ordered that he should be sent to the Sudan; and he was flown from Entebbe in a Sudanese plane early in January 1971.

Thus with Steiner due to go on trial in Khartoum the extent of Amin's involvement with the Anyanya was bound to emerge publicly. But another trial due to start in Kampala at the beginning of February threatened Amin even more. Detectives investigating an armed hold-up had stumbled on a group of men who in statements had admitted murdering Brigadier Okoya. They said they had been paid to do so by an air force officer who told them he was acting on Amin's instructions because Obote intended to make Okoya head of the armed forces in place of him. Obote doubted Amin's involvement and the only 'evidence' was the statements of the men who admitted killing Okoya. The *coup*, however, prevented the trial taking place and the way in which the files were destroyed and all the senior police officers involved in the investigation murdered in itself provided additional evidence.

Obote, before leaving for Singapore on 11 January, added two other ingredients to the *coup* recipe. The day before flying from Entebbe he called in Amin and Onama and demanded that on his return from Singapore written explanations should be on his desk stating what had happened to £2,500,000 of army money which the Auditor-General said had disappeared and how guns missing from military armouries had been found by police with Ugandan armed robbers known as *kondos*.

Then Obote flew out to Singapore. He had loaded the gun and pointed it directly at his own head. To survive, Amin had no other choice but to pull the trigger.

Radio Uganda played martial music throughout the morning of 25 January. Then at 3.45 p.m. East African time, Warrant-Officer (Class II) Wilfred Aswa, began in laboured English to read an eighteen-point announcement stating why the army had taken over. Amin was not mentioned in that first broadcast, but thirty minutes later it was announced he had been asked by the armed forces to take over the country.

2 The *Coup d'état*

The harsh jangle of the phone cut into the muted conversation in the office of the Inspector-General of Police in Kampala's Parliament building. The time was 9.30 p.m. on 24 January 1971. The delayed call from Singapore had been anxiously awaited by the eleven assembled men who forty-eight hours earlier had formed themselves into an 'anti-assassination committee' to protect Uganda's President Obote.

Interior Minister, Basil Bataringaya, lifted the receiver and spoke to his Permanent Secretary, Christopher Ntende, who had flown to Singapore two days earlier to report to Obote that a plan by Amin to assassinate him and seize power had been discovered. Bataringaya said his committee believed from further intelligence reports that the story of an assassination-*coup d'état* attempt timed for Tuesday, 26 January, was genuine. Army officers, known to be anti-government, were in contact with dissident civilians.

Since Ntende's arrival in Singapore's Hilton Hotel at 6.00 p.m. on Saturday he had been the only official contact between there and Kampala relaying instructions from Obote to Bataringaya.

But during the Sunday night call the Army Chief of Staff, Brigadier Suleiman Hussein, said he wanted to speak to the President personally. Obote agreed that if it was really necessary they would speak in Swahili which both of them knew. Instead the Army Adjutant and Quartermaster-General, Lieutenant-Colonel David Oyite Ojok, took the phone in the Parliament building and for two minutes spoke with Obote in Luo.

Obote asked Ojok only one question: Had Amin yet been arrested following his order from Singapore earlier in the day? The Colonel, who had been unable to locate the General, answered that arrangements were in hand and that Amin might be arrested before dawn. 'You are too late,' Obote said. 'Get out of the Parliament building. If you don't move now you will find it too late.'

It was already too late. The *coup d'état*, which ousted Obote and his civilian government, had begun thirty minutes earlier at the barracks of the Malire Mechanised Regiment in Kampala, the headquarters of the country's only unit equipped with armour—six Second World War Sherman tanks captured by Israel in the June 1967 war and given to Uganda, some American obsolete half-tracks and a number of Czechoslovakian armoured personnel carriers. Unbeknown to those in the Inspector-General's office, troops were already moving in to surround the Parliament. Bataringaya and Ntende spoke for a few more minutes with the Minister giving an assurance that loyal troops backed by police special units were already moving in to guard strategic points such as the radio station, Entebbe Airport and, ironically, the Parliament building. In Singapore, Ntende replaced the receiver and recalled later in a written report that Obote 'remarked that action which was being taken by loyal forces was too slow for his liking and might be too late'.

The Ugandan *coup* provides a classic example of the dangers of underrating the enemy once he has been identified. Obote is generally credited with being a shrewd politician yet all the ingredients of a *coup d'état* existed when he turned his back. Kampala had been alive with rumours of an impending *coup* attempt when Obote left for Singapore. Originally he had not intended to go, as Uganda's first General Election since independence and first ever Presidential Election were scheduled to be held before 15 April. To understand why he went to Singapore against the backdrop of *coup* rumours and the work he had to do on the election, it is necessary to understand the importance that black African leaders attach to the liberation of southern African countries still under white minority domination.

At the time Obote set out for Singapore there seemed every likelihood that Britain was intending to sell arms to South Africa over and above the Simonstown Agreement. This agreement derived from an exchange of four letters between the then British Minister of Defence, Mr. Selwyn Lloyd and his South African counterpart, Mr. F. C. Erasmus on 30 June 1955. The focal points of this exchange covered the need for international discussions on regional defence; agreement on defence of the Cape sea route; agreement on the further use of the Simonstown Naval Base at Cape Town; and financial and administrative details on the transfer of the Naval Base.

South Africa undertook between 1955 and 1963 to purchase six anti-submarine frigates, ten coastal minesweepers and four seaward defence ships from Britain at an approximate cost of £18,000,000. Within that time-span South Africa took delivery of all but two vessels (on which she cancelled orders) and thus any 'legal' obligations which arose under the Simonstown Agreement had been fulfilled prior to the 1963 United Nations Security Council resolution calling on member states 'to cease forthwith the sale and shipment of arms, ammunition of all types and military vehicles to South Africa'. France and Britain abstained from the resolution while affirming their repugnance for apartheid.

In 1964 the Labour party led by Mr. Harold Wilson ousted the Conservative government by winning a narrow three-seat majority. Mr. Wilson had already stated Labour would abide by the UN resolution and this was taken to include the Simonstown Agreement. But when Labour was defeated in June 1970 one of the first things that the new Prime Minister, Mr. Edward Heath, did was to make it clear that in British 'defence interests' arms sales to South Africa would resume. The decision was announced on 20 July, and the importance attached to the decision by progressive African leaders is demonstrated by the fact that within forty-eight hours Tanzanian President, Julius Nyerere, Zambian President, Kenneth Kaunda, and Obote held a mini-summit in Dar es Salaam. All three decided they would leave the Commonwealth if Britain supplied arms to South Africa.

In the ensuing weeks an angry confrontation developed. Both Nyerere and Kaunda went to London to try to dissuade Heath. At the Prime Minister's country residence, Chequers, on 10 October, the Tanzanian leader and Mr. Heath clashed sharply. Mr. Heath is said to have angrily pounded the table insisting Britain

would act in what she regarded as her interests and would not be
pushed around. Incredibly he is reported to have said just before
the meeting broke up: 'We will drop Africa and Africa will not
be able to pick up the pieces.' Kaunda reacted more emotionally
to this sort of harassment by storming out in the middle of a
dinner in his honour at 10 Downing Street. The less diplomatic
Obote bluntly refused even to go and discuss the issue with Mr.
Heath, although he was sent to try to persuade President Jomo
Kenyatta to support them.

The Africans argued that they accepted Britain must make
decisions in what Mr. Heath regarded as British interests. But in
turn they also would be forced to make their own decision, and
that was simply: if Britain sold arms to black Africa's enemy—
South Africa—they would have no alternative but to leave the
Commonwealth. These arms, which Britain argued were to
protect the vital Cape sea route, could be turned on the African
states supporting the liberation movements in southern Africa to
win the freedom they were being denied in that last white bastion.
And as the amount was so small, and therefore meant little to
the Indian Ocean military balance of power, what Britain was
in fact doing was giving Pretoria the moral support she was being
denied by world opinion.

In the following weeks angry reaction continued in Dar es
Salaam, Kampala and Lusaka. Predictably Ghana, Lesotho and
Malawi leaned towards supporting arms sales. But just as important, even if they were not apparently prepared to go as
far, Kenya and Nigeria were also outspoken in opposing the
sales. Outside Africa, support for the opponents came from
Canada, India and Pakistan, and so as Singapore approached,
Heath's increasing obduracy drew the predictable mounting
storm.

Nyerere was convinced of the need for a united front at
Singapore. He could not count on the Kenyans if it came to the
test, and Canada's Prime Minister, Pierre Trudeau, the link between the 'old' and 'new' Commonwealth groups, had only gone
along with a compromise put forward by Kaunda which sought
to lay out an ethic for the 'Club'.

The fourth paragraph of Kaunda's Commonwealth Declaration read:

'We recognise racial discrimination as an unmitigated evil of society and racial prejudice as a dangerous sickness threatening the healthy development of the human race; we therefore seek every means of combatting these scourges; we shall deny all regimes which practise them any assistance which can consolidate or strengthen them.'

The Zambian leader's point was clear. And Mr. Heath was not expected to accept it. The British argument was that there was a mounting Russian threat in the Indian Ocean, and British interests had to be protected. But the reality, as emerged during Nyerere's Chequers talks, was that the British Foreign Secretary, Sir Alec Douglas-Home, who had been Prime Minister of the 1963 Conservative government which abstained from the UN resolution, was as much, if not more, worried about the possibility of the French taking over at Simonstown.

Obote had twice said in Uganda that he would not attend the Singapore meeting. Sections of the British press chose to interpret this as pique over the arms sales issue. By all accounts from his intimates of that period, it was not. He tended to regard hopes of blocking arms sales as a lost cause. But all of his speeches of that period clearly shows his preoccupation with the forthcoming elections. Finally, however, the Ugandan Cabinet decided that Obote should go to Singapore to present as united an African case as was possible.

He flew to Singapore on 11 January, apparently secure in the belief that if Amin decided to move he would not get support from the bulk of the army. As the Kabaka before him had discovered it was predominantly Acholi. In broad terms this assessment was correct but two critical factors had been overlooked.

The first news of impending trouble came on Friday, 22 January, soon after the Commonwealth Premiers' meeting had ended in Singapore. The Inspector-General of Police, Mr. E. W. Oryema, telephoned from Kampala to the Minister of Internal Affairs, Bataringaya, saying that he had a most serious report to make. The Minister, with his Permanent Secretary, Ntende, drove immediately from Entebbe to the capital, arriving at the office of the Inspector-General soon after noon. The head of police had brought with him four other senior officers: the Head of the Criminal Investigation Department (CID), Mr. Mohamed Hassan, the Commanding Officer of Buganda region, Senior Assistant Commissioner of Police, Mr. Suleiman Dusman, the Acting Head of the Special Branch, Superintendent of Police, Mr. Obong, and the Police Bandmaster, Mr. Oduka.

Oryema said he had received a report from the Bandmaster to the effect that the President was to be assassinated on his return from Singapore on Tuesday and that a number of other leaders were also to be killed.

The Bandmaster said that a man named Juma Mafale, who used to be a police bandsman, had joined the army and now held the rank of lieutenant. Mafale was married to the elder sister of Oduka's wife and he was believed to be a relative of Amin.

Because of their wives, Mafale and Oduka met often, and the Bandmaster said that during the previous week the Lieutenant, during a call at his house, had said he was tired because he had been attending a meeting throughout the previous night. Oduka asked him what kind of meeting it had been to take all night, and the Lieutenant said it had been attended by Amin but gave no further explanation.

Then at 9.30 a.m. on 22 January, Mrs. Mafale called at the Bandmaster's office. She said she had pretended to be ill and had persuaded her husband to take her to Mulago Hospital. From there she walked to the Bandmaster's house but found he had left and took a taxi to his office. Her story was that meetings had taken place at her home on the nights of 19, 20 and 21 January, and these had been attended by Amin, the Minister of Defence, Onama, a Muganda Minister with a small moustache, three army officers, including a captain, and three non-commissioned officers. Details of what Mrs. Mafale said she overheard and saw at these meetings are contained in the written report of Ntende, made to Obote in Singapore.

Mrs. Mafale had reported a plan to kill Obote at Entebbe Airport on his return from Singapore as well as a number of other prominent figures. She was afraid that her brother-in-law would also be killed as he would be conducting the band at the airport welcoming-ceremony. At the previous night's meeting the plotters had clustered around a model of Entebbe Airport on a large table, and the positions the three NCOs were to take up to shoot the President had been agreed. They had also been instructed to throw hand-grenades.

The woman had told Mr. Oduka that among those also to be killed were a number of Ministers whose names were listed: some senior army officers, including the Commander of the Army, Brigadier Suleiman Hussein, and the Commander of the Air Force, Colonel Juma Musa; the former Commander of the Army, Shabani Opolot (who was in detention), the Inspector-General of Police, Oryema; the Commissioner of Prisons, Mr. Okwaare; and five former Ministers. Luzira Prison in Kampala was to be seized and some detainees killed, including Opolot and the former Ministers who had supported the attack on Amin during the gold and ivory scandal.

Mrs. Mafale had seen the model at the previous night's meeting, which had gone on until 3.00 a.m. on 22 January. While serving food and drinks she had overheard much of the plot, including the plan to seize strategic points in Kampala, such as the radio station and main post office. She recalled that during the previous week, just after Obote left for Singapore, that her husband had told her that the President had given orders that Amin was to be shot while he was away.

Bataringaya decided that the Vice-President, Mr. John Babiiha, must be informed immediately and that an 'anti-assassination committee' should be formed and meet that afternoon at the Inspector-General's office. Ntende was sent to get details of plane connections to Singapore so that he could fly there immediately to report verbally to the President.

The committee began meeting at 2.00 p.m. under the chairmanship of Bataringaya. Those who were present at the beginning were Ntende, Oryema, Dusman, Hassan, Oduka, Bernard Olila from the General Service Department, and Obong, the number three in the Police Special Branch. Efforts were still being made to contact Brigadier Hussein, and Lieutenant-Colonel David Oyite Ojok, who arrived late and was briefed on the details of the plot. It was decided that there would be maximum security at Entebbe Airport for Obote's return, and a subcommittee comprising Ojok, Olila and Dusman was set up to survey the airport and work out a security plan to protect the President.

In his report, Ntende noted here that Lieutenant-Colonel Ojok said that Amin had been very quiet since the reorganisation of the army and air force in October—breaking up the command structure—but that in the past week he had done two things indicating a tougher attitude. The first of these was that on 20 January, and the significance of this was that it was the day after Amin learned Steiner had been deported to Khartoum and not West Germany as he had expected, Amin had called a meeting of all officers and men working at army headquarters and had made the following points:

1. That he was still the boss.

2. That Lieutenant-Colonel Nyangweso was responsible for staff affairs at the army headquarters, and all other officers had no right to interfere with Nyangweso's duties. He would take action against any officer who intended to interfere with those duties.

3. That he had saved the country from a most serious situation in 1966. He supported the government and in actual fact he was so close to the President that he used to give the President a lift between Kampala and Entebbe on many occasions.

4. That some people were making all sorts of false and wild allegations against him. Those people were after something.

5. That the country had experienced the worst type of instability through the activities of 'kondos'. It appeared that the government was not taking any serious steps to try and provide a solution to this menace.

6. That he would convene another meeting, but of officers only, the next day, Thursday, 21 January 1971.

From this several points about General Amin's thinking emerge at this juncture. In the first place Mafale had told his wife that Obote had given orders that the General was to be killed. If the Lieutenant believed this then it is clear the General had given him the impression that he did also and in fact he was to claim immediately after the *coup* that the President had ordered his death. Whether Amin really believed this or simply used it as his justification for seizing power is unclear, but the latter is much more the plausible explanation.

The appointment of Brigadier Hussein as Army Chief of Staff and of Colonel Musa as Chief of the Air Force had left Amin as little more than a figurehead. He was angered by this, and had remarked as much publicly on a number of occasions since the reshuffle which became effective on 1 November. He must have recalled how in 1966 he had been made Army Chief of Staff. This had been the prelude to Brigadier Opolot being sacked eight months later. Even if Obote was not planning a similar fate for Amin it is highly likely that the General thought he was.

Thus his headquarters staff address on 20 January, which had the same theme as he adopted with officers on the following day, was the attempt of a man who saw time running out, to reassert his position. Brigadier Hussein proved ineffectual in his brief period as Army Chief of Staff, and Amin saw Nyangweso as a more malleable officer. The fact that Nyangweso has been Acting Commander of the Army since the *coup d'état* bears this view out.

Amin's contention that wild allegations were circulating against him was basically correct. An example of this is that during November it was widely rumoured in Kampala that he was under house arrest although Obote has denied this. In fact it is believed he was bedridden through gout caused by excessive drinking and was being treated with a new medicine by a young American doctor at Makerere. Whatever the truth, when the General appeared in public for the first time at Makerere University for a ceremony installing Obote as Chancellor, there was no special seat for him and the students jeered him as he walked in. He waved back good humouredly with both arms raised.

There is little reason to believe there is any truth in General

Amin's claim that Obote had ordered he should be murdered. In the same way that the finger of suspicion pointed at Amin when Okoya was murdered, so too would it have been directed against Obote had the General met a violent end. Nor was this Obote's style. If there is one outstanding lesson about his nine years in power it is that he was a courageous politician to whom killing was abhorrent. British correspondents being briefed by their High Commission in Kampala the day after the *coup* were told that Obote even refused to endorse death sentences passed by the courts. That was about the only good thing the British had to say about Obote at that point.

Lieutenant-Colonel Ojok told the meeting that he had gone to Mubende on the road between Kampala and Fort Portal and had missed Amin's second speech. Returning towards Kampala that night at about 10.30 p.m. he had been challenged as normal by a soldier near Mbuya, Kampala. He had left his car and identified himself when he noticed about forty soldiers in full battle dress around the area. The sergeant in charge said they had been ordered to carry out a night exercise, but he declined to say who gave the order. Lieutenant-Colonel Ojok said he had threatened the sergeant with arrest and he had then said the order had been given by Amin. The soldiers were all military policemen, and when Ojok contacted their headquarters he said he was told a night-long exercise had been ordered because a group of alleged British soldiers were supposed to be staying at a camping site near the city. Ojok went immediately to the camping site where he found about seven small tents but satisfied himself that the occupants were tourists.

It was decided that Ntende would leave that night, arriving in Singapore about twenty-four hours later after twice changing planes, to inform the President immediately. Bataringaya saw him off at the airport and gave him instructions. Ntende's written report gave them as follows:

1. To verbally report accurately to the President.
2. That the mere fact that the plan to assassinate the President had been discovered would ensure its failure.

3. That the President should be assured it would be safe for him to return to Uganda.

4. That maximum security would be provided at Entebbe Airport by trusted members of the army and police.

5. That the President should stop over in Nairobi on the way back using the pretext that he was informing President Kenyatta about the Singapore meeting.

6. That an official would be sent to meet him at Nairobi to inform him of the latest developments and plans.

7. That everyone at the airport for Obote's return would be searched.

8. That Ntende should inform Bataringaya from Singapore whether the President had decided to return through Entebbe or would use the alternative route through Tororo.

When Ntende arrived at the Singapore Hilton, Obote was in bed asleep after an all-night session at the Commonwealth meeting. Obote assumed that Ntende had come to report on discussions in Kampala with the British government that week over the question of Ugandan Asians holding British citizenship. Ntende sent in a note saying he had arrived to report on a secret matter on instructions from Bataringaya. He delivered his report verbally and was then told by Obote to put it in writing and was ordered not to tell anyone else in the Singapore delegation. Obote subsequently recalled that he was not surprised by the report but that there were aspects of it about which he was unhappy. He could, for instance, not understand why Oryema had taken four senior police officers with him to report to Bataringaya, and he felt that the story of Mrs. Mafale needed to be more carefully checked before any action was taken. Members of Obote's delegation in Singapore who still live in exile are convinced that Ntende disobeyed one part of his instructions and told Obote's Private Secretary, Henry Kyemba, about the plot. Kyemba, they believe, called Uganda from Singapore and passed on the news to his friend and tribesman, Wanume Kibedi, who became Minister of Foreign Affairs after the *coup d'état* and whose sister was married to Amin. Ntende's initial report was published fully in the Tanzanian official government newspaper the *Standard* on 16 February 1971. But his four additional reports on 24 and 25 January on conversations with both Obote and Bataringaya have hitherto been kept secret. Yet they are important for they shed considerable light on Obote's initial reaction and the instructions Ntende transmitted to Kampala from Singapore in four separate telephone conversations.

In Kampala on Saturday morning, while Ntende was flying, Ojok, with Olila and Dusman, had travelled by road to Entebbe Airport to carry out their reconnaissance and draw up security precautions. But when they arrived at the airport they found Amin and a group of soldiers, including some privates, already there, apparently carrying out their own survey for the assassination. One other notable person was at the airport, possibly coincidentally, although if this were so the remark he made was very strange. In the VIP lounge at the airport Ojok found Colonel Bolka Bar-Lev, head of the Israeli military mission to Uganda, who said he was seeing off another Israeli officer, who was said to be leaving for West Africa via Zaïre. Ojok recalled afterwards that Colonel Bar-Lev told him he was a good officer and urged him not to act in a manner that might endanger his life. When the Ugandan questioned how his life might be in danger, the Israeli answered that lives were endangered in thousands of ways including motor accidents. Flippantly Ojok assured Bar-Lev he would drive slowly and until after the *coup d'état* thought no more about the incident.

Ojok's committee completed their plans, deciding that the police would be in charge of security for Obote's return and that army personnel should be kept away. A strong police cordon would be thrown around the airport and nobody would be allowed in the buildings which might give a vantage point for a sniper.

The 'anti-assassination committee' reassembled at 2.00 p.m. on Saturday in the Inspector-General's office but the meeting was delayed for some time because Bataringaya was late.

Obong said that the Police Special Branch had received a reliable report to the effect that Amin and his fellow plotters had surveyed the airport that morning. This, coupled with Ojok's group having seen the General at the airport, convinced the committee that the assassination plan was still definitely on and it was decided that Brigadier Hussein should station troops, whose loyalty was certain, near the airport for the President's return in case the police needed help.

The reasons why Ojok had been unable to locate Amin to arrest him on the Sunday after Obote's orders from Singapore was because he had left Kampala. Amin, in the first of several contradictory versions of how the *coup d'état* occurred, claimed he was away on a hunting trip and that army personnel learning of Obote's alleged plan to have him murdered had decided to seize power and had only then asked the General to become President. But there is no reason to suppose this version is true for there is evidence that Amin on the Saturday night, only twenty-four hours before the *coup d'état*, had left Kampala and gone to a meeting north of Lwero, some forty miles from the capital.

Bernard Olila, the number three in the General Service Department, reported on Sunday that an informer had infiltrated the meeting. Amin, Onama and about forty other people had attended including a number of Anyanya leaders—members of the southern Sudanese guerrilla movement who had been fighting for years for full autonomy for the south. The informer had said that it had been decided to go ahead and stage a *coup d'état* rather than wait until the following Tuesday to assassinate Obote before seizing power.

It seems fairly certain that by Saturday night Amin was aware that his plans had been discovered. Ojok's reaction to finding Amin at the airport that morning was to take it as confirmation that the assassination claim was true. Amin must have similarly wondered what Ojok was doing. But even more important is the strong view that both the 'anti-assassination committee' and Obote's own delegation in Singapore contained people who were reporting back to Amin. Two of them, the head of police and the head of prisons, became Ministers in the post-*coup* government. Yet it seems unlikely that either of them acted as double agents and that Amin in the early days wanted to give his

seizure of power greater credibility by incorporating all branches
of the military and para-military. The Inspector-General of
Police, Oryema, appears at first to have considered moving his
men against Amin but decided not to after speaking to Bar-Lev
and after troops shelled his house, killing his father-in-law. Obote
supporters believe the informer was Suleiman Dusman, the
Buganda Police Commander, although again there is reason to
doubt this. Although registered in Lango he was Nubian-Muslim
and the only one on the committee, and the Nubian link-up had
not been appreciated at that time by Obote or his government
as a co-ordinated threat. But Dusman was retired during 1971,
and when last heard of was running a shop at Lira, which certainly does not smack of the generosity with which Amin
normally rewards fellow conspirators.

The briefing of senior officers by Hussein and Ojok had taken
place shortly before the 'anti-assassination committee' reassembled
at the Parliament building soon after 8.30 p.m. on the Sunday
night. The Commissioner of Prisons, Fabian Okwaare, had been
co-opted because of the plan to kill some prisoners and release
others held at Luzira. He insisted he could not secure the prison
with only warders, and the Inspector-General of Police was
instructed to send extra men from the Police Special Branch to
strengthen the guard.

Obote's prophetic call came through as they met. Within
minutes of it ending the committee realised troops were surrounding the Parliament building. Hussein rang the commander
of the Malire Mechanised Battalion only to find the unit had
already been overrun and that the adjutant, Lieutenant-Colonel
Augustino Akwango, had been arrested and severely beaten up.
The commander had personally held the keys to the armoury
and armoured personnel carriers. But troops, believed by Obote
supporters to be backed by Anyanya guerrillas, had pulled the
door off the main armoury with an armoured personnel carrier
they had managed to start.

What had gone wrong with Bataringaya's assurance to Obote
that the plan to assassinate him and topple the government was
doomed to failure because it had been discovered?

In the first place the committee had concentrated on the initial report that Obote would be assassinated at the airport on his return on Tuesday. They had done so until it was too late to a degree that excluded the possibility of Amin advancing his time schedule. That alone might not have mattered had it not been for the probability that their own ranks were infiltrated and the clumsy way in which Hussein called senior officers into Kampala on the Sunday morning where they were bound to be seen. If Amin was suspicious after meeting Ojok at Entebbe Airport, the Sunday meeting must have confirmed his suspicions that he had been discovered. Given that, he had no alternative but to act earlier.

Amin's meeting at Lwero with Anyanya leaders on the Saturday night and the decision that there would be a *coup* without an assassination first tends to confirm that by that point Amin knew he had to act quickly. The claim that a letter ordering his murder had been taken from Obote's office is untrue, for even the unpredictable General has never claimed it existed. Certainly if such a letter did exist, even if it were a forgery, he would have long since made it public. Another claim that can also be dismissed is that a Sergeant Musa in Jinja overheard a telephone call from Obote in Singapore to Ojok ordering him to kill Amin. Ntende's report makes it clear they only spoke on one occasion, and then in Luo which Sergeant Musa did not understand.

Hussein's decision to call in army officers from various units around the country for a briefing on the Sunday could not have escaped the notice of Amin's supporters. The officers, dressed in civilian clothes, were briefed in Kampala. Those who attended were Colonel Tito Okello, Commander of the 2nd Infantry Brigade stationed at Masaka; Colonel Mesusera Arach, Commander of the 1st Infantry Brigade stationed at Mbale; Colonel Albertino Langoya, Commander of the Infantry School at Jinja; Lieutenant-Colonel Hillary Abwala, Commander of the 3rd Battalion at Mubende; Lieutenant-Colonel Akwango, Commander of the crucial Malire Mechanised Battalion stationed in Kampala; Lieutenant-Colonel Oyite Ojok and Brigadier Hussein. They were given details of the plot, of the counter-plans and told to put their units on standby.

While this was going on Ntende was again trying to reach Bataringaya with a list of fifteen instructions from Obote. The Minister could not be located so he passed the instructions to Obote's Permanent Secretary, Justus Byagagaire, who was told to find Bataringaya and pass them on. The important ones were:

1. That Mafale's house was to be raided, he and his wife arrested and interrogated separately and any arms seized.

2. That a letter, which Mafale alleged had been stolen from Obote's office and contained instructions to kill Amin, should be located, if it existed.

3. That the names of anyone who attended meetings at Mafale's house should be obtained and the people detained.

4. If Bataringaya was satisfied after the interrogations the story was untrue the original sources of the information should be arrested and it should be ascertained who they were working for.

5. In the meantime certain strategic points should be guarded. These were given code-names, with the radio and television station becoming 'Ojera', which was the surname of the Minister of Information. The airport was code-named 'The place we reside in' because Bataringaya and Ntende lived there. Murchison Falls Dam and the reservoirs were simply 'water', and finally the Uganda Electricity Board installations were code-named 'Erisa' after the chairman.

6. All army units had to be led by reliable officers under the overall command of Brigadier Hussein, code-named 'the golfer'.

7. Bataringaya was given a free hand to act as he saw fit and Ntende arranged to call back in four to five hours.

Ntende, on Obote's instructions, had spoken to Bataringaya first of all at 7.00 a.m. and again at 1.30 p.m. Uganda Time on the Sunday. The first conversation added little other than that the Inspector-General of Police wanted to see the Minister immediately. But there had been several developments by the second, which Ntende lists in his first 'additional' report as follows:

1. That Brigadier Hussein had briefed a number of trusted officers who had been told to return to their units and put them on standby.

2. The Bandmaster, Oduka, had visited Mafale's house, whose wife had overheard the plot, and the Lieutenant had told him there would be a *coup d'état* on Tuesday, 26th January, whether or not Obote had returned.

3. Oduka said he had seen uniforms and equipment— which was taken to mean firearms—at Mafale's house.

4. Mafale had warned Oduka to be careful to remain out of trouble.

5. Dusman, the Buganda Police Commander, had seen Amin near the Veterinary Institute in Old Entebbe, apparently carrying out reconnaissance.

6. That Mafale had also told Oduka that apart from local supporters of the Major-General there would be others helping in the *coup* operation who would be coming from the southern Sudan, and white mercenaries including Israelis who had been contacted for the purpose by Steiner.

The latter point was critical, apparently confirming the informer's report of a meeting north of Kampala on the previous night attended by Amin and Anyanya leaders. Obote gave these instructions which Ntende says he passed on to Bataringaya:

1. That Bataringaya must weigh the situation very carefully and take whatever action he considered appropriate to contain the situation.

2. That he must co-ordinate with Brigadier Hussein who would have overall command of the security forces to be involved in any exercise that may be necessary.

3. That the Brigadier would ensure that all units of the army were well under control.

Obote's advisers had been convinced that even it Amin attempted to stage a *coup d'état*, he would not receive support from the army. But here two factors were overlooked. The first was the West Nile–Nubian–Muslim link and the second the possibility of an external force being involved.

Since the *coup d'état*, Obote's supporters have insisted that the
critical factor which turned the tide against them was the involvement of at least 500 southern Sudanese Anyanya guerrillas.
According to this version several hundred of the guerrillas had
been transported from the southern Sudan in lorries and buses
supplied by a company partly owned by the Minister of Defence,
Felix Onama. The guerrillas had been taken to a camp near
Bombo, and the original plan was presumably to help Amin
seize power after Obote had been assassinated on the Tuesday.

There are several factors which lend credence to the broad
view. As Steiner's diaries showed, Amin was having considerable
contact with the Anyanya without the knowledge of Obote. He
had met the guerrilla commander, General Joseph Lagu, in the
southern Sudan on at least two occasions and was helping to get
arms and other supplies to him. Obote became aware of this in
the latter part of 1970, and at about the same time the head of the
Israeli Central Intelligence Organisation, General Zamir, visited
Uganda. He asked permission for Israeli planes flying arms to the
Anyanya to refuel at Entebbe or Gulu and for guerrilla training
facilities in Uganda, but Obote refused. The Israeli then approached Akena Adoko and suggested that the General Service
could co-operate, referring to other arms of government which
were clandestinely used in the United States on matters of this
nature. When this also failed he approached Amin.

Thus there are two reasons why the Anyanya would have
involved themselves in the Ugandan *coup d'état*. Firstly because
there was a danger of their supplies being curtailed because of
Obote's attitude and secondly because they had reason to be
personally grateful to Amin. Even so there is considerable difficulty in ascertaining the degree of Anyanya involvement, but
further points I have discovered independently make me con-
clude that Obote's claim is correct.

Ironically a year after the Ugandan *coup* the Anyanya's need to
have a sympathetic figure in Kampala ended with the settlement
of the sixteen-year-old war and a peace agreement with gives
the southern Sudan a generous degree of autonomy. Sources in
the southern capital, Juba, who had had close ties for years with

the Anyanya told me that soon after the Ugandan *coup* almost 1,500 Anyanya fighters were recruited into the Ugandan army. Many of these, they said, had taken part in the *coup d'état*. The second point which tends to verify the claim is that soldiers I have spoken to, who were in the barracks of the Malire Mechanised Battalion on the night of 25 January say that a large group of men attacked the camp. The men were armed and those who escaped insist that they were not Ugandans but southern Sudanese. Warders at Luzira Prison, who four days later saw Brigadier Hussein and others beaten to death by men in Ugandan army uniforms, say categorically that the killers were not Ugandans but southern Sudanese because of their tribal markings and distinctive features.

The meeting that evening of commanding officers, which must have affected Amin's decision to move earlier than planned, was to have a further repercussion. Few of the commanding officers had returned to their units when the fighting began at Malire, and therefore the troops were far from being on a state of alert. Lieutenant-Colonel Akwango was the only commander to have reached his unit. Colonel Arach was in Jinja on his way back to Mbale. Colonel Langoya had also reached Jinja but had not returned to his unit. Colonel Okello and Lieutenant-Colonel Abwala were in a car on their way to Masaka. So most of the units were left without their commanders and the officers in the barracks had no idea what was happening .The lack of leadership at this crucial moment was compounded by the fact that half the officers in the army were simultaneously on leave. A considerable accumulation of back-leave had built up and there had been some dispute in the government how this should be wiped out. One proposal had been that the officers should receive money in lieu of leave, but the Ministry of Finance objected to this. It had been finally agreed that the leave must be taken on a staggered basis after March. But after Obote left for Singapore Onama ordered that all back-leave was to be taken immediately or it would be forfeited. The result was that on the Monday morning a few hours after the *coup* began there were forty army officers at Gulu, of whom only one, a major, was on duty. The bewildered

officers, unable to contact their commanding officers for orders—
as by this point most had been arrested—decided to send a delegation to the Minister of Defence, Onama, who was also in Gulu.
The delegation was told there was nothing to worry about and
that everything was being brought under control.

After seeing troops surrounding Parliament, the Bataringaya
committee, with the exception of Hussein and Ojok, had scattered. By telephone, the two officers swiftly discovered that all
the army units around the country, with the exception of the
2nd batallion at Moroto, had been taken by surprise and that
there had been no resistance. Almost all the officers, other than
those from West Nile, had been rounded up and the killing of
Acholi and Langi officers and other ranks had already begun.
The critical factor was that Amin's fellow Nubians had seized
all the armouries.

Hussein and Ojok, both armed only with pistols, locked the
office door on the inside. Twice troops came to the door and
banged on it, shouting that if they came out and surrendered they
would not be harmed. It appears that the troops were not certain
whether the two officers were still in the building or had escaped
with the others. Early on Monday morning Amin arrived at
Obote's office only thirty yards away while the officers were still
hidden. Outside troops amused themselves shooting up Ojok's
car and then finally ramming it with an armoured personnel
carrier. Occasionally they shouted through a loud-hailer telling
the officers to surrender, but none of them seemed anxious to
come inside and hunt them down.

However, Hussein and Ojok realised it was only a matter of
time before they were found, and soon after dark on Monday
night they moved from their fourth-floor hideout to another
office on a lower floor. Just after midnight they crept downstairs
to a back door facing the National Theatre. There was a soldier
standing guard at the door and around 2.00 a.m., while they were
debating whether to shoot him, he shouldered his rifle and
wandered off, apparently bored with his job. The two officers
were in civilian clothes and they walked through the streets un-
molested until they arrived at a small cinema near the railway

station. Then two soldiers challenged them and they split up, with Hussein running off along the Kampala road towards Entebbe. Ojok was captured, and when he identified himself, one of the soldiers said: 'Oh, they want you very much.' He also said that it was rumoured in the ranks that whoever killed Ojok would be promoted to be the next man to Amin. Yet remarkably the soldiers let him go, advising him that he was less likely to meet troops if he took the Jinja road. Ojok hid at the homes of two friends before finally making his way out to Tanzania from where eighteen months later he was to take part in the abortive invasion aimed at overthrowing the General.

Four of the others on the Bataringaya committee were not so lucky. The Minister was subsequently dismembered alive and his head put on display at the end of a pole at the garrison town of Mbarara in south-west Uganda. CID Chief Hassan, was among several hundred killed in the Mutukula Massacre in January 1972. Apart from Ojok, the only other person still alive outside Uganda is Bernard Olila. Oryema and Okwaare both became Ministers in Amin's post-*coup* Cabinet, but were sent on leave early in 1973 with the rest of the Ministers and only Oryema was reappointed nine months later. Ntende became Permanent Secretary in the Ministry of Religion but was later sacked. Obong died in a car crash and Dusman is retired.

But the most tragic and terrible story of all is about the Police Bandmaster, Oduka, who had brought the details of the assassination plan to the committee. He escaped from Uganda and went to live at the Indian Ocean port of Mombasa in Kenya. Amin sent Senior Assistant Commissioner of Police, Peter Adroni, who has himself since fled to Britain, to Mombasa to persuade him to come back assuring him that he would be safe. Oduka returned to Kampala and met Amin at the Parliament building. Their discussion was friendly and the Bandmaster was asked to go to Makindye Military Prison to record a statement before going on fourteen days' leave. The Bandmaster left after shaking hands and Amin immediately ordered Lieutenant-Colonel Ochima to take him instead to the barracks of the Malire Mechanised Battalion. Then he turned to a Minister and invited him to go and watch the Bandmaster being killed. When the Minister reached Malire thirty minutes later, Oduka was already dead, his skull crushed with a club. Three men wearing long red robes who described themselves as 'judges' were standing by the body. They had killed the Bandmaster.

Of the military commanders who attended the Sunday army headquarters briefing all were murdered except Ojok and Okello who escaped to Tanzania.

Thus of the sixteen men who attended the two meetings, eight were murdered, three escaped into exile, one died in a car crash and three others were either sacked or retired, and one is a Minister.

3   The Aftermath

On the end of Singapore Airport's main runway, East African Airways Super VC10 pilot, Captain John Winston, faced a dilemma as he carried out his final checks ready for take-off for Bombay. On the high-frequency radio linking him with his final destination, Nairobi, headquarters of EAA, news had just come through instructing him to inform Obote that fighting had broken out in Uganda.

Obote was in the first-class section while most of his delegation were in economy. The reason for the Captain's dilemma was that this was a scheduled flight, diverted through Singapore from Hong Kong, with many passengers other than the Ugandan delegation aboard. Correctly he guessed that Obote's bodyguards would be armed and he feared that in desperation the Ugandans might try to hijack the plane.

Colleagues in EAA say that the Captain told them later he refused to tell Obote while the plane was on the runway with the engines running. He told Nairobi he was willing to go back to the terminal, close down the engines and then tell Obote in the VIP lounge. Finally after some argument it was agreed he would take off on the three-hour flight to Bombay and at his own discretion tell Obote once there.

More news kept coming through as they headed for Bombay, indicating to the cockpit crew that there had been an army take-over. After take-off from the Indian airport, Captain Winston asked Obote to come to the cockpit and briefed him on the messages. Colleagues say that the Captain told them Obote took the news calmly, put his hand on the pilot's shoulder and asked whether he had known at Singapore. It was indicated that the news came through after they were airborne.

What Captain Winston did not know was that Obote learned an hour before boarding the plane that there had been a military

take-over. At 6.00 a.m. Singapore Time, about four hours after
fighting started, Ntende and another member of the President's
staff had come into his room weeping and told him Amin had
moved. Bataringaya, who had taken refuge in Kampala's Apollo
Hotel, was contacted by phone. He told Obote all was lost. Amin
had moved the heavy armour into Kampala and Brigadier
Hussein's loyal troops had been overpowered. Bataringaya said
he wanted to go back to the Parliament building and he did not
care if he was killed. Obote's only instruction was to order him
not to. Then before they drove in a Presidential motorcade to
the airport, Obote briefed the whole delegation on the situation
in Uganda and the report Ntende had brought.

At Bombay during refuelling Obote detached one of his aides
to go to New Delhi to report to Nyerere who was on a state
visit to India after the Singapore meeting. The Ugandan leader's
information at that point was that in the tradition of African
coups, Amin had seized only the capital. There were no reports
of support for the General from other outlying army units.
Obote's plan was to get to East Africa as quickly as possible,
assess the situation and draw up counter-plans.

Many of the Kenyans who had emerged in profitable leadership positions in the post-independence period after December
1963 had little reason to like the socialist policies of Obote or
Nyerere. In many senses they represented a threat to their own
positions, for students and the growing urban unemployed tended
to look to Tanzania and Uganda for ideological leadership.
There was a tendency also to fear what was seen as the Tanzanian-
Ugandan political alliance against Kenya in the East African
Community.

Thus on Monday, 25 January, there were clearly those in
Kenya who were far from unhappy about Obote's downfall.
The reaction in Tanzania was one of shock. At that time I was
Acting Editor of the Government newspaper and remember
vividly an argument that ensued at lunchtime on the day of the
coup over the main headline—'Attempted *Coup d Etat* in Uganda'
—which we were putting up in a special edition. The senior
Tanzanian editorial member argued that we should not use it.

There could not have been a *coup*. To him and many other Tanzanians a military take-over in East Africa was unbelievable. In the decade since the first of the former half-dozen British colonies and trusteeships in the area attained independence they had been spared the debilitating effects of army take-overs. The flurry of mutinies in Kenya, Tanzania and Uganda, in the wake of the civilian revolution of January 1964 in Zanzibar, had all been crushed and despite some of the limitations of *de facto* or *de jure* one-party rule, the civilians of East Africa realised that military dictatorships offered even less democracy.

When Obote flew into Nairobi's Embakasi Airport at 7.00 p.m. that night it was already obvious from the lack of traditional fanfare that he was viewed as a fallen Head of State. Vice-President Daniel Arap Moi and Foreign Minister Njoroge Mungai, were there to meet him and he was swiftly whisked away to the Pan Afrique Hotel. But at Nairobi's Airport Obote managed briefly to make contact with some of his old friends from the days when he was a trade union official in Kenya before Ugandan independence.

He told them to hire seven large fast saloon cars immediately and have them ready to drive back into Uganda that night. He intended to make a quick assessment of the situation at his hotel by telephoning contacts inside Uganda and then drive back to link up with loyal troops by one of two routes. The simplest was to head north-west from Nairobi through Nakuru and Kitale, crossing into Uganda to the east of Tororo. Ugandan army units were located at Mbale to the north and Jinja to the west, and Obote felt if these had not joined Amin he could use them to march to Kampala to dislodge the mutineers. The second—and most likely route—was again through Nakuru and Eldoret but heading northwards from there to link up with the 2nd Battalion stationed at Moroto. The advantage of taking this longer and more difficult route was that the unit at Moroto was fully self-contained, because of the remote nature of the barracks with adequate fuel stocks, anti-tank guns, other support weapons and plentiful small arms and ammunition.

Obote's plans to assess the situation by phone and then quietly

slip out of his hotel and head across the frontier were effectively
blocked by the Kenyans. Moi came to the hotel with him and
phoned President Kenyatta who was on holiday at the coast.
The Kenya leader said he would like Obote to stay. Then when
Obote's aides tried to get through to Uganda they were told the
phone lines were out of order. However when he sent some of
them quietly to town they found the phones working. Later,
when Moi returned, the phones in the hotel, which had also been
out of order, were working again and he once more called
Kenyatta and Obote told him he planned to go to Dar es Salaam
on the following day and make arrangements for his wife and
three sons who were inside Uganda. A little later the hotel
phones were again officially out of order.

The Kenyans had thrown a huge security cordon around the
hotel making it impossible for Obote to slip out when a call from
Tanzania's Second Vice-President, Rashidi Kawawa, offered a
less inhibited base from which to plan the next move. Kawawa
had called an emergency Cabinet meeting in Dar es Salaam and
from the State House phoned Obote at his hotel to tell him that
Nyerere was flying home immediately and that if he came to
Tanzania he would be given whatever assistance he needed.

The reception the Ugandan was given at Dar es Salaam
Airport was in marked contrast to that of a day earlier in Nairobi.
Nyerere had sent two of his Ministers from India to join Obote
in Nairobi and on the one hour flight to the Tanzanian capital
he chatted casually with the crew of the chartered EAA Super
VC10 about a new type of aircraft that was due to go into service.
The Ugandan Presidential emblem was broken at the masthead
as Kawawa embraced Obote. Then with his official flag on the
wing of the black State Rolls-Royce he was driven through
streets lined with thousands of cheering people to Dar es Salaam's
State House, residence of the last British Governor and now
Nyerere's offices.

Nyerere arrived back in Dar es Salaam a day after Obote and
was greeted by the most amazing emotional demonstration since
independence a decade earlier. Tens of thousands of people met
him at the airport and lined the route through the city waving

banners reading: 'Give us the arms to fight.' Immediately he issued a statement saying Tanzania would continue to recognise Obote as Uganda's legal President: 'We do not recognise the authority of those who have killed their fellow citizens in an attempt to overthrow the government of a sister republic.' Tanzania, he said, was not contemplating invading Uganda, as Amin claimed, although there is reason to believe that this may not have been entirely true.

Now the Tanzanian leader, noted as one of Africa's most astute political manoeuvrers, swung into action. Diplomatic initiatives began in the region to block recognition of the Ugandan military regime. Five days after the *coup* Nyerere told a huge rally in Dar es Salaam: 'How can I sit at the same table with a killer? Jomo [Kenyatta] is speaking for the people who elected him. I am speaking for you. Whom will Amin be representing? I cannot sit with murderers.'

For Nyerere the Ugandan military take-over was a traumatic experience. He had always abhorred the increasing African tendency towards 'elections' through the barrel of a gun rather than the ballot box, especially when progressive African leaders were the victims. But in Obote's case there was a further factor. Kenya, Tanzania and Uganda were linked in the East African Community, an economic grouping comprising a common market and common services which tentatively began in 1902 under British rule between Tanganyika, Kenya and Uganda. The supreme body of the Community was the Authority consisting of the three Presidents, who, in theory at least, met quarterly, and resolved difficulties which inevitably arose within the group. In their countries they enjoyed the image of the 'Fathers of the nation'. They had led their countries to independence and, despite stark differences in approach thereafter, a close bond existed. For one of them to fall to a military *coup* affected the others emotionally, and, perhaps more important, it underlined the frailty of their own positions. Altogether the Ugandan *coup* was just too near to home.

Obote set out on a series of visits to countries in the region with two major purposes in mind. In the first place he wanted to persuade members of the sixteen-nation East and Central African 'Good Neighbours' group to deny Amin recognition, and secondly he was canvassing to see what support, both moral and material, he could get. At Kenyatta's Mombasa beach-house, accompanied by Kawawa, he saw the Kenya President. Kenya's Foreign Minister, Njoroge Mungai, was to tell Parliament in Nairobi a month later that Kenya would not recognise Amin until she was satisfied the people of Uganda accepted him and that anyway Kenya recognised countries and not regimes. That was one outcome of the Mombasa meeting. The other was that Kenyatta promised Obote anything he needed, and this was taken to mean material support if requested, but Kenyatta stressed there must be a quicker solution.

The fallen Ugandan leader flew next to Zambia to see President Kenneth Kaunda. Here again there was a strong emotional tie, for Kaunda, Nyerere and Obote were members of what was known as the 'Mulungushi Club'—an affiliation of the ruling parties of the three countries. There was little need even to ask Kaunda for support. Obote went on to see Ethiopia's Emperor Haille Selassie. Future historians will have great difficulty in putting the Emperor's role in perspective in reviewing the first decade of independent Africa. He is a total enigma, black Africa's only monarch and the head of a virtually medieval feudal country. The Emperor promised Obote he would not recognise Amin.

Obote's third trip was the most difficult superficially, for he was seeking to recruit the support of two African leaders who were themselves soldiers and who, like Amin, had seized power through the gun. That he received this support from Somalia's General Siad Barre and Sudan's General Jaafar Nimeri has been much misinterpreted for the point about this is that both, like Obote, and unlike Amin, were in the progressive African bloc. Barre, in a statement, prophetically warned that the *coup* could lead to increased difficulties in Eastern Africa, urged other African leaders to take a strong position against Amin and added: 'The Somali Democratic Republic unreservedly declares its moral and material support for Dr. Milton Obote and his government and recognises him as the legitimate President of the Republic of Uganda.' The Sudan adopted a similar position although less publicly.

Well-informed sources in Dar es Salaam at that time told me that Nyerere was unhappy about the vigorousness of the Somali statement. Then it seemed inexplicable, yet now on reflection it is probable that Barre's public announcement of material support for Obote proved embarrassing to the plans which it is believed were being drawn up in Dar es Salaam. This cannot now be proved, but it is believed that on 4 February originally and then on 6 February a joint attack on Uganda was being planned by Somalia and Tanzania, as well as possibly by others in the area, to put down what was regarded as a mutiny by sections of the army led by Amin. As mentioned earlier, Obote had gone to Singapore to support the African case against British arms sales to South Africa. One of Amin's earliest speeches made clear he would not leave the Commonwealth over the question, which in his view was an internal matter for Britain. The plan is believed to have been a simultaneous attack by Tanzanian troops and 1,500 Somali troops along the southern Uganda border with Tanzania. Some Obote supporters protest that from the beginning they never wanted troops from other states to reverse the *coup*; they only wanted arms. But Obote at this point had no organised force and the loyalists who supported him were generally widely scattered. Nyerere is said in the final analysis to have withheld landing permission for the Somali troops, and Chinese Premier, Chou-en-Lai, may have indirectly influenced events. After Nyerere's 'I will never sit with a murderer' speech, at the beginning of February, the Chinese leader sent an urgent message through his Ambassador in Dar es Salaam making two points to Nyerere. He drew his attention to the principle of non-interference in the internal affairs of other countries, which is theoretically accepted by all nations. Secondly he warned that if African countries intervened to unseat Amin, whom the British initially preferred to Obote, they were creating the risk that British troops stationed in Kenya and elsewhere might be put in to support the Ugandan soldier against them.

Chinese sources confirm that such a message was delivered, which tends to give credibility to the whole story, but what influence it had on the outcome is problematic. Nyerere is very much his own man, yet in the emotional furore which followed the Ugandan *coup*, Chou-en-Lai's note may well have struck a chord. Certainly, if such an attack had occurred at that time, it would have been a bad decision, for Nyerere would in some quarters, including Uganda, have been judged to be as guilty as Amin of trying to rig the ballot. When eighteen months later the Tanzanian sponsored an attack by Obote supporters, both the left and the right were prepared to accept on Amin's record the need to remove him. But in February 1971 the international mood was very different and Britain's recognition of Amin on 4 February could have seriously affected plans.

Malawi's President, Dr. Kamuzu Banda, who had diplomatic links with South Africa, and Ghana's Prime Minister, Dr. Kofi Busia, who advocated a dialogue between the independent black states and minority white southern African governments, both followed quickly. At this point it seemed that Amin would firmly align himself with these leaders. First he announced he would be happy to go to South Africa and Rhodesia, which led to open condemnation by students at Kampala's Makerere University. Then he congratulated Banda publicly on visiting South Africa and Portugal's East African colony of Mozambique while the rest of Africa was condemning the Malawi leader. Then Amin cut off Ugandan contributions to the Organisation of African Unity special fund in support of the guerrillas fighting in southern Africa. A year later he was talking of plans to liberate white-ruled southern Africa and offering Ugandan troops, and two years later he was demanding Malawi's expulsion from the non-aligned group of nations because of Banda's links with southern Africa.

While the ripples of the Nyerere–Obote initiative to block recognition of Amin were widening, the General's situation inside Uganda was far from consolidated. The usual bevy of 'instant experts' jetted in to keep the Europeans informed. In Kampala they found massive rejoicing. That was predictable enough in Baganda country. But elsewhere the story was different. Killings had already begun in Acholi and Lango. And Baganda jubilation soon subsided when they found that Amin, despite allowing the Kabaka's body back for burial, had no intention of restoring the monarchy which he had been the blunt instrument in destroying. But for the journalists Amin was readily available at his home, a local hotel swimming pool, or taking telephone calls from newspapers in London. He was none too bright but he was available, which Obote had been only to a handful. In this mood the growing contradictions passed unnoticed. Amin had said his would only be a caretaker administration, but within four weeks he had declared himself President for five years and promoted himself to General. The first reason given for the *coup* had been detention without trial by Obote, and Amin released fifty-five people. But in early March he reintroduced detention and by late March 1,000 people were being held. The army was given the power of search and detention and a sentence of seven years' imprisonment introduced for people who gathered in groups of more than three.

That the *coup* could have been overturned within the first week is quite possible. The 2nd Infantry Brigade under the command of Colonel Okello in the south and the 2nd Battalion of Moroto on the north-east frontier with Kenya remained loyal. But they were gripped with the ineptitude and indecision which characterised moves to check the *coup* once it had been discovered. A decisive move by Obote at this point could well have rallied his scattered and confused supporters. Yet for vastly different reasons both Kenya and Tanzania failed to act as the springboard for the counter-offensive.

The story of the 2nd Infantry Brigade as related to me by Colonel Okello is, in the critical hours and days after the initial uprising, a tragic tale of the failure of a leader to lead. Okello had left Kampala at 9.15 p.m. on the Sunday evening after being briefed by Brigadier Hussein on Amin's plot. The Colonel was ordered to put his unit on standby and told that Amin was to be arrested that night by a Malire platoon. Okello was to send one company immediately to Kampala and the commander of the

1st Infantry Brigade, Colonel Arach, was ordered to send another. Both were to report to a hill at Buya in Kampala where they would be briefed.

Okello reached his headquarters at Masaka at 10.45 p.m. and called an officers' conference at 11.30 p.m. to brief them. An officer was detailed to remain by the phone throughout the night and Senior Sergeant-Major Gabriel to man the wireless and keep it open. The 3rd Battalion at Mubende and the 4th Battalion at Mbarara were both put on alert and a company of the 4th Battalion detached on guard duty at the ordnance depot at Magamaga near Jinja were ordered to Kampala.

Shortly after midnight at his home Okello received a call from the quartermaster of Malire Mechanised Battalion, Lieutenant Okot. He said his commanding officer and his adjutant had both been arrested by troops and severely beaten up. The quarter-master had gone to see the air force commander, Lieutenant-Colonel Juma Musa, to ask for help but this had been refused. About ten days earlier the Malire commander, Lieutenant-Colonel Akwango, at a senior officers' meeting in Kampala had complained about certain officers spending the night in his barracks among the other ranks without authorisation. His complaint followed Amin's arrival at the unit one night bare-footed, wearing running shorts and a singlet and staying over-night with the paratroop unit known as 'Amin's Suicide Squad'. Akwango had been authorised to bar officers not stationed there from staying overnight in his unit and had communicated this to the troops. One of Amin's Nubian supporters, Sergeant-Major Musa, had challenged him saying: 'You don't want Amin to come here . . . that is why you are telling us this. But he is the Major-General.' The Sergeant-Major was on leave in Kampala on the night of the *coup* but he was one of the leaders of the group estimated to number 500 which attacked Malire around 9.00 p.m. People at the barracks say that many of them were Anyanya guerrillas or Nubians. About two hours earlier Akwango had completed a briefing of officers and men on instructions from Brigadier Hussein. The Brigadier's orders had been explicit. They were: (1) that Akwango should personally select a platoon of trusted men, command it himself and arrest Amin at dawn on Monday; (2) to ensure that all the armouries were guarded, the officers and men were briefed to remain calm and that he held the keys to the armoury and starting devices for the armoured vehicles.

When the Anyanya and Nubians stormed Malire they went first to Akwango's office and then to the officer's mess hunting for him. They found him in the canteen briefing the platoon which was to arrest Amin and Musa immediately challenged him again about the order forbidding unauthorised personnel from remaining in the barracks overnight. Sergeant-Major Musa was promoted to lieutenant-colonel immediately after the *coup* and it is said that the attacking force would be promoted to the ranks of the individuals they killed. Akwango was badly beaten and taken to hospital but was later dragged from his hospital bed and murdered. A further noteworthy point about the Malire unit at this time is that records show that between September 1970 and the *coup*, Amin had transferred twenty-two officers of either Nubian origin or from his own West Nile area to Malire. On the day of the *coup*, of the Unit's forty-three officers, the number who were Nubian, Kakwa or Lugbara was thirty-two against five Acholi, three Langi, two Baganda and one Karamojong.

Despite the Malire setback, Okello was still in a position to reverse events. In the 2nd Infantry Brigade he had 2,000 men under his command and they did not come out in favour of the *coup*. About 10.30 a.m. the next day Okello sent a section of seven men a few miles up the road towards Kampala to see what was happening. Apparently they went little more than two miles from Masaka and found Baganda celebrating. The company ordered to move from Magamaga to Kampala arrived at their rendezvous point after the *coup* started and there was no one there to give them any orders. Okello called up a forty-two man platoon from Mubende and sent them towards Kampala with orders, if they met any Amin troops, to send a message back and hold the road. Mbarara was ordered to send a full company to guard the Brigade headquarters at Masaka but the commander said he did not have enough transport and neither he nor Okello appear to have thought the situation urgent enough to commandeer private buses or trucks. The platoon sent towards Kampala met Amin troops for the first time in an armoured personnel carrier on a roundabout five miles from Kampala. The platoon commander, Lieutenant Okema Lajongo, was ordered back by the crew of the APC and he withdrew eight miles and radioed for instructions. Okello told him to withdraw a further eighteen miles to Mutiana and set up an ambush position on the road.

On Wednesday the commander of Mubende objected to his personal jeep being taken away for so long with the platoon and they were recalled to Masaka and sent back to their unit. On Friday Amin ordered Okello to report to Kampala, but having been warned he would be killed if he went, Okello remained at Masaka. Then on Sunday, with 2,000 loyal troops still under his command and fighting going on elsewhere in the country, Okello and an official driver climbed into his private grey Mercedes car and drove across the frontier at Mutukula into Tanzania. Not a finger had been lifted to resist the *coup*. Brigadier Hussein's instructions to him on the previous Sunday had been to await further orders. And despite the fact the Brigadier was initially missing and then murdered when he was captured, this is exactly what Colonel Okello did all that week.

Amin and his supporters from Malire had seized the capital, and as in all African *coups* that was critical. In the north he faced some difficulties, however. Fighting and killing continued around Gulu for some days. But the most important potential seat of resistance was the 2nd Battalion at Moroto. The danger here for Amin was that as long as they held out against him, and the country was therefore not 'pacified' and supporting him, Obote could justifiably request troops from neighbouring countries to put down a 'mutiny' in his army. The approach to the newly constructed barracks at Moroto was through difficult terrain and the unit with its anti-tank weapons could easily hold out indefinitely against the Malire armour. About a week after the *coup*, Amin rang Moroto and spoke to a fellow Nubian,

Captain Ozo. The conversation was tape recorded and the tape later smuggled out of Uganda to Tanzania. Amin appealed to Ozo—promoted after the *coup* to lieutenant-colonel—to persuade fellow Nubians and West Nile troops at Moroto to turn on the other defenders, particularly the Acholi and Langi, whom he said Obote was using to maintain increasingly tribally orientated rule. As resistance at Moroto ended three days later and Ozo was promoted two ranks it is presumed he responded to Amin's appeal.

Meanwhile Nyerere's and Obote's joint diplomatic offensive was having considerable success in Africa. It was unprecedented to try to mobilise African opinion to continue to recognise a fallen leader in this way, but only Ghana and Malawi recognised Amin in the first month. Britain's attitude was regarded as decisive and Nyerere called in the High Commissioner, Horace Phillips, to ascertain Whitehall's thinking on 4 February. Britain, with 50,000 holders of United Kingdom passports and other interests in Uganda, would have to deal with Amin, the High Commissioner said. That was understood, but it fell short of recognition. Amin meanwhile, in addition to saying it was up to Britain and no one else if she sold arms to South Africa, had said he would denationalise all British firms in which Obote had said the government intended to acquire a controlling interest. It is not hard to imagine the reaction of the British Prime Minister, Edward Heath and his colleagues, to these friendly overtures after their bruising confrontation with Kaunda, Nyerere and Obote.

The mood of the British press also was violently hostile towards Obote and pro-Amin, who was from the outset cast as a model soldier and a jolly, gentle giant.

'One good reason that might be advanced for holding Commonwealth conferences more often is that the number of undesirable rulers overthrown as a result of their temporary absence, as has now happened to Dr. Obote of Uganda, would thereby be increased.' (*Daily Telegraph*, 26 January 1971.)

'I cannot say I learnt of the overthrow of Dr. Milton Obote of Uganda with any great regret: if a choice is to be made

between quiet military men and noisy civil dictators then I
prefer, in Africa at least, the military.' (*Spectator*, 30 January
1971.)

'So far as Britain is concerned, Amin will undoubtedly be
easier to deal with than the abrasive Obote.' (*New Statesman*,
29 January 1971.)

These three quotations give a sample of reactions from three
sectors of the British press of varying political hues. The *Telegraph*
was to become the crusading paper of Fleet Street in late 1972
over the massacres by Amin's supporters which had begun when
the above comment appeared. If Obote was noisy, as the *Spectator*
thought, then Amin strode into the international political arena
with all the accompanying thunder of Thor. And certainly he
was not to prove easier to deal with for Britain, as the *New
Statesman* asserted, when eighteen months later he summarily
expelled 40,000 Asians holding British passports and seized all
British firms.

Phillips went back to see Nyerere again late on 4 February to
tell him he had just received a message from London that Whitehall had decided to recognise Amin. It was a stormy meeting.
Phillips said that the High Commissioner in Kampala, Ronald
Slater, had been invited to attend a ceremony there on the following day when Amin's new Council of Ministers would be
sworn in. It had been decided he must attend and Whitehall
argued as this was tantamount to recognition it would be
hypocritical to pretend otherwise. The belief in Dar es Salaam
was that recognition was a calculated move by Heath to undermine Nyerere's diplomatic campaign in Africa and rally support
for Amin. The next morning both the official government and
party press in Dar es Salaam carried the same editorial written
by one of his aides and approved by the President, saying: 'By
its hasty recognition of Amin the British government has tried
to replace an independent African government by a British
stooge; a government which always says "yes Sir".'

The United States adopted the position that Nyerere sought
and a statement released by their Embassy in Dar es Salaam read:
'The United States believes that initial acceptance and recognition

of the Amin regime to be an African matter and does not anticipate any formal steps towards the regime in advance of action by African states.' The American Ambassador, and a number of others whose countries insisted they did not recognise Amin, attended the swearing-in ceremony in Kampala, without, as Britain had done, finding it necessary to announce recognition, while the Chinese Chargé d'affaires was the only head of mission to boycott it.

Amin's unpredictable behaviour was already becoming apparent in these first few days, although the euphoria in Britain which greeted Obote's downfall led the press and politicians alike to ignore it. The soldiers, in an eighteen-point justification of seizing power, gave as one of their reasons the fact that there had been no elections for eight years—although both Presidential and Parliamentary Elections were scheduled before 15 April. Amin on the day of the *coup* promised a 'free and fair' General Election soon. But three weeks later he suspended all political activity in the country and said there would be no elections for at least five years.

The major success in Nyerere's campaign to bar recognition to Amin came in the Ethiopian capital, Addis Ababa, on 20 February. Kampala had been scheduled as the venue for the OAU summit in June and a conference hall costing several million pounds was being constructed when the *coup* occurred. The OAU's Ministerial Council, which meets traditionally in February for what is largely a budgetary session, faced an unusual problem as they gathered in Addis Ababa.

Amin had sent a thirty-man delegation headed by his Foreign Minister and brother-in-law, Wanume Kibedi, who had trained in London as a lawyer and who had been regarded by the Obote regime as a progressive. Obote had also informed the OAU Secretariat that he would be sending a delegation headed by his Foreign Minister, Sam Odaka, who had been with him in Singapore.

The progressive African bloc, with which Obote had been closely associated and who were the strongest force for the liberation of southern Africa, adopted a common strategy for the

Sixteenth Ministerial Council on the Uganda question. Their maximum target was to get Odaka seated as the legal representative of Uganda and Obote, but they realised this would not be easy. The minimum goal was to keep Kibedi out and thereby deny Amin OAU recognition.

The critical factor in favour of the progressive bloc was that one of their members, Somalia's Foreign Minister, Omar Arteh Ghalib, was to chair the session. As chairman he could allow or prevent discussion and had he, for instance, ruled that it was out of order to discuss the composition of a delegation from a sovereign state, the Amin opponents would have been in serious difficulty. But there was no question of that occurring, for Somalia was one of the two countries which had announced it still recognised Obote.

That Obote had been removed by a military *coup* was, under the OAU Charter, outside the purview of members. A third of the governments represented had come to power the same way, and as the OAU, unlike the United Nations, has no credentials committee, there is no forum to question this means of seizing power. Many delegations made it clear they still recognised Obote and that they would not sit in the same hall as Kibedi. They argued that fighting was continuing in Uganda, that the army therefore was divided and that Obote had sacrificed a great deal in the cause of African liberation by going to Singapore. These were the main arguments raised during the informal meeting of leaders of delegations in the normally allotted hour or so before the Emperor's formal opening of the meeting. The OAU Secretariat had refused to give either delegation accreditation pending a decision by the Ministers and finally it was unanimously decided to proceed with the opening ceremony without either Ugandan delegation.

Immediately after the opening discussions resumed in closed session in Africa Hall. The opponents of Amin had scored a clear strategic victory by keeping Kibedi out of the opening, which now made it doubly difficult for his supporters to have him admitted. The supporters argued that it had been normal OAU practice to accept representatives of regimes who came to power through army take-overs and it was pointed out that Libya's Colonel Qadhafi had overthrown King Idris in the middle of a session and one team had gracefully withdrawn and another taken its place. The pro-Obote group were basically playing for time, with the situation inside Uganda confused, in the hope Obote would be able to stage a comeback. But so violently divided was the Ministerial Council on the issue that they could not proceed with the agenda, and finally the meeting was acrimoniously adjourned until June when the venue for the OAU summit, to Amin's anger, was shifted from Kampala to Addis Ababa.

With resistance fragmented and disorganised inside Uganda, the slaughter of senior officers mainly from Acholi, Langi and Iteso under way, and the possibility of intervention by an African neighbour apparently past, an alternative plan to eject Amin began to formulate in Dar es Salaam.

In late February or early March a training camp was established for Obote supporters at Kingolwira to the east of the town of Morogoro 122 miles inland from Dar es Salaam. At the time of the *coup* there were 114 Ugandan students at Dar es Salaam University and of these about eighty were members of the branch there of Obote's ruling Uganda Peoples Congress Party. Many of the students supported the idea of joining the training camp, but on 22 March only five of them—two from Lango and three from Eastern Region—went to Kingolwira. They travelled with seventeen other people who had fled from Uganda to join the Obote forces and found fourteen people at the camp when they arrived.

Training began in late March and after a week the Obote supporters were issued a few automatic rifles used by warders at a nearby prison. More and more people arrived at the camp and by the time they had completed basic infantry training in late June there were three platoons with thirty-two men in each. Two Ugandan Captains, Oyile and Okot, did most of the training, assisted by a Tanzanian sergeant and a corporal on support weapons. Late in June 200 new automatic rifles were issued as well as uniforms consisting of Tanzanian army shirts and National Service trousers. Support weapons arrived next. First there were ten Chinese-made 75 mm recoilless rifles and then a fortnight later a consignment of 106 mm recoilless rifles. The group trained also on 82 mm mortars and 18 mm medium machine-guns.

At Kingolwira the training was very rigorous, and one man from Bugisu died from over exertion during this period. Ideological difficulties arose within the group, with a UPC member from Eastern Region named Omongin advocating political education and guerrilla warfare instead of the conventional campaign they were being prepared for. Odaka accompanied by a young Ugandan militant, Yoweri Museveni, was sent to try to resolve the dispute but Omongin finally collected his Mao books and disappeared with a dozen supporters from his Teso tribe.

By 3 August the group at Kingolwira had increased to 294. It was a tough, well-trained unit, able to handle an array both of small arms and support weapons, that moved out secretly by truck and Land-Rover on the night of 3 August to Morogoro Station. A special train was waiting, and as they headed northwest across Tanzania they were feverishly excited. They had been told they were going in. Their arms, taken off them at Kingolwira, would be waiting at the border where they were heading via Mwanza and Tabora. They arrived at a tiny wayside station called Igalula, fourteen miles before Tabora at 4.00 a.m. on 5 August and there a convoy of trucks was waiting. They were driven to a disused National Service camp at Kigwa. The camp was rather dilapidated and they were the first arrivals, but they set about rebuilding the tumbledown houses and constructing others with vigour still fired by the expectation of going home.

But it was to be thirteen months before they moved across the frontier. In the interim period they handled no weapons and did precious little training. The enthusiastic and fit group which had arrived at Kigwa camp on 5 August 1971 were mentally and physically ill-equipped to go into action on 17 September 1972.

4   Amin's Reasons

On 19 December 1969, as Obote walked out of the conference of his ruling Uganda People's Congress after introducing his 'move to the left' policy, a gunman rushed out of the crowd. He fired a single shot which set in train a sequence of events leading directly to the Ugandan *coup d'état* and the slaughter of the past three years.

Obote was taken to Mulago Hospital. While rumours spread that he was dead, it was found he was not seriously injured. The bullet had entered his right cheek, smashed through his bottom teeth and gone out of the other side. Fortunately, a hand-grenade, which landed at Obote's feet, thrown by another of the group of would-be assassins, had failed to explode. But Obote was unable to speak and as he sat on a hospital bed with people crowding around him in the corridor, he indicated he wanted a pen and paper. A pen was found and Oyite Ojok handed the President his diary. Obote wrote: 'Have you told my wife, the General, Akena and the Inspector-General?'

None of them had been at the conference when he was shot, but his wife, Miria, the Inspector-General of Police, Oryema, and Head of the General Service Department, Akena Adoko, had all been summoned. Ojok, accompanied by Bernard Olila, a senior GSD officer and an army lieutenant, were sent to Amin's house in Kampala's Prince Charles Drive to brief the General. The house was surrounded by a high barbed-wire fence and the trio were stopped at the gate by sentries. Ojok said he had come to see Amin on urgent business and a sentry phoned the house. Ojok was told the General was in and would see him. They rang the bell for several minutes and knocked on the door but there was no reply. Mystified they returned to the gate where the sentry, who said he had spoken to Amin, could offer no explanation.

Ojok then telephoned the next most senior officer, Brigadier
Pierino Yere Okoya, the forty-five-year-old Commander of the
2nd Infantry Brigade of the Ugandan army who had his headquarters at the southern town of Masaka. The Brigadier was
known to be staying that night at Jinja preparing for an army
shooting contest on the following day which Obote was
scheduled to attend. Okoya was contacted soon after 11.00 p.m.,
told that Obote had been shot and Amin had disappeared. He
drove immediately to Kampala reaching the capital soon after
midnight. From headquarters he put the army throughout the
country on standby and ordered all commanding officers to
attend a briefing in Kampala at 6.00 a.m.

When the commanding officers gathered there was still
confusion as to whether the shooting of Obote was an isolated
act or the prelude to an attempted *coup d'état* which had gone
wrong. Amin was still missing and it was feared he had been
kidnapped or murdered, which lent support to the view that the
shooting had broader implications. But at about 10.00 a.m., as
officers were taking their coffee break in the mess at army
headquarters, the General strolled in. He had apparently gone to
Mulago Hospital around 6.00 a.m. where after receiving treatment for barbed-wire cuts on one hand and a leg, he had gone to
see Obote at around 8.00 a.m.

Some of the officers were inclined to treat their commander's
disappearance as a joke, and from then on some referred to him
by his father's name, Dada—'sister' in Swahili—which was a
clear reference to his manhood. He in turn suggested that he
thought that the group who had come to his house the previous
night were there to kill him. But as details of the circumstances
of his disappearance began to emerge, Brigadier Okoya and a
number of other senior officers were not prepared to dismiss it
lightly. It transpired that after the guards called to say Ojok and
two others were at the gate Amin had fled out of the back of the
house and cut himself climbing over the fence. He had then
stopped a passing Uganda television van and ordered the driver
to take him to Bamunanika about thirty miles from Kampala.
The two television employees in the van subsequently said that

Amin had told them he thought that young officers had seized power and he feared for the President's life. From Bamunanika he had telephoned senior NCOs telling them to send an armoured personnel carrier to fetch him and warning them not to take orders from their officers.

During the night while this was going on, an intriguing scene had taken place at the Uganda Club, the popular gathering place of politicians, civil servants and other prominent people. The Defence Minister, Onama, like Amin from West Nile, had expressed the view that Obote was dead. An Asian, Dr. Masser, said this was not true and said he had seen the President writing a note at the hospital. The Minister was unwilling to believe this and finally Dr. Masser was sent to the hospital to check. At the hospital he put on a white doctor's coat and was in time to see Obote, very much alive, being wheeled into the operating theatre. Onama had also ordered a hunt for the 'assassin' and is believed to have been responsible for a statement broadcast at about 1.00 a.m. by Radio Uganda on 20 December stating that at least one 'assassin' had been arrested. Why at this point both Onama and Amin were erroneously convinced Obote was dead is not clear, although later events offer an explanation.

Onama's third intriguing move during the night following the shooting came at an emergency Cabinet meeting. The Vice-President, John Babiiha, aged fifty-six, was known to react badly under pressure. He was unwell and had gone to bed, and Onama said that in the absence of both the President and Vice-President he would chair the meeting. This was challenged and a heated debate ensued which was only resolved after the constitution was consulted. The constitution laid down that in the absence of the President and Vice-President the chair should be taken at Cabinet meetings by a Minister designated in writing by the President. Nobody had this authority. The security committee of the Cabinet met with Bataringaya in the chair and Onama pressed for marshal law to be declared which, with both Obote and Babiiha incapacitated, would have left the Defence Minister in an extremely powerful position, but it was decided that only a state of emergency would be declared.

The Defence Minister had contacted Lieutenant-Colonel Juma Musa and told him to take command of the army in the absence of Amin. Musa was the most senior officer in Kampala, but it is noteworthy that Brigadier Okoya was an hour's drive away by road and it seems improbable that Onama was not aware of this. Okoya, called to Kampala by Ojok, ordered all troops back to barracks after he arrived in the capital, and by 4.00 a.m. the streets had been cleared of soldiers. Then Okoya, Ojok and Musa went to report to Onama. The Minister is said to have demanded to know why Okoya had come to Kampala 'without my knowledge' but he did rescind Musa's temporary appointment and put Okoya in charge.

Angry rumblings began among senior officers about Amin's disappearance, and finally on 17 January, Obote, who had been discharged from hospital, was forced to call a meeting of senior officers. Only commanding officers were supposed to attend but a number of Amin's friends such as Lieutenant Marella Dodi (now Lieutenant-Colonel in command of military police) and Lieutenant Avudria, then commandant of Gulu Air Base, were also present when Obote arrived.

At this meeting many people believe Okoya was unwittingly signing his death-warrant: bluntly he accused Amin of desertion and cowardice; he said that the General had disgraced the army by running away and had made it appear that the army was involved in the attempted assassination. Amin's behaviour, in his view, smacked of involvement by the General in the shooting. The Brigadier demanded that Amin explain why he had run away and in particular why he had ordered other ranks not to take orders from their officers. Officers who attended the meeting say that Amin denied that he had deserted but did admit an error of judgement. With the meeting becoming increasingly acrimonious Obote decided to adjourn it and ordered that when it resumed two hours later only commanding officers would attend.

In a letter after the *coup* in 1971 addressed to the then Chief Justice of Uganda, Sir Dermot Sheridan, Obote described what took place:

'The exchanges at one stage were extremely hot. The officers accused Amin and gave examples of his mismanagement of the armed forces. Some of the accusations were that Amin used not to follow the proper chain of command and a number of instances were cited where Amin sent messages to NCOs in various units to do things which only the commanding officers should order. That Amin used to promote privates and NCOs without the knowledge or recommendations of the commanding officers. That Amin effected transfers of NCOs and posted them to various units without the knowledge of commanding officers. That recruitment, a matter which was under an embargo due to lack of accommodation, was, nevertheless, being carried out by Amin and that persons so recruited were either from his own district and county or southern Sudanese. That Amin did not allow even senior officers to know what was going on or to visit the unit then stationed at Bamunanika, north of Kampala. That Amin never consulted senior officers as to which officer or NCO should go for further training overseas but made selections alone. That Amin bypassed officers of the rank of major or captain and appointed lieutenants to be in charge of units. Two examples were cited. There was Lieutenant Dodi in charge of a unit at Bamunanika and Lieutenant Avudria in charge of Gulu Base.

'On the matter of relations with the Sudan—the officers accused Amin of activities which were in direct opposition to the government policies of not giving assistance to the southern Sudanese rebels who are sometimes called Anyanya. It was alleged that from time to time Amin ordered officers in charge of units near the Sudan border to allow supplies which included weapons and food to go from Uganda to southern Sudanese rebels and that there were cases when medicines bought with the Uganda funds for the Uganda armed forces were diverted, on Amin's orders, to the southern Sudanese rebels. It was further alleged that Amin made many trips to visit the Sudanese rebels inside Sudan or to meet the Anyanya leaders in West Nile, and that the pilot who was always a foreigner participated together with Amin in various meetings held in West Nile or inside the Sudan between leaders of the Anyanya and Amin.

'Brigadier Okoya demanded an explanation as to why and in what circumstances Idi Amin ran away from his house on 19 December 1969 and hid himself for several hours while at the same time contacting only NCOs. Amin was not able to give any explanation. There were other accusations including one that in various meetings with the troops, Amin had told the troops to be careful of what the officers say and he named certain officers in those gatherings and told the troops to consider the named officers as persons who were likely to bring trouble. The Minister of Defence, Felix Onama, proposed that since the allegations were so grave and since some of them could be dealt with administratively, the meeting should not go into them on that day but that he be given the opportunity to meet senior officers in his office to sort out which of the allegations required the attention of the Defence Council or the Cabinet and the others which, he, as Minister of Defence, could deal with. The proposal was accepted but realising the grave nature of the allegations, I invited, at the close of the meeting, the commanding officers only, together with Onama and Amin, to meet with me at another place on the same day. That meeting took place about an hour later and Amin told the meeting that he had realised that some of the things he had done were wrong and further proposed that after the meeting with the Minister, he himself would hold a meeting with senior officers in order to straighten things out. The meeting ended and that was the last time I saw Brigadier Okoya alive.'

At the resumed meeting Amin had adopted an apologetic attitude. Okoya, he said, was his 'best friend', and had been since they served together in the King's African Rifles before Ugandan independence. He had made a grave mistake by running away at a time of crisis and proposed that he should personally meet commanding officers on the following day when they could air their grievances and make recommendations to be sent to the Minister of Defence. Amin chaired that meeting and some proposals, including one on promotions, which the officers argued were being held up, were drafted. A further meeting was arranged for 26 January 1970. But that meeting never took place. Just after 11.00 p.m. on 25 January at his home at Koro village a few miles from Gulu, Okoya and his thirty-year-old wife, Anna, were shot dead.

Okoya had been shot once, with the bullet entering the right-hand side of his chest, passing through both lungs and brushing the heart before coming out of his back. His wife, who was naked and taking a bath when she was killed, had been shot twice. A Chinese-made 7·62 mm assault rifle was lying unfired by Okoya's body. The murder weapon was probably of the same calibre on general issue in the Uganda army.

He and his wife, in an army Mercedes staff car with a driver, had travelled from his brigade headquarters at Masaka to Gulu on 23 January where he intended to pay his children's school fees. Before leaving Masaka a message had been sent to general headquarters, Uganda armed forces, notifying them of his movements. The day before his death another message had been sent to headquarters informing them of his intention to drive back early the next morning for the resumed meeting on Amin's disappearance. Intriguingly, although only a few days earlier Amin had declared that Okoya was his 'best friend', he did not attend the funeral despite having told Obote he would. Already rumours were circulating linking the General's name with the Brigadier's murder.

For months police inquiries met a blank wall. People living near by had heard the shots and had about that time seen a Mercedes, a Peugeot car and an army Land-Rover, registration number 66 BT 14, in the area. Detectives went from house to house and visited bars questioning people and offering a reward of almost £3,000 for information leading to the arrest of the killers. Rumour held that it was an internal army killing and Okoya's driver, Private Edward Ssenkaayi, and house servant who had been fetching beer when the murders occurred were closely questioned. The Private said in his statement they had been away longer than the journey to a nearby bar took because he had stopped quickly to have intercourse with a girl on the way back. Even so he did not think they had been away for more than fifteen minutes. Most of the neighbours said they had heard three shots followed immediately by an army Land-Rover driving away at high speed.

There the investigation remained for eight months. Then on 21 August came the first break in the case. Detective Assistant Superintendent Athanasius Kayondo, was interviewing a Ugandan called Bumali Ssekamanyi suspected of being a member of a gang of armed robbers who had held up a bank van on the road from Mubende to Kampala a few days earlier.

Amin was to claim after the *coup* that Obote and Akena Adoko had had Okoya murdered so that they could blame it on him. But that makes no sense at all in the light of the eight-month delay before the police inquiry began to make any progress. Nor does it explain Amin's desperate hunt for all the files on the Okoya murder immediately after the *coup* and the murders of almost every one of the investigating police officers and of many of Okoya's male relatives.

One of Obote's secretaries, who worked for Amin for some time after the *coup*, told me that about forty-eight hours after the General seized power a man named Ismail, a private, who was a State House driver in the 'close escort unit' came into her office and said he wanted, on orders from Amin, everything on the Okoya case. This included the complete police file as well as memorandum from Obote to the Director of CID, Mr. Hassan, and while he was away in late 1970 attending an Interpol conference in Tokyo, memorandum to his deputy, Mr. Festus Wauyo. All of these documents were locked in a cupboard and Ismail took the keys. Files from the office of the Attorney-General and from the police as well as Interior Ministry were also seized. A few days later Ismail was promoted to Captain.

What Amin did not realise was that, with the Okoya case due to go to court a few days after he staged the *coup*, a considerable number of copies of the file had been produced together with police pictures. As far as I know two have survived. One was smuggled out of Uganda for me and the other has been put in a place of safe keeping in the hope that the case can be resumed one day. The 400-page case file contains the statements of ninety-six people. They include five *kondos*—a Ugandan word for armed robbers—who admit taking part in the killing. They said they were briefed by Captain Smarts Guweddeko, a pilot then stationed at Entebbe, who, twenty-two days after the murder, was promoted to Commandant of Gulu Air Base. His rapid rise has continued ever since and today he is commander of the Ugandan air force with the rank of lieutenant-colonel.

Ssekamanyi's statement on 21 August brought the breakthrough in the eight-month investigation. In the case file Superintendent Kayondo in a statement says: 'He (Bumali) said that he had information to give me concerning the murder of Brigadier Okoya and the person who was responsible for it.'

The officer immediately called in Detective Senior Superintendent Wauyo who was in charge of the Okoya case. Bumali, and another prisoner, Twaka Katumba, also a suspected *kondo*, implicated a number of men in the Okoya murder, including one who was in prison facing a death sentence after being found guilty of murder. Then on 30 August a man named Siperito Kapalaga was arrested on suspicion of being involved in the Mubende robbery and murder. The Okoya case file shows that he named the alleged killer of the officer as Patrick Wambuzi who, he said, since the murder had adopted the title of 'Brigadier'. Acting on information from the first two prisoners, Wauyo had already put out an alert for Wambuzi and he received information that he was staying at the Ripon Falls Hotel at Jinja. A group of policemen led by Detective Superintendent Anthony Ochungi had in fact arrested Wambuzi at the hotel the day before Kapalaga's claim.

According to Ochungi's statement, Wambuzi apparently thought he was being arrested in connection with some other alleged offence. He told the detective that he wanted to discuss the matter with him in private. But when, according to Ochungi's statement, he asked Wambuzi about the Okoya murder in front of two other police officers, Wambuzi said: 'How did you know this also. I am now in big trouble.' Ochungi said that subsequently Wambuzi offered him shs 10,900 in cash to drop the inquiry.

On the following day, 31 August 1970, Silvesiteri Patrick Mukwaya, alias Wambuzi, aged twenty-eight and unemployed, after describing his arrival at Okoya's house, said in his statement: 'The Brigadier opened the door, got outside and stood on the verandah. He first turned and looked facing Kampala direction. Then he turned and faced Gulu. At this stage I jumped near him and shot him with a gun. He fell down after staggering.' A British forensic expert had in fact said eight months earlier that Okoya had been shot at a distance of probably not more than two inches.

Wambuzi told police officers in his statement that he had led the *kondo* group who killed Okoya. The others, he said, were Siperito Kapalaga, alias John Katabarwa, a nineteen-year-old Muganda taxi driver; Samwiri Kiyima Gombya, alias Sam Teen, a twenty-nine-year-old Muganda mechanic; Sebastiano Lukaaga, alias Teenager and Willy Lukaaga, a seventeen-year-old Muganda taxi driver; and John Mbuku, a twenty-seven-year-old Muganda taxi driver.

By piecing the story together from the statements it appears the plan began late in 1969, although there is some doubt as to whether it began before or after Obote was shot. A twenty-eight-year-old Muganda office supplies salesman, Moses Kasozi Njuki, a one-time police special constable, said in a statement he had met Captain Smarts Guweddeko in a bar in late November, although it seems possible that it was in fact December. The air force officer, Njuki said, asked him his tribe and said he wished to discuss a confidential matter. 'He told me that he had been assigned by the army Major-General [Amin was the only one] to carry out a plan and if that plan was successful it carried a lot of money and that the plan needed courageous men. He asked me whether I knew any courageous men who would carry out the plan. I promised that I would try to get some.'

For his efforts Njuki said he was promised a big post and he said he contacted Mbuku who went to meet Captain Guweddeko at Entebbe Airport with Wambuzi. On 29 August 1971, Njuki made his third statement in a fortnight. The theme and basic facts of his story were much as before but he added on this occasion that Captain Guweddeko had told him at one meeting: 'When something has the backing of the Major-General of the army, automatically it has the full backing of the President.'

All the men said in their statements that Guweddeko had told them that Amin wanted Okoya killed because Obote intended to replace him as head of the army with the Brigadier. The amount they said they were paid for the murder varied, ranging from shs 16,000 to shs 25,000 and the explanation for this may well be that Wambuzi held out on his fellow *kondos*. One of them said that in fact he received nothing for his part while Njuki complained he never received the big post he was promised.

Captain Guweddeko denied the whole story and meeting the five, but he was picked out at an identification parade at police headquarters on 28 September by Mbuku. Their statements spoke of meeting with other army personnel and at the time of the *coup* a number suspected of being involved were in detention. Accompanied by the *kondos*, police retraced their journey to Gulu and collected a number of items which were to be used in evidence including a petrol receipt.

Other details in the case file mention a white Peugeot 404 being stolen from a European woman in Kampala in the second half of January and of a number of *kondos* visiting a witchdoctor named Diro who gave them medicine to protect themselves and the car. Police later traced it when it was sold by a brother of one of the accused. Okoya's fateful final message to head-quarters notifying them of his intended return on 25 January for the meeting with Amin and other commanders was, police believed, the signal for the *kondos* to move. The *kondos* said they set out for Gulu on 25 January in the stolen Peugeot and an army Mercedes. Four of them later reconstructed the journey in considerable detail for police officers, showing where they had stopped for petrol and to change into army uniforms collected from the barracks at Gulu. At the Brigadier's house they said they were accompanied by two army lieutenants and they entered the compound in two groups, one through a break in the fence and the remainder by a small gate. Once inside they fanned out. The Brigadier's wife was shot outside in a tin bath. He was killed when he ran out on to the balcony. Wambuzi and others were photographed as they demonstrated to police officers where they had been when the shooting took place and where Okoya fell.

As soon as news of the murders became known rumours began to circulate linking Amin's name with them. It was well known both in army circles and outside that eight days earlier Okoya had accused him of being a coward and a deserter. When the break in the case came eight months later, Guweddeko, detained during October and November at the maximum security prison at Upper Luzira under the Emergency Regulations stuck to his denials. The thirty-four-year-old Muganda pilot insisted he only knew Gombya and Amin was never questioned. Secretaries who typed memoranda from Obote to Hassan and Wauyo said these made it clear that Obote could not and did not believe Amin was implicated.

Obote's secretaries who typed what were known as 'blue minutes' recall that he was very troubled at the allegation by the *kondos* implicating Amin. He could not understand why Amin would have used *kondos* and not commandos in the army he could depend upon. Amin set up a Board of Inquiry chaired by Brigadier Hussein which interviewed many witnesses. Hussein presented his open report to Amin and the Defence Minister, Onama, who gave a copy to Obote. But unbeknown to either Amin or Onama the Brigadier presented a second secret report to Obote after requesting a private interview.

'Hussein told me that in his view Brigadier Okoya had been murdered in order to advance the interest of a foreign country which wanted to have greater influence in the control and management of the Uganda armed forces,' Obote said later in a letter to the Chief Justice. The country referred to in the small typed memorandum he handed Obote that day was Israel.

'He accused Felix Onama and Idi Amin of being in the pay of the foreign country in question and of being responsible for the murder of Brigadier Okoya. Suleiman Hussein, who did not attend the meeting I had with senior military officers and Minister Onama in January 1970, said that the stand which Brigadier Okoya took at the meeting occasioned the murder. He said he himself was very worried for his life and that during the Board's inquiry he had noticed the same feeling among many officers. The substance of the memorandum was the same as what I was told verbally. I did not accept the accusation levelled by Brigadier Suleiman Hussein and I told him so.'

While it is true that there was no evidence against Amin at this point Obote knew enough about his personal background and the clash with Okoya to be a great deal more circumspect than he was. The break through in the case came while Amin was in Cairo and he returned secretly after telephoning from Egypt to tell a group of senior NCOs to draw arms on the pretext that they were going on border guard and to be waiting at the airport as a bodyguard to meet him. He slipped secretly back into the capital, and later that day, when Obote had found he had returned, denied all knowledge of Okoya's murder. Asked why he had returned secretly he said that his cable notifying his arrival had been delayed. It is true that a cable did arrive after Amin but it gave no details of his flight, expected time of arrival or even the day of return.

However, the police, pursuing their own separate inquiries, were becoming increasingly suspicious about Amin. They had discovered that the night before the murder he had moved a 'safe' Nubian unit to Gulu on guard duty, cancelling the movement of the company originally ordered to go. They regarded as unusual the interest he was taking in finding how far their inquiries had gone. And then after Guweddeko was detained Amin pressed for his wife to be allowed to visit him. Her first meeting was in private but during the second, lasting little more than a minute, police overheard her say: 'Do not implicate anyone.' She was immediately arrested but refused to say who had given her the instruction.

But still there was no evidence at all against Amin other than the word of five men who admitted being murderers. The final statement on the Okoya case file was made on 12 January by Hassan. Thirteen days later the *coup* took place. A week after that the trial should have begun.

In Dar es Salaam at a press conference in the State House, Obote, flanked by Ministers of his deposed government, accused Amin of seizing power to cover up a number of crimes ranging from 'murder to corruption'.

'Exactly a year ago—that is on 25 January last year—a senior army officer, indeed the Deputy Commander of the Ugandan armed forces, was murdered together with his wife at night. The police later found out that he was murdered by persons we call in Uganda *kondos* and in the statements which these people made to the police, they claimed or alleged they had murdered that Brigadier because Major-General Idi Amin told them to do so. The case was due to go to the court next week . . .'

What had happened in Uganda was an attempt to cover up these murders, Obote charged.

Amin responded by ordering an inquest into the Okoyas' murders instead of the planned trial. He appointed a judge, Mr. Justice Arthur Dickson, to hear it, and the inquest opened at Gulu on 23 February. What Amin wanted to establish was that the statements of the *kondos* had been made as a result of torture and a string of witnesses were trotted out to say that they had heard screams of agony or had actually seen the accused being tortured at the offices of Hassan and Wauyo in Parliament building.

So far as the inquest was concerned, the unusual course was taken of appointing a judge to head the inquest when it would normally have been a magistrate. Then a British barrister, Mr. Percy Bloomfield, was briefed to examine the witnesses. How much value can be put on the evidence of witnesses at the inquest given the reign of terror which had already started in Uganda is problematic. The charges of police brutality and procedural malpractice may well contain some truth. That sort of police behaviour is not peculiar to Uganda. Two witnesses at the inquest I have interviewed allege they were prevented from bringing out all the relevant details of what they knew. Some who said they had made statements under duress were in detention and able to see the daily killings that were going on. Of senior African police officers involved, only Wauyo stuck to his guns, denying impropriety. And he, like the CID chief, Hassan, was murdered a few months later at Mutukula Prison, having been in detention virtually since the *coup*.

Bloomfield made much of the fact that soon after the case was transferred to Wauyo there was a major break through. All lines of inquiry were utterly dead and Bloomfield said he found it incredible that such a sudden break through had been achieved after months of stagnation. Wauyo countered that this had occurred because one of a group of men arrested for the Mubende robbery had confessed involvement in the Okoya murder and led police officers to the other members of the gang.

The British barrister's incredulity apparently had limitations for he indicated no surprise at the sudden appearance of a letter purported to be written by Obote ordering Adoko to implicate Amin in the Okoya murder. At Gulu on 21 March, Amin security forces had without warning seized a letter from Obote giving these instructions. Although this document was of vital importance to the inquest on 8 April, Mr. Bloomfield requested an adjournment until 14 April when he hoped to be able to produce it in court. Surprisingly, he apparently did not find it incredible that it was to be twenty-four days from the time news of the document first broke and forty-three days since it was 'found' before he was able to produce it to an inquest set up by Amin. Bloomfield had observed in reference to the break through in the case in the previous year: 'Suddenly the wall of silence crumbled away and over its ruins there rushed a flood of evidence which prima facie indicated a conspiracy by a high-ranking army officer and others to liquidate Brigadier Okoya.'

The document written in Luo and purported to be from
Obote to Adoko read:

'The Mzee plan which you have been working on must now
be treated with utmost urgency. Shortly you and I will be
away from the country on conferences and we must make
sure that matters are put on a proper sound basis. Olila, who
will be acting in your place, must himself take charge of
the boys and our goods in Kioga when you are away.

'You assured me that the training has been proceeding
well, but before I send any of the boys to Kenya I have to be
sure that they are in topmost condition. You have to take
absolute care and details of the central plan have to be con-
fined to the five people you know already. Our friends
however will be kept fully informed. It is a matter of life and
death.

'Although we cannot send any big group now it would be
a good idea to dispatch some of our boys to Kenya as advance
guard. They can travel by road through Busia, but the idea
is to maintain our contacts in K. Kikuyu as you know are
ruled out. Luos can work with us easily and Kisumu is
therefore an important area. Once there is confusion in K
we shall be all right. Mzee is a complete nuisance.

'Since we have now shelved plans to arrest Amin we must
do something quickly before things get out of hand. The
army is, as we assessed, at least 95 per cent loyal and opposed
to Amin but Amin's contacts with K at official level is
disturbing. You know he made similar contacts with Egypt
when he was there in December.

'With the recent promotions all key positions are now
under control, and after your Okoya trick the Acholis are
now after him. But I doubt whether they will act in time.
Other plans must therefore work before it is too late.
Ogwal, C.O. Artillery, Masindi, and Obote, C.O. Air
Force, Gulu, are charged with special recruitment. Oyite,
Ojok and Arach have to take personal charge of the goods.
I am trusting you completely on this. Brief Olila fully on the

direction of the funds. Okello Ojok has told me that he needs more funds on his job and I told him I could contact you on this question.

'Immediate report on latest position required. Send messages by hand of bearer who must proceed here direct. Time is 1.45 p.m.

'Copies of this message go only to Olila and Oyite Ojok.

Milton

The letter had been found by Lieutenant Isaac Maliyamungu, who told the inquest it was with a quantity of arms in one of two trucks abandoned by their drivers in the Kioga area. There are many reasons for being quite certain it is a forgery. In the first place a British correspondent inexplicably referred to it briefly in a broadcast from Kampala in the BBC African Service programme, 'Focus on Africa', the day before Lieutenant Maliyamungu said he found it on 2 March. Amin's announcement of the document detailing a plot by Obote to overthrow President Kenyatta in neighbouring Kenya came immediately after the Kenyan Foreign Minister, Dr. Mungai, had announced his country would not recognise Amin until they were sure the people of Uganda accepted him.

The objective in trying to prove Obote was plotting against Kenya was obviously to try to stop support for the deposed President when not a single country in the region was willing to recognise Amin. Henry Kyemba, Obote's Private Secretary for eight years, who the delegation in Singapore suspect had passed information back to Kampala that the planned assassination of Obote and *coup d'état* had been discovered, identified the signature 'Milton' as being Obote's. Kyemba, after the *coup* had been promoted by Amin to Permanent Secretary in the Office of the President and Secretary to the Cabinet, and several people who knew his writing, said that it was remarkably like Obote's.

Nearly a month later Bloomfield called a handwriting expert who was given five specimen signatures of Milton Obote. The signature on the document Maliyamungu had produced and those known to be written by Obote showed 'basic dissimilarities' from the specimen signatures in letter proportions, writing skills and habits, the expert said. Because of these 'observable dissimilarities' he could not say that the signature on the document and the specimens had been written by the same person. Bloomfield dropped the matter.

Each of the *kondos* was brought to the inquest and claimed their statements had been taken after torture, that they did not know the contents when they signed and they knew nothing about the Okoya murder. And Mr. Justice Dickson ended the matter finding, as everyone knew, that Okoya and his wife had been murdered by a person or persons unknown. But he did reject as inadmissible the statements of the alleged *kondos* which had been mentioned in the inquest and published in the press as having been made after improper pressure or manufactured. The men who were to have faced trial went free, including one already convicted of another murder, and the senior policemen who investigated the case were murdered in detention.

Whether or not Amin was involved in the Okoya murder as the statements claimed will probably now never be proved. But there is no doubt that the shooting of Obote, Okoya's accusations and then his death set in motion the principal strand leading to the *coup*. However there are some other important subsidiary reasons.

Corruption within the Ministry of Defence was a further critical factor. At his press conference in Dar es Salaam three days after the *coup*, Obote had this to say:

'There was a person very close to Major-General Amin as the Commander of the [Jinja] depot; he ordered or is alleged to have ordered materials worth shs 40,000,000 (at that time about £2,500,000). There is no document, no copies of the invoices, no copies of any delivery note. On the same day I left for Singapore, I asked General Amin, on my return, to give me a written report on how the shs 40,000,000 was to be spent. I have no doubts at all that what is now developing in Uganda is another attempt to hide the loss of shs 40,000,000 and an attempt to prevent me getting back to the country and punish the culprits.'

Michael F. Lofchie, an Associate Professor of Political Science at the University of California, Los Angeles, writing in 1972 in the *Journal of Modern African Studies*, observed of these remarks: 'The post regnum speech of a deposed president, can, of course, easily be dismissed as an attempt to castigate the dubious morality of his successors and, by implication, to vindicate his own administration. If it were not for the availability of additional, more authorative evidence of corruption, it might be necessary to disregard Obote's allegations as self-justifying.' However, he goes on to note: 'Rampant corruption within the Ugandan army during the period preceding the *coup* has been dramatically documented in the report of the Auditor General for the fiscal year ending 30 June 1969.' But what Lofchie did not realise, and Obote already knew when he demanded an explanation from Amin, was that the accounts for the fiscal year ending 30 June 1970 had revealed even grosser discrepancies.

The 1968–9 audit showed that of the government's total excess and unauthorised expenditure of shs 45,355,067 a total of shs 29,955,215 was incurred by the Ministry of Defence. Here are some of the Auditor's comments:

'Excess expenditure: The actual expenditure on the Ministry's recurrent and development budget exceeded the amount provided by Parliament by shs 24,900,000.

'Control of expenditure: The Appropriation Accounts reflect unauthorised expenditure of shs 23,828,995 on 15 subheads of the recurrent budget and shs 6,126,220 on two items of the development budget.

'Accounting standards: Accounting standards have deteriorated. During the year an investigation team was appointed to look into and suggest a simplified accounting system and the report is being studied. The main cashbook was not written up and balanced daily and three bank accounts were overdrawn to a total of shs 48,520,815. Ledger posting was many months in arrears so that I have been unable to ascertain monies due or owing by soldiers to whom advances were given on demand.

'Unauthorised expenditure: A sum of shs 5,800,000, suspended by the Treasury during 1968, was released on 30 June 1969. It is inconceivable that the money was spent on the last day of the financial year.

'Unvouched and improperly vouched expenditure: 310 vouchers to a total of shs 4,816,800 which were missing in 1967–8 have not been found. I have been unable to reconcile wages paid with amounts appearing on vouchers and have requested the paymasters be instructed to return muster rolls to headquarters after payment.

'Army establishment: I have still made no progress in the matter of being provided with details of the army establishment. I have invited attention to the Armed Forces Act (Cap. 295) which vests in Parliament the prerogative to determine the strength of the armed forces and asked whether the present strength was so determined.

'Ordnance stores: I have again been refused access to the stores and arms and ammunition records. Thus, for payments amounting to shs 35,000,000 during the year, I am unable to certify either that they are correct or that I have received all the information and explanations that I have required.'

From this it is clear that not only was there gross financial mismanagement and corruption in the armed forces but also that there were grave doubts as to the real strength of the army. The following extracts from the Auditor's report for the fiscal year ending 30 June 1970 are even more revealing.

The 1969–70 audit showed that of the government's total excess and unauthorised expenditure totalling shs 41,834,630 a total of shs 35,956,693 was incurred by the Ministry of Defence. Lofchie assumed erroneously that Dr. Obote's remarks in fact related to the 1968–69 accounts. But in fact they referred to the 1969–70 audit published three months after the *coup*, as the deposed President had been made aware of the situation by the Treasury. It is noteworthy that while in the first report eleven Ministries or departments had been involved in the excess only three plus the Ministry of Defence were involved in the 1969–70 over expenditure. Thus there clearly had been some tightening up. But none the less Obote's concern—and demand for an explanation—are shown by some of the Auditor's remarks in the second report about the army:

'Appropriations Accounts: The Ministry has not forwarded to me its Appropriation Accounts for the year under review.

'Excess expenditure: Despite the non-submission of the Appropriation Accounts I have ascertained that at year's end expenditure in excess of funds appropriated by Parliament on the recurrent vote amounted to shs 35,956,693. Under expenditure on the development budget was shs 86,942. These figures do not include payments of shs 6,545,053 or bank debits or unpaid invoices of shs 7,025,855 which have not been reflected as voted expenditure.

'Control of expenditure: The cash-books reflected at year's end bank overdrafts totalling shs 78,192,703 of which shs 4,108,669 related to paymaster's bank accounts which were closed following the introduction of imprest accounts.

'Audit correspondence: I have not received a single reply to forty-seven letters issued on the accounts for the year under review.'

The Ugandan Auditor, Mr. G. H. Kabiswa, probably wisely, as a military government was in power and had already killed several thousand people when the report was released, refrained from resurrecting the question of the army establishment and ordnance stores.

Thus the financial irresponsibility and fiscal corruption within the military was clearly spelled out when Obote demanded written explanations from Onama and Amin. The attitude was that the army was not accountable to the civilian government, or indeed to the public, and it was unashamedly involved in prodigious misuse of funds and profiteering. That it had been able to do so for so long is partly Obote's fault, for an aura of impunity had gathered round the military establishment's financial behaviour. By demanding a written explanation he indicated that the era of impunity was over.

What happened to much of the missing money—as well as guns and ammunition from the armouries—is unknown. But there is reason to believe that a portion of it found its way to the Anyanya in southern Sudan. While Obote's government, as links with Jerusalem waned and those with Khartoum strengthened following the seizure of power on 25 May 1969, by Major-General Nimeri, refrained from supporting the southern cause, Amin definitely did not.

In January 1971, just before leaving for Singapore, the Ugandan Cabinet Security Committee chaired by Bataringaya, had decided that the West German mercenary, Rolf Steiner, should be deported to Khartoum. The forty-year-old Steiner had had a chequered career fighting on the losing side in seven wars. His losing streak began in the Second World War as a 'Wolf Cub' in the Hitler Youth in the last desperate days of the Third Reich. Next he joined the French Foreign Legion and fought in Korea, Indo-China, the Middle East and Algeria. Then he became a mercenary in the Biafran civil war where he is remembered for his brutality and the Nazi death's-head pennant he flew on the wing of his white Mercedes. Finally in the late 1960s he became a mercenary in southern Sudan.

Steiner expressed amazement that he should have been arrested during a visit to Uganda, for he thought Uganda backed the Anyanya. His diaries showed that on at least two occasions Amin, accompanied by Israeli officers, had visited the southern Sudan. Nimeri's government had said they would put Steiner on trial, which meant the embarrassing details about Amin's involvement were bound to emerge publicly and which could have forced Obote to act. Steiner was finally sentenced to death in late 1971 but Nimeri commuted this to twenty years' imprisonment.

In addition to Okoya, corruption and Steiner there was the growing wave of *kondoism* in Uganda. Police had arrested a number of *kondos* and arms they had found with them came from the armouries of the Ugandan army. Again whether Amin was involved was problematic but none the less that was a further immediate point of difficulty.

After Obote was shot in December 1969 Amin had fled to the unit at Bamunanika near Bombo. During the angry confrontations before Okoya's murder, officers had complained that this unit was to them something of a secret Amin force of Nubians. As a result late in 1970 Obote decided to break it up and ordered Brigadier Hussein to do so. The camp was commanded by a Sudanese, Lieutenant Marella Dodi, who today with the rank of lieutenant-colonel heads Amin's military police and is one of the most feared men in Uganda. The breakup of Bamunanika came while Amin was in Cairo and must have been seen by the General as another sign of his impending eclipse. Arms from Bamunanika were transferred to the Ordnance depot at Magamaga where the Commander was Major Michael Ongoga, a cousin of Mrs. Kay Amin, the General's second wife. The Major was replaced as commander of Magamaga late in the year and a check of the armoury revealed that twenty-two of the Bamunanika submachine-guns were missing and that six of these had been captured by police from *kondos*.

Another reason given by some people for the *coup* was that Obote had decided to publish the report of the 1966 gold and ivory commission. This comprised judges of the High Court of Tanzania and Kenya, chaired by a judge of the East African Court of Appeal. The commission had been set up in response to charges that Obote, Amin and Onama had embezzled gold, ivory and other items from the Congo nationalists fighting in the early 1960s. The report had never been published and with opponents resurrecting the issue Obote had decided to publish it before the planned April election to block the rumours. All of those against whom allegations were made, except Amin, were exonerated and in his case it was found that he had been stupid and not criminal in banking money belonging to the nationalists. As Amin knew the report's findings, and allowed its publication to go ahead after the *coup*, I do not accept that this was a reason. Okoya was the main reason, with Obote's demands for written explanations on missing money and arms and Steiner's impending trial strong secondary reasons. Against this background, in November 1970 he had seen an army and air force chief of staff appointed, thereby diluting his absolute rule over the armed forces and he would have been much less shrewd than he obviously is not to interpret all of this as a conspiracy of events which meant that time was fast running out.

Why Obote did not act before going to Singapore remains a mystery. However, in fairness to him the charges implicating Amin in the Okoya murder, Steiner's arrest with his diaries showing Amin's involvement in the southern Sudan, and the missing arms and money were all matters which came to light in the last quarter of 1970. At that point, in none of these cases was there conclusive proof against Amin, although Obote had detained people in the past on lesser grounds. However, that he was beginning to move is indicated by the appointment of an army chief of staff, an air force commander and the closure of the Bamunanika unit, although all of these had been demanded by the senior army officers. To detain an army commander is not a decision to be taken lightly and, in part, Obote's slowness to act must be attributable to the role Amin had played against the Baganda in 1966 and from then on. But Amin could not have failed to see the storm gathering around him and like a wounded cornered animal he lashed out in the only way he could.

5   Britain and Buganda

That Obote trod a tightrope for over eight years from independence on 9 October 1962 until his overthrow by a military *coup d'état* is undoubtedly true. No other East African Commonwealth leader faced such an unenviable task at independence. That he survived as long as he did is a tribute of sorts to his political skill. That he fell when he did was a bitter irony.

In part the reasons for his fall began long before Obote was born. The British and Germans divided East Africa between them through treaties signed in 1886 and 1890. Britain's share was Kenya, Uganda and Zanzibar. The Kaiser's—named German East Africa—was mainland Tanzania (known as Tanganyika until the 1964 union with Zanzibar), Burundi and Rwanda. Germany's defeat in the First World War saw the breakup of her colonial empire. Tanganyika, came under British rule, and Burundi and Rwanda were administered by Belgium, initially under a League of Nations mandate and later as United Nations trusteeships.

These arrangements by the European powers were not accepted by the Africans without considerable opposition. From 1905 to 1907 southern Tanzanian tribes, spearheaded by the Wahehe, fought the Germans in a bloody rebellion known as the Maji Maji uprising. An estimated 100,000 Africans died, largely from starvation.

In Uganda the British found the powerful and well-organised kingdom of Buganda straddling the equator and stretching inland from the north-western shores of Lake Victoria. The first Arab trader had reached Buganda in 1848, where the Kabaka, Mutesa I found Islam a useful weapon against the traditional gods in his struggle with the chiefs. The explorer, Captain John Speke, searching for the source of the Nile, was the first European to visit the Kabaka's court in 1862. Protestant and Catholic missionaries followed in the late 1870s. The Kabaka had encouraged his courtiers to embrace Islam and he began to wear Arab clothes and adopted the Muslim calendar, although he never became a Muslim. But as the belief in the old gods had challenged his authority, so too did Islam and in 1879 he had 100 Muslims put to death.

Anglo-American explorer, Henry Morton Stanley, visited the court in 1875, four years after his famous meeting with Dr. David Livingstone, and the Kabaka is reported to have said afterwards: 'I say that the white men are greatly superior to the Arabs, and I think, therefore, that their book must be a better book than Muhammad's.'

The first Protestant missionary arrived in 1878 and the Catholics in the following year. Soon they were publicly denouncing each other at the court. The Kabaka, who once more sought to use religion for his own political ends, faced a dilemma as to whether the God of the Catholic White Fathers or that of the Anglican Church Missionary Society, was the more powerful. Both won converts and the problem had not been resolved when Mutesa I died in 1884.

Mutesa I had done much to consolidate and shape the kingdom. He was impressed by the white man's power and particularly his guns. His great-grandson, Sir Edward Mutesa (ousted as Kabaka and Uganda President in 1966 by Obote), recalls in his book, *The Desecration of my Kingdom*, that his great-grandfather was reputed to have called a courtier and told him to take Speke's gun out and shoot one of the crowd. A shot was heard and the courtier returned to report that the gun worked well. Death was an almost daily occurrence at the court and one of the earliest Anglican missionaries, Scotsman Alexander Mackay, said in a letter in 1879 that executioners waylaid people on all the roads around the court and he referred to 'the terrible Baganda grin of pleasure in cruelty'.

Mutesa was succeeded by his son, Mwanga, who had far less faith in the motives of the white men. In June 1886, after criticism of the practice of sodomy, which he had adopted from the Arabs, Mwanga had thirty-two Christian converts burned to death. Many Christians fled into the bush, but it is an ironic commentary on the whims of the Kabaka that when they emerged from hiding, Mwanga formed three regiments of musketeers, one officered by Muslims, another by Protestants and the third by Catholics. These he used to attack the chiefs who continued to follow the old gods, thereby challenging his authority as Kabaka. By 1888 his religious machinations had turned full circle once more and he turned on the religious leaders and in a clumsy plot tried to isolate them on an island in Lake Victoria where he intended to leave them to starve to death. In the rebellion which followed he was forced to flee. An infant prince was put on the throne and a Muslim-Christian coalition ruled.

In the same year the Imperial British East African Trading Company had received a royal charter in the wake of the first Anglo-German treaty giving it full administrative powers over the domain with the right to acquire territory and levy taxes. Captain Lugard was sent to Buganda in December 1890, by which time the coalition had collapsed and Mwanga was back on the throne. But the religious rifts led to a further crisis in 1892 and Mwanga and the Catholics were defeated in a battle with Lugard and the Protestants at Mengo, the site of the Kabaka's palace. Many Catholics fled and Mwanga only survived by hastily becoming a Protestant. Captain Lugard reported in February 1892 that the country had been 'pacified'.

In 1897, apparently opposing Christian rule and British colonial supremacy, Mwanga again fled his capital and led a revolt against the British. At the same time Lugard's Sudanese mercenaries, a tough and vicious group who formed the backbone of his tiny army, mutinied. Finally in 1899, with most of Christian Baganda backing the British against the Kabaka and the mutineers, Mwanga was captured. He was deported to the British colony, the Seychelle Islands in the Indian Ocean, where he died in exile in 1903 and his infant son, Daudi Chwa, was placed on the throne.

Two important points should be made about Lugard's activities in Uganda at this point, for they were to play a crucial part in the crisis which gripped Uganda after independence.

The neighbouring Banyoro had long been traditional enemies of the Baganda and in 1894 Captain Lugard, to quote from Sir Edward Mutesa's book, 'marched west from Kampala with 180 Sudanese; 160 Zanzibaris; 300 porters and possibly 25,000 Baganda against Bunyoro'. Resistance by the Banyoro was crushed, the Omukama (king) forced to flee and all the land in the Bunyoro kingdom south of the Kafu River ceded to the Baganda. This included Mubende district and parts of three counties as well as the graves of the Banyoro Omukamas. The 'lost counties' were to become the focal point of an emotional political dispute within Uganda for the next seventy years until they were returned in 1964 following a referendum. The second point is that Lugard's Sudanese mercenaries were to provide the origins of the Nilo-Hamitic/Sudanic group who have held the power in Uganda since Amin overthrew Obote.

The 1899 exiling of Mwanga led directly to the 1900 Uganda Agreement which divided Buganda into twenty counties; established a *Lukiiko* or Parliament, which began functioning in 1902 and was referred to in the Agreement as a 'native council'; and established indirect British rule over Buganda. Clause 6 stated that as long as the Kabaka, his chiefs and people abided by the laws and regulations laid down by Her Majesty's Government and co-operated loyally, 'Her Majesty's Government agrees to recognise the Kabaka of Uganda (stated for Buganda) as the native ruler of the province of Uganda under Her Majesty's Government's protection and overrule.' As 'native ruler' the Kabaka would be assisted by three Ministers—a Chief Minister, Chief Justice and Treasurer.

Buganda had been the most significant and developed kingdom the British found at the end of the nineteenth century and the next sixty years served to entrench the Baganda's position. While in the 1870s Mutesa I had recognised the power that the gun gave the European, and his son had discovered the dangers it posed, the Agreement of 1900 put the seal on the relationship between the British and the Baganda. Apolo Kagwa ruled as Chief Minister of Buganda from 1889 to 1926 and after the Agreement relations proceeded comparatively smoothly. Britain regarded a railway as essential to strengthen her position in Uganda and in 1901 the tracks reached the shores of Lake Victoria, some five years after work had begun at the Indian Ocean port of Mombasa. Cotton was introduced to Buganda as a cash crop in 1903 and then coffee. The Baganda prospered. The British took the Baganda, as the favoured recipients of colonial patronage, to other parts of the country as their subordinate officials.

The Devonshire Declaration of 1923, although referring to neighbouring Kenya, was seen by the Baganda as further assuring their future. It read: 'Primarily Kenya is an African territory... the interests of the African native must be paramount and if and when those interests and the interests of the immigrant should conflict, the former should prevail.' The immigrants, and in particular the Kenya European settlers, ignored this. But in Uganda there was no substantial settler group. Daudi Chwa had become Kabaka while an infant and thus the reality of power lay with the Kitikiro (Chief Minister) and in turn elevated the *Lukiiko* to a position of power it might never otherwise have acquired.

The *Lukiiko*, consisting of neo-traditionalists, worked continuously to reduce the Protectorate government's supervisory role over Buganda and to preserve privileges and autonomy. They also opposed a central Legislative Council fearing it might undermine their position. But the most passionately felt issue was East African Federation between Kenya, Tanganyika and Uganda, for the Baganda felt they would come under the rule of the Kenya British settlers. Backed by liberal allies in London, they managed to block Federal proposals in the 1930s, but failed to stop the East African High Commission being formed in the 1940s, which established common services such as railways, airways and harbours, as well as a common currency.

With the death of Kabaka Daudi Chwa in 1939, his son, Mutesa II, became Kabaka at the age of fifteen. During the forties he spent about four years in Britain, first at Cambridge University, and later in the Grenadier Guards, where King George VI gave him a commission as a captain. It was a period which moulded his life, making him the most inept Kabaka in memory.

Relations between the British and Baganda began to deteriorate during the 1940s. Rioting twice broke out in Buganda with the Kabaka's government and the *Lukiiko* under open attack over a series of political and economic complaints. Then in 1952 a new Governor, Sir Andrew Cohen, was appointed.

He was a highly able colonial administrator and in a number of ways he set out to try to do exactly what Obote did a decade later. The Governor decided that Uganda must have a strong central government and a national Parliament. The Kabaka's position had been weakened by the 1945 and 1949 rioting and Sir Andrew formulated his policy on the basis of a government memorandum on the report of Mr. C. A. G. Wallis of an inquiry into African local government in the Uganda Protectorate. The critical part of the memorandum said:

'The future of Uganda must lie in a unitary form of central government on Parliamentary lines covering the whole country. . . .'

The special characteristics of the component parts would be taken into account, but the memorandum added:

'The Protectorate is too small to grow into a series of separate units of government, even if these are federated together. The different parts of the country have not the size, nor will they have the resources, to develop even in federation with each other the administrative organs which modern government requires. This can only be done by a central government of the Protectorate as a whole with no part of the country dominating any other part but all working together for the good of the whole Protectorate and the progress of its people.'

Relations between Sir Andrew Cohen and the Kabaka, Sir Edward Mutesa (he was knighted later), deteriorated sharply. In March 1953 the Governor announced his proposals for constitutional reform, including that the *Lukiiko* should have an elected majority and that the Buganda government should assume responsibility for primary and junior secondary education and for most health and agricultural services in the kingdom.

Then on 30 June 1953 came one of those chance remarks which make history. The Conservative government's Secretary of State for the Colonies, Oliver Lyttelton, at a time when the Central African Federation was being imposed, despite nationalist protests, on what is now Malawi, Rhodesia and Zambia, in an after-dinner speech in London referred to:

'still larger measures of unification and possibly still larger measures of federation of the whole East African territories'.

The remark might have passed unnoticed had it not been for the Kenya settler newspaper, the *East African Standard* seizing upon it and giving it splash treatment. The Baganda traditionalist leaders were already up in arms about Sir Andrew Cohen's constitutional reforms, and now they feared that the federation which they had opposed for thirty years would be imposed from London. The Governor tried to allay their fears, which he described as 'groundless' promising that local opinion would be fully taken into account in any future development.

The Kabaka and the British Governor held a series of meetings at which the former demanded independence for his kingdom and the latter refused. Under pressure from his government and the *Lukiiko*, the Kabaka refused to nominate any Baganda to the Legislative Assembly and the Governor called him to Government House on 30 November. Mutesa II made it clear he would not give way and Sir Andrew Cohen fell back on the 1900 Agreement, which demanded acceptance of British policies and withdrew recognition of the Kabaka as 'native ruler' of Buganda. As the Governor walked out two policemen entered through another door and the Kabaka was taken straight to Entebbe Airport, put aboard a diverted Royal Air Force plane and deported to Britain.

Sir Andrew clearly feared disturbances in Buganda, and a state of emergency was imposed. But in fact there was precious little reaction, which is indicative of the Kabaka's popularity at the time. Indeed, one widely held view is that Mutesa II was so unpopular in Buganda that he would have been deposed in the coming months. Many Baganda nationalist politicians disliked Mutesa II intensely, regarding him as little more than a British agent. The Conservative government defended Sir Andrew's actions in Parliament in the face of a motion of censure from the Labour opposition. The motion did not represent support for a feudal Buganda state of the type that Kabaka and neo-traditionalists sought to sustain, but rather opposition to federation, which was consistent with Labour's position over the Rhodesias.

A compromise of sorts was arrived at in September 1954 after an Australian, Sir Keith Hancock, had been appointed as an independent mediator. The 1955 Agreement replaced the 1900 Agreement and Article 1 laid down that Buganda would continue as an integral part of Uganda. In Article 43 the *Lukiiko* agreed to Baganda elected participation in the *Lukiiko*. To an extent, Sir Andrew Cohen's unitary state had now been constitutionally underwritten and the Kabaka returned to Uganda on 17 October 1955. Whereas in November 1953 his position was increasingly being questioned by the Baganda, he was now a hero.

A series of factors had inhibited the emergence of a strong national political party up to this point. There was no common language in Uganda. Religion had caused considerable polarisation. The country had been divided into districts on tribal lines, thereby encouraging tribal, rather than national politics. The dearth of elections had discouraged national political activity and finally the bulk of the country's potential leaders were in the civil service and therefore barred from political activity.

The Uganda National Congress (UNC), formed in 1952, began as a multiracial party under the slogan 'self-government now'. But it soon adopted an anti-European and particularly anti-Asian stance and never formulated an action programme. The UNC protested at the Kabaka's expulsion and took up a number of other local-tribal issues, but never gathered national momentum. The United Congress party was formed in 1957 by a breakaway group two years after the largely Protestant Progressive party. Neither really got off the ground. The mainly Roman Catholic Democratic party (DP) had been formed in

1956 with backing from bishops and priests, and in 1958 Benedicto Kiwanuka took over as its President.

The Uganda Legislative Council, formed in 1921, had its first African members appointed in 1945. By 1958 over half of the sixty-three members were Africans. It was at this point that Milton Obote emerged into national political prominence, albeit from a tribal base. In October that year he was elected with 40,081 votes as Member for Lango.

Milton Obote, born in 1925, in Akokoro village in Lango, was the third of nine children of a northern chief. He spent a year in Makerere University studying English, economics and politics, but left in 1949. Efforts to get into universities elsewhere were blocked by the colonial government and he moved to Kenya to learn trade unionism, working first as a labourer on a sugar plantation and later for a construction company. He was involved in Jomo Kenyatta's Kenya African Union (KAU) until it was banned in 1953 at the start of the Mau Mau emergency, and finally returned to Uganda in 1957. In the following year he won a seat in the Legislative Council as a Uganda National Congress member. In 1960 he broke away to form the Uganda People's Congress (UPC) of which he became President-General.

It was now clear that the Baganda bid for separate independence had failed and 'the wind of change' signalled by the British Prime Minister, Mr. Harold Macmillan, was blowing briskly across the continent. Nine states were independent by 1960 and eighteen others followed by the end of 1961, including neighbouring Tanganyika. In 1959 the Uganda Protectorate government recommended direct elections to the Legislative Council on a countrywide common roll, to be followed by the establishment of a central government consisting mainly of Africans and led by an African Prime Minister. The then British Governor, Sir Frederick Crawford, feared the Baganda reaction and a commission was established to consider Buganda's relationship with the rest of the country. In February 1960, to the fury of the other tribes and political parties, the Relationship Commission recommended a special relationship between Buganda and the remainder of the country.

At the end of 1960 the *Lukiiko* decided that Buganda would terminate its 1955 agreement with Britain, and on 1 January 1961, in a symbolic but utterly futile gesture, the *Lukiiko* declared Buganda independent. They decided to boycott the March 1961 Legislative Council elections, which none the less went ahead. However, the decision turned the election into a complete farce. In Buganda only 35,000 out of an estimated 1,000,000 Baganda people registered. The UPC, during campaigning, demanded a unitary government and declared its opposition to Buganda pretensions, thereby alienating even those Baganda who had registered. The UPC won thirty-five seats throughout the country against forty-three won by Benedicto Kiwanuka's staunchly Catholic anti neo-traditionalist Democratic party. But nineteen of the DP seats were won in Buganda where the boycott was 97 per cent effective and only 20,000 people voted. Elsewhere the DP victories were mainly in Catholic strongholds, where UPC Protestant domination was feared. On the basis of the popular vote the UPC was ahead polling 488,334 against the DP's 407,416. Benedicto Kiwanuka became Prime Minister at the head of a DP government, but it was clear new elections were vital and he lasted only eight months in power.

In the wake of the DP victory a new political organisation emerged, meeting for the first time in June 1961. As a Catholic, Kiwanuka was unacceptable to the Protestant establishment at Mengo. Although a Muganda, he was a commoner, and it was totally unacceptable to have a Prime Minister whose role in Uganda seemed more important than that of the Kabaka. The new grouping, known as the Kabaka Yekka, meaning 'King only', insisted that it was not a political party and the hardcore comprised Baganda separatists who had been known as the 'King's friends' during his exile in Britain. In some senses the Kabaka Yekka never was a political party, for it sought no national base and was formed primarily to bring down Kiwanuka, who, the Baganda argued, had committed treason by ignoring the Legislative Council election boycott. However Mutesa clearly saw the KY as an instrument to control the twenty-one members of Parliament from Buganda as well as to use them as a bargaining point with other parties.

The power of the Baganda traditionalists at this point is amply demonstrated by the fact that during the February 1962 *Lukiiko* elections, the KY won sixty-five of the sixty-eight seats. But even then the traditionalists feared revolution from within by the KY radicals and an executive committee was established with comparable powers to the chiefs, chaired by the Katikiro, Michael Kintu, which effectively blocked all reform.

Much of this Obote watched from the wings. The DP was cast as a Catholic party bent on destroying the Kabakaship. The KY appealed for Protestant anti-Catholic support and the UPC support in the 1961 election had been largely Protestant or animist.

The UPC–KY alliance—or rather marriage of convenience—which followed, arose on the eve of the September 1961 London Constitutional talks. While superficially the arrangement bringing together the Baganda with the only party which had been able to attract national following might have had its attractions, there can be no doubt that both sides were using each other.

However, Mutesa II badly underestimated Obote, as this passage from *The Desecration of my Kingdom* shows:

'At the time I had heard little of him and certainly had never met him. There were a number of stories about him. He was said to have been a herd boy and been wounded by a spear throw. Deciding that life was too vigorous, he went to school and followed that with a brief career of one year at Makerere. I do not know why he cut short his studies. A spell in Kenya as some sort of clerk under Kenyatta during the time of Mau Mau came to an end, and it was on his return to Uganda that his fortunes started to mend. Up to this point his career had not been a conspicuous one.'

Despite this regal disdain for a commoner, Mutesa II made it clear he intended to use Obote:

'After the election Kiwanuka was puffed up with pride and success. He must have understood as clearly as everyone else that almost half his support was fictitious, the result of the boycott . . . until then I had seen him as a friend from whom I had drifted apart. Now he became intolerable. He made personal attacks on me and said that I had arranged the boycott.'

Mutesa II recalled that not long after the election Obote was brought to see him:

'An alliance between Buganda and UPC was suggested with innumerable promises of respect for our position after independence. He would step down, and I should choose whomever I wished to be Prime Minister. Though I did not particularly like him, for he is not a particularly likeable man, I agreed to the alliance without misgivings. He understood our fears for the position of Buganda; we shared his hopes for a united, prosperous and free Uganda. Kintu was alone in opposing this new friendship. Obote had said that he meant to crush the Baganda and Kintu would not forgive or trust him. We waved it aside as an impetuous remark made to please the crowds. Now we thought him reformed, the obvious and best ally against Kiwanuka and the hated DP.

'Moreover he was the only ally. The tiny vote in Buganda had shown that a party supported by myself and the *Lukiiko* could sweep our country. Our bargaining power was therefore based on the twenty-one seats inside Buganda we would win in the next election if we took part. It was clear that there would have to be another election.'

Dr. Obote's explanation of the marriage of convenience equally demonstrates his underlying strategy.

'The alliance came about because Buganda could have blocked early independence and the UPC felt that it was to the best interest of the country to have early independence; to have MPs representing constituencies in Buganda at the time of independence and MPs who although indirectly elected enjoyed the confidence of the electorate in Buganda more than those twenty-one MPs elected in 1961. Lastly the UPC felt that the "Buganda issue" could not be solved by the British but by Ugandans after independence.

'The arrangement was for the electoral college—the Buganda *Lukiiko*—to have sixty-eight members themselves directly elected by adult suffrage. We insisted on that provision and it was agreed. . . .

'The UPC had no illusions that things would work out smoothly after the April 1962 elections with the UPC and KY in Government. However, we had banked on having a majority of our own in the National Assembly—a majority over all other parties put together. The alliance itself was to deny us that majority. We lost all of the two seats in Bunyoro, one of our strongholds. And we lost two seats in Toro. All four on account of the alliance. Other seats which were ours for the taking went to the DP on account of over confidence on the part of our candidates. In two constituencies, for instance, our candidates gave beer parties to thousands of voters on the eve of the elections. Thousands did not vote the next day including the two candidates. They were tight. Our opponents got through in each case with a margin of less than a thousand votes. There were other incidents of this kind but even if we had obtained our own majority, we were not going to break the alliance without good cause before 9 October 1962. Thereafter it was to be anybody's guess.'

In the National Assembly elections in April the UPC won thirty-eight seats and the DP twenty-three. There was no national election in Buganda so that the DP lost twenty seats and the UPC one. Dr. Obote had failed to get his Parliamentary majority by four seats but the KY had achieved their objective by ousting Kiwanuka and the DP. It had previously been agreed that the winning party should appoint nine special members and as the UPC held two-thirds of the alliance seats, six went to Obote's party and the remaining three to the KY. Thus at independence on 9 October 1962 the UPC had forty-four seats in Parliament against twenty-three for both the KY and DP.

6   Obote and Buganda

With the wisdom of hindsight it is easy to see that the marriage of convenience had little chance of working. The UPC stood for a unitary state with a strong single government and a representative Parliament, and there were already some indications of the socialist policies which were to emerge fully in 1968. In direct contrast the KY stood for the Kabaka, Buganda privilege and autonomy. Yet for both it acted as a device to get rid of the DP and a platform for them to manoeuvre against each other from the centre.

None the less the argument that the alliance avoided independence being delayed is a reasonable one. Equally it brought its own problems. The British Protectorate became an independent state with the four traditional kingdoms of Buganda, Ankole, Bunyoro and Toro, plus Busoga district, merged in a loose federal arrangement with supreme legislative power resting with a single National Assembly. Obote became Prime Minister, five months before independence, of a country heavily tribal-orientated politically, where the other thirty-six tribes looked to the Buganda position with jealousy and envy. The determination of the Baganda to retain their separate identity, either through ruling the whole country, or through secession, dominated Ugandan politics as much immediately after independence as it had before.

The privileged position of the Baganda in 1960 is amply demonstrated in Nelson Kasfir's *Cultural Sub-nationalism in Uganda*. In both economic and educational terms the Baganda, first exposed to the missionaries and nearest the country's administrative centre, were and remain the nation's most developed group.

In 1960 the Baganda, whose population represented 16·3 per cent of Uganda's total, had 29 per cent of the places in secondary schools and 46·6 per cent of the places at Makerere College, the country's University. A 1967 regional breakdown of employees in private industry showed that 75,000 were from Buganda and the total from the north, west and east regions was 75,100. In the public sector the comparative figure was 109,800 from Buganda against 132,100 from the other three regions. Only in the army and police force—a fact later to prove important—were the Baganda underrepresented. No accurate statistics are obtainable giving a tribal or regional breakdown for the army but two factors proved critical in leading to northern military dominance.

The first is that in Uganda, as elsewhere in Africa, certain tribes show a marked preference for military or para-military professions. The Baganda tended to regard uniform service as beneath their dignity and the disproportionate representation in both the army and police came from West Nile, Acholi, Lango, Teso and Busoga. Kasfir's statistical analysis shows that in 1961 Buganda supplied only 3·8 per cent of serving police officers. Teso, which had 8·1 per cent of Uganda's population had 15·2 per cent of police officers; Lango, 5·6 per cent of the population, had 7·5 per cent; Acholi, 4·4 per cent of the population, 15·5 per cent; and Kakwa and Madi, whose shares of the population were 0·6 per cent and 1·2 per cent respectively, had 1·6 per cent and 3·8 per cent of the police force. At independence about three-quarters of the army is believed to have been Acholi with the bulk of the remainder from West Nile and Lango.

But in 1962, in Uganda as elsewhere in Africa, the question of military ethnic affiliations was little appreciated. It took a spate of army *coups* to demonstrate to the civilian politicians the reality and instability of power. Mutesa II in *The Desecration of my Kingdom* observed after he had fled into exile in Britain:

'I was sadly and vividly aware that he [Obote] had from that moment on complete control of the army, which was filled with northerners from his own stock. . . . The Buganda police force could be controlled by Obote if he wished. We knew that from this time on if it came to force, we could not hope to win.'

The built-in privileges of the 1900 Agreement had served psychologically to demilitarise the Baganda. Under the British they became the nation's economic and educated élite dominating the administration, while the Nilotic people of the north dominated military fields.

But if the alliance was an uneasy one based on insecure foundations there was little public sign of this through 1963. Mutesa II became Uganda's President during the year, with Obote's support, which appeared to have the effect of confirming the alliance. A point of significance was that in 1963 a number of KY members of Parliament joined the UPC and in 1964 floor crossing began from the DP with the leader of the opposition in the house, Basil Bataringaya, joining the UPC on 31 December 1964. Although DP members abstained from voting on the referendum laws, the floor crossing gave Obote the majority he had narrowly missed at the polls. Of additional importance here is that the constitution was amended in 1963 so that when Mutesa refused to sign the referendum bills, Obote was empowered to do so and this is what occurred.

However a divisive swell was already mounting behind the scenes. In a closing address in Kampala on 9 August 1970, to a seminar on 'Law in a Developing Country' Obote observed:

'Soon after independence the government of Uganda began to receive petitions, demands and representations from various capitals of the tribal governments within the country, for greater power than what was already given to them by the constitution. Readings of the provisions of the 1962 constitution to those who made the petitions, demands and representations, were brushed aside with, so to speak, a wave of the hand. To them it was not the constitution, but it was the very existence of a tribe, and if the tribe had a ruler, it was the importance of that ruler that mattered. Insofar as they were concerned it was the ruler and the tribe and not the constitution that had to decide and determine what was to be done.'

Some of the local, or tribal, governments argued, Obote said, that the only central Ministry should be Foreign Affairs with a subordinate Ministry of Finance whose only role would be to distribute funds to the tribal governments. Defence, internal security, health and education would all be autonomous matters, locally controlled. 'The issue was whether Uganda was to be a balkanised state with the parts of the country exercising more power than the centre, or was it to be a united country with the centre having more power than the parts,' Obote asked.

The first real breach came in 1964 over the 'lost counties', the large part of Bunyoro kingdom conquered by Captain Lugard in 1894 and 'colonised' by Buganda. A political group, called the Mubende-Banyoro committee, had been formed in Bunyoro in 1921 to agitate for the return of the counties. There had also been violent clashes in the early 1960s. The British government had consistently refused to consider the return of the 'lost counties' and on the eve of independence the Molson committee set up by the British government reported on the emotive question.

The population breakdown given by Molson at that time is important. In Buyaga County there were 33,000 Banyoro against 3,300 Baganda; in Bugangazzi 16,700 Banyoro and 4,200 Baganda and in Buwekula 4,800 Banyoro to 21,700 Baganda. The Molson committee said that those counties where there was a Banyoro majority should be handed back, and where there was a Baganda majority, the *status quo* should be maintained. The Kabaka immediately rejected the proposals which were laid before the final constitutional conference in London in June 1962.

The problem of the 'lost counties' proved insoluble. Mutesa II had flatly said the Baganda would never return them and the Banyoro would accept nothing but their return. A compromise was proposed which deferred the question until two years after independence when a referendum would be held so that the people of the 'lost counties' could themselves choose whether they wished to be governed by Buganda, Bunyoro or be established as a separate district. Again the two sides rejected this, but Obote finally persuaded them to accept, arguing that no other solution existed.

Immediately after independence, without a Parliamentary majority and involved in an alliance with the KY, Obote had to move cautiously on the 'lost counties' issue. The floor-crossing by DP and KY members of the National Assembly to give the UPC an absolute majority was an important factor in strengthening his hand for the 1964 referendum, which led directly to the final confrontation with the Kabaka and *Lukiiko* in May 1966.

Some Baganda politicians immediately after independence tended towards the view that even if it came to a referendum the Banyoro would vote to keep the 'lost counties' where they had been for the past seventy years. That was not the view of Mutesa II. In mid 1963 he began establishing a camp at Ndaiga on Lake Albert in the 'lost counties'. At least 8,000 Baganda, mostly former Second World War servicemen, were moved into the area. It was a most blatant attempt to rig the ballot in the coming referendum. The Banyoro responded by grouping their ex-servicemen at the capital, Hoima, and arming them.

The Kabaka's actions at this point need to be carefully considered, for Obote has been cast as the abrogator of the 1962 independence constitution. In the first place, at the London constitutional talks, the Kabaka, as the leader of the Baganda, had accepted the referendum. Secondly, he had accepted the Presidency of Uganda in 1963. Against this background his attempt to rig the referendum can only be seen as indicative of his lack of respect at that time for the constitution he signed and oath of office he took.

There were some clashes between the Banyoro and Baganda, and the Kabaka burned down a village market where Sunday meetings had been called to back the return of the counties. In an article published in October 1968 in the *East African Journal*, entitled 'Footsteps of Uganda's Revolution', Obote accused Mutesa II of 'squandering and embezzling public funds' during his resettlement programme. He then goes on to mention a charge frequently made against the Kabaka during this period:

'There is a third matter about the "lost counties". This was the brutality which a person who was the President and the

Kabaka displayed, by shooting to death a number of persons on a Sunday morning in a market place and in the process burning down the market. This he did fully conscious of the fact that the provisions of the constitution put him both as the President and as the Kabaka, beyond the normal criminal proceedings applicable to other citizens, thus abusing the privilege bestowed upon him by the state and the constitution. This callous behaviour and complete disregard for human life has been part of the institution of monarchy in Uganda. The association and extension of this characteristic with the office of President in modern times was bound to end in a revolution.'

Mutesa II openly admits loading the ballot in his book:

'With at least two years to go, it seemed possible that we might make the atmosphere more friendly, but if not, we would use the land and have more Baganda there when it came to a showdown.'

Thus, although the Kabaka and Baganda politicians had accepted a referendum during the final constitutional talks to allow the Banyoro to decide the counties controversy, they had almost immediately set out to rig the voting. The Kabaka had badly underestimated the Prime Minister who ruled that only people who had been on the 1962 voting register could vote in the referendum, thereby debarring the new Baganda 'settlers'. This decision was later upheld in the courts, and over 90 per cent of the inhabitants of the two counties affected by the referendum —Buyaga and Bugangazzi—voted in favour of being governed by Bunyoro.

Writers on Uganda have generally paid far too little attention to the importance of the 'lost counties' referendum as the crucial issue for Obote's showdown with the Baganda in 1966 and the new political phase which emerged after that until the *coup d'état* in January 1971. The crisis could only have been avoided if Obote either turned a blind eye to the vote rigging or simply decided not to hold the referendum. But whatever he did he was bound to clash with either the Baganda or Banyoro. As early as March 1963 his thinking was clear. In a speech he noted that the tribe 'has served our people as a basic political unit very well in the past. Now the problem of people putting the tribe above national consciousness is a problem that we must face, and an issue we must destroy.'

A further point which brought matters to a head was that Obote's UPC after independence began recruiting members in Buganda and opening branches and offices. The KY considered that this was in breach of the terms of their alliance for they considered Buganda their exclusive domain.

The façade of unity between the UPC and KY formally ended in the second half of 1964 over the 'lost counties' question with the UPC terminating the alliance, before the referendum. The Kabaka remained as President and throughout 1965 an uneasy truce prevailed. But one incident of considerable future significance occurred early in 1964. In January some units of the Uganda army had mutinied.

There were simultaneous mutinies, previously mentioned, in the Tanganyika and Kenya armies and British troops were called in to quell them. These all occurred in the wake of the successful Zanzibar revolution which toppled the Sultan and in that Cold War era, many viewed it as a chain reaction triggered variously by Havana, Moscow or Peking. While psychologically the mutinies may have been a reaction to the successful revolution, they took the form of protests against pay, conditions and the continued presence of British officers, rather than an attempt to oust the African governments. I had arrived in Dar es Salaam, the Tanzanian capital, about three weeks earlier, and had personal experience of the mutineer's objectives.

A few hours after the soldiers mutinied in Dar es Salaam, I was arrested by three of them while driving through the city to see what was happening, and forced at gunpoint to take them to Colito Barracks on the outskirts of the capital. Inside the barracks I was ordered out of the car and a group of soldiers led by a corporal came across. To my surprise they were very friendly and when I asked what was happening they said that they had intended a peaceful protest to force the government to increase wages and replace white officers. But there had been looting and shooting in the city which had spoiled this. It was not until two days later when dissident trade unionists linked up with the mutineers that there was a considerable likelihood of a *coup d'état*.

Yet none the less the mutinies revealed to East Africa's political leaders the power of the gun and the fragility of civil supremacy when based on the traditional British concept of the trusted neutrality of the military. African army commanders emerged in each of the three countries after the mutinies with Brigadier Shabani Opolot becoming commander in Uganda and Lieutenant-Colonel Idi Amin the deputy commander.

Amin was soon in political difficulty. Mutesa II claimed to have received a telegram from Khartoum from a Congolese nationalist leader, General Olenga, early in 1965 asking what had happened to nationalist money frozen in Uganda. Mutesa claimed he passed it on to Obote who dismissed the matter as of no importance. As already discussed, the question of the Congolese money, gold and ivory surfaced briefly in Parliament in March 1965, and in September the same year during a debate on the security situation in Uganda when the late Daudi Ocheng, a northerner, but close friend of the Kabaka, alleged Amin had banked £17,000 after a trip to the Congo border earlier in the year.

Ocheng claimed he had obtained a copy of Amin's bank statement showing the deposits because it had been delivered by mistake to a Kabaka Yekka office. But a subsequent inquiry showed the photostat of Amin's account had in fact been obtained in the bank. The Minister of Defence, Felix Onama, dismissed the allegation as untrue but promised an investigation and in September a preliminary report was given to the house.

But on 4 February 1966, three days after Obote had left on a tour of Acholi and West Nile which had been announced two months earlier, Grace Ibingira, Minister of State in the Prime Minister's Office, called a meeting of the Cabinet. Only nine members were present, while nine others, including Obote, were on up-country tours. UPC Vice-President Nadiope supported Ibingira's candidacy two years earlier for the UPC Secretary

General' when he defeated the leftist incumbent, John Kakonge. Since then, Ibingira had purged the left wing of the party. Now he set out to stage a 'palace revolution' in a bid to oust Obote.

Ocheng, a Member for the KY, had moved a motion demanding Amin's suspension pending an investigation of the gold and ivory affair. The UPC Parliamentary group in a caucus meeting had voted unanimously to reject the motion, which apart from any other consideration went beyond the constitutional powers of the Parliament. But Ibingira and his eight colleagues, with the Minister of Justice, Cuthbert Obwangor from Teso in the chair, decided on 4 February to support the motion which amounted to a vote of no confidence in Obote. The motion was carried with only one dissenting vote from the government bench and this ironically was by John Kakonge.

Now the confrontation began to develop at a rapid pace. According to the Kabaka, Brigadier Opolot was instructed to send some soldiers to ask Obote to return immediately to the capital. Akena Adoko argues in his book *Uganda Crisis* that they were sent to arrest Obote and bring him back to the capital 'dead or alive'. Whatever the truth of this assertion, troop movements and counter-movements began in Kampala. Here again the versions of Mutesa and Adoko vary dramatically. The former claims troops loyal to Obote were moved in. The latter says that Brigadier Opolot began moving in troops. Lieutenant-Colonel Okoya, the senior Acholi officer, countered this by moving in loyal troops. Whatever the truth of these allegations and counter allegations, it is perfectly clear the government and UPC had irreparably split into two factions headed by the Kabaka with Teso backing, and Obote. Thus at the beginning of 1966 Obote faced a major crisis.

Obote returned on 12 February, and at a press conference at Entebbe denied the charges against him stating: 'I have received no money, gold, coffee or elephant tusks or any gainful commodity.' A KY Member of Parliament put the matter in more perspective the same day saying the gold and ivory had been used to buy supplies, including guns, for the Congolese rebels with whom Obote and a number of other African leaders, including Kenya's President Kenyatta and Tanzania's President Nyerere, were in sympathy.

At a Cabinet meeting on 14 February, Obote demanded that any Minister who believed the Ocheng allegations should resign immediately. Despite the position adopted by Ibingira and his supporters only ten days earlier, none did so and Obote proposed that an independent judicial inquiry should be established. This began meeting in the following month, chaired by a British judge of the East African Court of Appeal assisted by judges from the Kenya and Tanzania benches.

But the crisis was far from over. Obote left for Nairobi on 17 February to attend a two-day meeting of the Authority, supreme body of the East African Community, consisting of the three heads of state. He returned on 19 February, when according to a report subsequently presented to a UPC delegates conference he learned of renewed unauthorised troop movements. The 'Constitutional and Political Report' to the UPC meeting in 1968 states:

'In the evening of that day (19 February) I came to know that without the knowledge of the Minister of Defence, without any information to me whatsoever, and without the knowledge of anybody, arrangements had been made for the 1st Uganda Battalion to go for training in Bunyoro for two weeks; for the 3rd Uganda Battalion to go for training in Bunyoro; 4th Uganda Battalion to go for training for two weeks in Kizinga, South Ankole. This came to me towards midnight on 19 February and troops were to begin moving to take their positions by about 21 February. I would not like to say very much at this stage but here is the actual document of this movement. I had to summon the Minister of State for Defence immediately and I had to write a letter that very night to the Minister and to the Commander of the Army cancelling these training arrangements.'

Later the report added:

'Then on Monday, 21 February, a senior police officer went

to Makindye to **report to the** President about the situation. After the police **officer had** reported to the President, the President asked whether the police officer knew what was going to happen on 22 February. Obviously the officer did not know, and then the President immediately said: "Oh, do not worry, this is one of the Kampala rumours." But the officer felt that this was important. So immediately after leaving the President he came to see me and he told me that he had been asked about the 22nd. I said that we had better find out what was going to happen on the 22nd, but as far as I know I have already cancelled the army movements. I moved therefore to Kampala and I found that this was really the day—it was to happen on the 22nd that most of the troops would be in training and just a small section would have been used.'

Obote had also learned that on 8 February the President had called in the British High Commissioner in Kampala and had asked him about the possibility of bringing in British troops. Mutesa says in his book:

'I sounded out the British High Commissioner and some African ambassadors as to whether it would be possible to fly in troops if the situation got out of hand. I did not invite a foreign force to invade Uganda. I had in mind something similar to the successful intervention by the British which Obote had authorised two years before. It seemed to me likely that a *coup* was imminent. Neither the Brigadier nor I as Commander in Chief had authorised the troop movements. . . .'

Exactly what Mutesa had asked of the British is unknown but it is extremely doubtful if he ever sounded out any African country. If a *coup d'état* began, military intervention would have to be swift and thus the Kabaka would only have consulted the countries in the region. As members of the community, neither Tanzania nor Kenya had High Commissions in Uganda so they must be ruled out. Rwanda had no army to send and like the

Sudan, Obote enjoyed good relations with the leaders of these two countries. Egypt, Ghana and Nigeria all had embassies in Kampala but were too far away to be able to intervene and certainly none of them would have done so for the Kabaka. This leaves only Zaïre and at that juncture Obote's relations with both Kasavubu and Mobutu were improving, so again an approach here seems unlikely. Mutesa in fact claims to have approached 'some' African embassies but it seems likely this was probably a cover for his having only approached Britain.

The Cabinet met again on 22 February. Obote revealed now what a ruthless and decisive politician he was. A dozen Ugandan policemen burst into the Cabinet room and arrested five Ministers, Grace Ibingira (Ankole), Dr. Emmanuel Lumu (Muganda), George Magezi (Munyoro), Balaki Kirya (Mukedi) and Mathias Ngobi (Musoga).

On 23 February, Amin, who had been deputy army commander was promoted to Army Chief of Staff, with Brigadier Opolot, the Army Commander, being made Chief of Defence Forces. While nominally Opolot was promoted (he was dismissed and detained eight months later), the move was intended to bring the command of the army more directly under Amin, who was regarded by Obote as loyal. The Colonel must have recalled this, when on 1 November 1970, he found himself the victim of a similar shuffle. The effect of the February 1966 crisis had been for Amin in the space of nineteen days to move from his suspension being demanded in Parliament to his being promoted.

That swift change of fortune—particularly as few knew Amin had been authorised to liaise with the Congo nationalists— amazed many. But had they known what was going on behind the scenes they would have been even more surprised. On the night the Parliamentary resolution was debated Amin went into hiding believing Opolot had ordered his arrest. There was some reason to believe his fears were well founded as two senior officers and a squad of armed soldiers were searching that night for Amin. Opolot on the other hand claimed rumours reached him that Amin was planning to have him murdered. On 5

February, the day after the resolution, the Attorney General advised Onama that it would be unconstitutional to suspend Amin, as this could only be done by the Defence Council and Opolot ignored an instruction from the Defence Minister to send Amin on leave pending investigations. Amin was armed and stayed in the homes of various friends during the next few days while Obote called a meeting of the Defence Council at Arua on 9 February. But earlier that day two majors and a dozen heavily armed soldiers arrived at Moyo where Obote was. Obote had been warned in advance that they were coming, met them with a unit of the Police Special Force and several thousand civilians armed with bows, arrows and spears. Whatever the squad's true intentions the majors now said Opolot could not attend the Defence Council because of the tense situation in Kampala and they produced a letter from the commander stating that Amin was intending to kill him. Onama and Bataringaya tried to resolve the confrontation between the two soldiers but neither Opolot nor Amin would attend a meeting together for fear of the other. Onama met them individually and Amin asked for a police bodyguard and although the Ministers accepted this, Opolot vehemently opposed it.

While all of this was occurring Akena Adoko had received a report that Amin was planning a *coup* and he promptly reported this to Obote and sent his own men to investigate. It was found that there was nothing in this charge and what has to be appreciated about the whole of this chaotic confrontation is that Obote knew throughout Amin's exact role with the Congo nationalists as he had authorised it, whereas the Prime Minister's opponents were seeking to use Amin as a Trojan horse with the ultimate objective of getting Obote. All of the details of Amin's involvement had in fact come out in the preliminary investigation but were unknown to the public and thus the allegations in Parliament on 4 February sent shock waves through Uganda.

The matter however did not end there. On 19 February Obote cancelled Opolot's order for a large section of the army to be sent for 'training'. On the following day both Onama and Opolot requested that 600 recruits should be allowed to leave

Jinja for Namalu in southern Karamoja for a passing out parade
and Obote agreed. They reached Namalu on 21 February but
according to reports reaching Obote they were immediately
ordered to return to Jinja and then move into Kampala to arrest
Obote and other leaders. As the recruits headed back towards
Jinja they were met between there and Tororo by the 1st
Battalion and were arrested and disarmed.

The gold and ivory commission began work on 7 March and
the three judges exonerated Obote and his fellow Ministers.
Daudi Ocheng could bring no evidence to substantiate his
charges made in Parliament and although Amin admitted banking £17,000, the Commission's lawyer noted: 'Amin never
denied the receipt of the money. It was manifestly clear from
what Mr. Nyati [the Congolese nationalist who handed over the
money] said, Amin discharged his trust to the full satisfaction.'
Even then one strange incident clouded the inquiry. The question
of Amin's bank account had first been raised in Parliament in
March 1965 when Onama promised an investigation and the
scandal had been revived by a cable from the Congolese
nationalist, General Olenga.

Inexorably the confrontation continued to unfold. Obote
called an extraordinary meeting of the National Assembly on
15 April and in what must qualify as one of the most remarkable
pieces of Parliamentary high-handedness in history, demanded
that Members should pass a new interim constitution—which
was still being printed—without debate or even seeing it. They
would find copies in their pigeon holes as they left, he told them.
Obote's followers tend to justify this by arguing that the new
constitution contained little change—other than what was
necessary. The new provisions made the Prime Minister Executive President, ordered that there would be direct elections from
Buganda to the central Parliament, instituted central Government
auditing of Buganda government finances and terminated the
practice in Buganda of payment in kind by way of land to
leading figures.

The Baganda reacted with predictable anger. On 20 May the
Lukiiko passed a motion stating they no longer recognised the

authority of the Obote government as it had abrogated the 1962 constitution and it ordered the central government off Buganda soil. The gesture was as futile and symbolic as Buganda's secession from Britain six and a half years earlier. Rioting broke out and six police stations were stormed with some loss of life. Three Buganda chiefs—Sebanakita, Lutaya and Matovu—who had been prominent in the *Lukiiko* motion, were arrested and the scene was set for the final act.

Trees were felled near the government lodge as road blocks on 23 May and Amin was ordered to clear the area. According to Akena Adoko, a first cousin of Obote and head of the General Service Department at the time of the 1971 *coup d'état*, in *Uganda Crisis*, some of those captured at the road blocks told police officers later that day they had been issued arms at the Kabaka's palace and ordered to go and fight. The Cabinet met and Amin was ordered to go to the palace at Mengo Hill to ascertain whether there were any illegal supplies of arms.

At dawn troops had surrounded the palace and there followed the second battle of Mengo Hill. In 1892 Captain Lugard representing British Imperial interests had effectively circumscribed Buganda's autonomy for all time. In May 1966 Obote effectively destroyed the 500-year-old kingdom. Accounts of the second Mengo battle vary wildly. The Kabaka under the 1962 constitution had been allowed a personal bodyguard of 300 men, but he states that in May 1966 he had only 120, many of whom were absent. They were equipped with Lee Enfield rifles and 'managed to get hold of three carbines, half a dozen Sterling submachine-guns and six automatic rifles'. Against a numerically superior, better trained and equipped force they had no chance. Officially the dead were put at forty-seven but the Kabaka implies it might have been as high as 2,000 which is deliberately misleading. After the *coup d'état*, when courting Baganda support, Amin said ten truck-loads of bodies were taken from Mengo, but as he was responsible for the original official figure of forty-seven this, too, is dubious. Certainly, based on the Kabaka's own account of the numbers in the palace grounds during the battle, it seems highly improbable that the dead could have numbered more than 100 at the very outside. During the battle the Kabaka fled with some of his bodyguards and finally made his way to Burundi and he was then flown to Britain where he died in 1969, aged forty-five.

His exiled courtiers in London put it out that he had been poisoned, but an official inquest found that the Kabaka, who it was well known drank to excess, had died from alcoholic poisoning. It was a month after the Kabaka's death, as he was leaving a UPC conference, which had adopted a resolution demanding Uganda should become a one-party state, that Obote was shot. His assailant and the rest of the would-be assassins were all Baganda. Uganda's British Chief Justice five months later sentenced six people to life imprisonment including a defrocked clergyman, the Revd. Erisa Sebalu, while five others received terms of fourteen years for conspiracy. Sebalu said the plot had begun in June 1969. After the assassination attempt, road blocks were set up in Buganda and the army behaved harshly towards civilians. The government said seven people were killed but it seems probable the figure was higher. Twenty-six people—twenty-one of them Baganda—were arrested including Members of Parliament and a former Vice-President, Sir Wilberforce Nadiope. Opposition parties were banned and Uganda became a *de facto* one-party state.

———•◆◆◆•———

Despite the severity of the outcome of the confrontation between Obote and Buganda between February and May, there was remarkably little reaction from the Baganda. In part the speed with which Obote moved contributed to this, as did the flight of the Kabaka. Only a handful of the 200 Baganda in the top echelons of the country's civil service left their jobs. The Baganda challenged the interim constitution, but it was upheld in the courts as a legal document, and Obote began immediately drafting a new republican constitution.

What Obote did in 1966 and 1967 was to move towards populist egalitarianism, crushing at the same time monarchist, separatist and minority élitist groups. It was not a move against the Baganda only, but against the neo-traditionalist establishment at Mengo, in the *Lukiiko*, and elsewhere in the country. Even after 1966 the Baganda were very heavily represented in the Parliament and in 1967 they had seven Ministers out of a total of seventeen in the central Cabinet. Before independence they had held two out of every five places at Makerere, and while their percentage declined in the first decade after independence as more places became available to more tribes, none the less their absolute numbers rose and they had one out of every three places, or double their share in proportion to the population.

The confrontation at Mengo had been between the forces representing on the one hand entrenched minority ethnic privileges and those who stood for national unity. Ali Mazrui notes that if the Kabaka and neo-traditionalists had won in 1966 it seems highly probable that the *coup d'état* of January 1971 would have come earlier.

Obote's approach with his republican constitution made public in June 1967 was radically different from his 'rubber stamp' demand in Parliament fourteen months earlier. The new con-

stitution was debated for three months before being adopted on
8 September, including a month by a Constitutional Assembly
of Members of Parliament, and a substantial number of amend-
ments were accepted by the government. Now the republican
constitution went further and three particular points in this must
be noted:

1. It confirmed the abolition of the kingdoms and, with
the exception of the Kabaka, the traditional kings were
pensioned off.

2. Buganda was divided into four districts with the same
status as those elsewhere in Uganda.

3. It considerably tightened the central government's
control over the districts, removing the autonomy which
had hitherto inhibited the building of a nation state.

Nelson Kasfir draws attention to three particular problems
that Obote faced at this juncture. Buganda had long been the
model for the other kingdoms seeking to assert their own
separatist tendencies and the *bête noire* of the northerners. Much
of what had now been achieved towards moulding a nation
state had been at the expense of the Baganda and there was no
way of telling how deep their bitterness ran. While many
Baganda civil servants stayed at their posts they were acquiescing
—for there was little else they could do—rather than supporting
Obote. Turning the former Buganda Parliament building into
offices for the Defence Ministry can only have exacerbated the
hidden resentments.

The republican constitution had laid down that elections to
the National Assembly must be held five years after the document
was made public—on or before 15 April 1971—and this again
raised the possibility of sub-national grievances resurfacing. In
part, however, this was blocked as all political parties, other than
the UPC, were banned after the assassination attempt on Obote.
Finally, despite the obvious trend towards socialist development
and national equality, wide economic and educational disparities
remained. To push ahead the underprivileged tribes and block
out the Baganda would have further embittered the latter. Yet

the solution here lay in Uganda's own development. By 1971 hospital beds were to have increased by 80 per cent from 1964, while from 1961 to 1968 secondary school places tripled and university places doubled. While Buganda's share, based on percentage of total population, fell, her absolute numbers rose and the allocation of beds and school places elsewhere tended to reduce the feeling of deprivation.

The latter part of 1966 through to 1968 was largely a period of consolidation. In 1968 Obote began a series of up-country 'meet the people' tours using the theme 'One State, One Government, One Parliament, One People'. However, an important factor affected his ability to communicate with the people and at the same time forge a sense of national identity. Uganda then—and still today—has no nationally spoken language and Obote and other politicians, outside their own vernacular areas, were often forced to communicate through interpreters, which inhibited their effectiveness. One of Britain's most far-sighted policies in neighbouring Tanganyika had been the encouragement of Swahili as a national language. This proved a critical factor in the nationalist struggle with a nation that spoke the same language if not always to the same ends.

Swahili has the advantage that, although it is essentially a Bantu language liberally mixed with Arabic, it is tribally neutral. At the British insistence it was taught in Uganda schools prior to the Second World War, but thereafter, largely as a result of pressure from the Baganda—who viewed it as a challenge to Luganda—it was dropped. Thus the possibility of employing language to merge tribal consciousness and identity in Uganda into a national character was lost. The question of Swahili was periodically resurrected but it was not until 1970, when the Language Association of Uganda adopted a motion calling on the government to promote Swahili as a potential national language, that it was given any real thrust. Obote responded to this in October 1970, in a speech after he had been installed as Chancellor of Makerere, by promising to introduce Swahili in schools. Three months later he was overthrown. Ironically it was the soldiers—who from British days had had Swahili as the language of command—who introduced Swahili as a domestic language on Radio Uganda soon after the *coup* and later as the national language.

A national language was essential to the egaliterian ethic that Obote was introducing. Yet why did he wait until as late as October 1970 to give it official blessing?

'For as long as Uganda was a dissected country with six governments: the central government; the Kabaka's government (Buganda); the Omukama's (Bunyoro) government; the Omukama's (Toro) government; the Omugabe's (Ankole) government and the Kyebazinga's (Busoga) government—and with Buganda in particular opposed to Swahili—it was not prudent to reintroduce Swahili. I had to deal with the constitution and the power of the centre first. When this was successfully accomplished in September 1967, the next task was, as I saw it, on ideological guidelines. The National Service and Swahili were my pet twins in the implementation of the ideological guidelines.'

Mazrui argues that 'Obote was looking for both socialist and intellectual respectability and from 1968 onwards these ambitions manifested themselves more sharply. It became clearer than ever that Obote aspired to a socialist revolution for his country and at the same time a reputation of intellectual innovativeness for himself.'

There followed a series of five important ideological policy guidelines under the collective title of 'move to the left'. The first in October 1969 was the 'Common Man's Charter', in many senses comparable to Tanzania's 1967 'Arusha Declaration' and Zambia's 1969 'Humanism'. The 'Common Man's Charter' was presented at an emergency UPC delegates conference in Kampala on 18 December 1969. It committed the country to socialist development, endorsed the republican constitution, rejected feudalism and capitalism, affirmed the UPC would be a mass party and made it clear that nationalisation of the major means of production and distribution was in the offing.

In a speech at the conference, Obote told the delegates: 'I

shall begin with telling you something I have never told you. I am not a coward. At this moment though I am afraid . . . I have a lot to fear.' He was referring to the policies he was about to introduce, but it was the policies of the past which proved almost fatal some hours later, when an attempted assassination took place.

The UPC conference had also adopted Obote's proposals for the establishment of National Service in Uganda, published on 1 October 1969, which were to become Document 2 in the 'move to the left' series. These proposals are of considerable importance, for they show the political path along which Obote was trying to guide Uganda. The objectives were listed as follows:

1. To mobilise all able-bodied persons to develop a real sense of individual and collective responsibility to society, within the overall national goal of 'One Country, One People'.

2. For those citizens who have little or no education or training (professional or technical) the Service will aim at providing expanded opportunities, developing their potentialities and enabling them to acquire skills.

3. The Service will further aim at the promotion of an intercourse amongst all the people of Uganda and provision of facilities for people of different backgrounds to participate in national and community projects, thereby affording to all participants in such projects opportunities to know more and more about Uganda and her people, and to develop new values and attitudes towards the nation.

4. Since the majority of the citizens of Uganda live in rural areas where the standard of living is low and amenities are few, it will be the principal concern of the National Service to encourage and promote new patterns of rural life that are compatible with modern requirements and standards. It is for this reason that it is proposed that the National Service should not be based on training in arms of war, but in arms for the sustained development of the economy, raising the

standard of living, and the inculcation of national unity, integrity and a spirit of dedicated service to the nation.

Basically then, the National Service was seen as a nation-building task-force to provide training and education as well as a meeting point for people from different tribes to merge them into a national identity through contact. A Ministry of National Service was established and every able-bodied man was required to go into the Service for at least one year. National Service or conscription is common enough in Europe and North America. But there the objective is military. In Uganda this would have been secondary. Four National Service camps were to be established initially, one located in each region and activities would include agriculture, animal husbandry and culture. Training centres for primary school leavers and youths aged fourteen to twenty-one were planned in every Parliamentary constituency.

The third document in the series came on 20 April 1970, as a 'Communication from the Chair'—a speech to the National Assembly by Obote. This was largely a review of the government's record and a pointer to the future. Its importance is somewhat limited here although in it Obote announced the appointment of an Electoral Commission, a Minimum Wages Committee, variation of civil service terms and developed the growing theme about the future in Uganda of immigrant minorities—in particular, those of Asian origin.

The fourth document, known as the Nakivubo Pronouncement, was made in a Labour Day speech on 1 May 1970, when Obote referred to the country's need to win economic independence. Major means of production and distribution were taken over with all import and export business placed in the hands of state corporations; and 60 per cent holdings taken in oil companies, banks, credit institutions, insurance firms, transport companies, the copper mines and 'every important manufacturing industry and plantation'. In all eighty private companies were involved and compensation was to be paid from profits 'within a period of time not exceeding fifteen years'. The Uganda government, in fact, proved more flexible when it came to negotiations, both with regard to the percentage holding and the repayment period.

The fifth document in the series, published on 24 August 1970, was entitled 'Proposals for New Methods of Election of Representatives of the People to Parliament'. In some senses it is the most important of the series, for with these proposals Obote sought to break down the final vestiges of tribally based national political representation.

The republican constitution passed in September 1967 had ended the practice of Parliamentary constituencies being based on tribal boundaries. It envisaged would-be Parliamentarians having to appeal to at least two ethnic groups. Obote's 1970 proposal went considerably further. Mazrui noted: 'In many ways Document 5 is the most original piece of constitutional theory to have emerged from independent Uganda and one of the most challenging political experiments to have been seriously considered anywhere in Africa.' It was, he says, a 'brilliantly stimulating idea'.

Certainly the proposals were a unique, although somewhat complex, means of combating tribal politics. Each candidate for Parliament had to stand in a basic constituency of his choice where there would not be less than two or more than three contenders (it was later amended to only two). After he had been nominated in his basic or home constituency he was required to stand also in three other constituencies in the country's other three regions. The electorate would be asked to cast a vote for the representative for that constituency as well as for three other national candidates, each from a different region. The popular votes were then computed on percentage with those 'for' and 'against' each candidate in four constituencies totalled and the candidate with the highest number of votes nationally being declared the winner.

Mazrui describes this as 'electoral polygamy in both a metaphorical and literal sense'. Yet, despite some counter-arguments to the proposals, there was no denying that as Document 5 states, it is aimed at freeing the election process from the dangers of the pulls of tribal loyalties. It notes the absurd degree of tribal

Map 1. The region.

Map 2. The area of conflict.

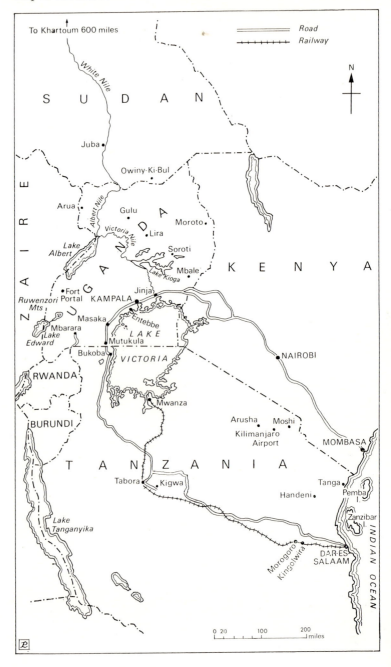

1. Amin with Union Jack in King's African Rifles.

2. Major-General Amin watched by President Obote (on his right with a walking-stick).

3. Amin drives into Kampala, after having seized power

4. Soldiers lead away a civilian.

5. The body of Sebastiano Namirundi against the tree to which he has been tied for public execution in Mbale.

6. Body of Brigadier Okoya as found.

7. Body of Mrs. Okoya as found.

8. Patrick Mukwaya (centre) at the scene of the murder of Brigadier and Mrs. Okoya.

9. Hans Poppe.

10. Amin congratulates Sergeant Musa.

11. Amin addressing a press conference.

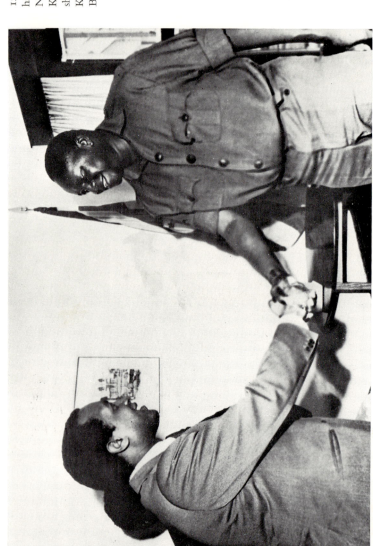

12. Amin shaking hands with ex-King Ntare of Burundi in Kampala (taken shortly before the King was arrested in Burundi).

13. President Idi Amin and British High Commissioner Richard Slater.

14. David Martin tape recording an interview with survivors of the Mutukula massacre.

15. Chancellor of Makerere University.

influence on Ugandan politicians, which had reached a point where a leader would argue that all projects in his constituency were there irrespective of tribal considerations but that others located in other tribal areas were there only because of tribal considerations.

One of the strongest arguments made against the proposals was that it would be possible for a candidate to lose in his basic constituency but be elected on the basis of votes he obtained in the three national constituencies. Mazrui argues that this could disfranchise the basic constituency voters who were represented by a minority candidate. Yet in a sense this is the very thing which happens in Britain: many of the candidates elected to Parliament fail to secure over 50 per cent of the votes in their constituency because the fight is among three or more candidates. The electorate is not disfranchised because their Member of Parliament does not represent the majority of the voters. The very point about Obote's election proposals was that candidates should not be elected on a tribal vote but rather on a national vote and to change this to meet the criticism would have entailed undermining the whole principle.

Document 5 also contains the proposals for the election of the President and considerable confusion exists over Obote's intentions here. Mazrui asserts that the UPC sought to protect Obote from campaigning and wanted the President of the UPC automatically made President of Uganda. As Obote had been elected by the UPC delegates conference in late 1969 for a seven-year term the effect of that was clear. Obote opposed this in a memorandum arguing that the President must face the electorate. The UPC National Council maintained this position at a meeting in September and Obote called another meeting in December where his opposition was finally accepted. The final proposal was based on a Presidential Election by acclaim, with the electorate voting for or against a single candidate put forward by the ruling party, as is common in most African countries. In Uganda, where one-third of the constituencies disagreed with the UPC choice of a Presidential candidate, they would be allowed to put forward their own rival candidate in a two-way contest. That required thirty-two dissenting constituencies which as far as Obote and Uganda were concerned in late 1970 was highly improbable.

Obote sheds some further light on some of the questions Mazrui raises and in particular the question of candidates taking a 'bride' in each constituency to give them, so to speak, a home base:

'The electoral proposals (1970) were widely discussed. I had very many long meetings with members of Mazrui's department at Makerere and of course with other groups. I recall that the point of electoral polygamy was first argued by the late William Kalema at a meeting in my office; Mazrui and others were present. Two days later Mazrui gave a public lecture on it—electoral polygamy. He assumes in the book that the basic constituency and the national constituencies which were to be "married" for the 1971 elections were to remain so "married" in any following future elections. That was not to be so. Constituencies were to be linked afresh for every General Election. In that case any person who went on acquiring wives as suggested by Mazrui, and if elected to two or three Parliaments, will end up with either six or nine wives from the national constituencies. I did not see that as a distinct possibility.

'There is also an assumption in the book about nursing the national constituencies. One of the objectives of the proposals was for prospective candidates to "nurse" the whole country. It would have been futile for anyone to have gone on acquiring brides without knowing whether his basic constituency was to be linked with what constituencies. The linkage was to be done afresh only weeks before nomination day for every general election.'

Obote had entered the Uganda Legislative Assembly in 1958 as a young unknown militant elected on a Lango tribal ticket. In almost his first speech on 6 May 1958 he spoke out strongly against the colonial, tribally orientated electoral system:

'If the government is going to develop this country on a unitary basis, how on earth can the government develop another state within a state? Does the government really think that, when self-government comes to this country, the state of Buganda will willingly give up the powers it has already got now, in order to join with other outlying districts or provinces? I do not think so.'

Within three and a half years he became Prime Minister. The British legacy was a country divided on the basis of position, tradition, constitution, tribe and religion. When he was overthrown in January 1971 he had removed most of these barriers. Elections were scheduled to take place within eighty days that would have gone even further towards cementing the unitary state he had spoken of thirteen years earlier. If history judges him harshly for some individual acts, equally it must judge him as having laid the foundations of a nation state from the scattered pieces of a jigsaw left by the colonial era.

8   Amin's First Repression

———◆•◆◆•◆———

Even when Amin has gone and the present reign of terror in Uganda ends it will probably still not be possible to document fully the horror of his tenure. Today, while he is still in power and fear grips Ugandans, the picture of repression can only be painted in a fragmentary manner. For fear of their own lives people inside Uganda who have given details of the killings cannot be identified. And even those in exile fear to be named in case of reprisals against their relatives at home. But none the less from the accounts of massacres and individual murders that are known, it is now possible to understand the nature of Amin's first three years.

Selective killings have continued since the *coup*. But the major phases of repression broadly break down into two periods. The first came in the twelve months after the *coup* when Amin genuinely feared the influence of three tribes—the Acholi, Langi and Iteso—who for historical reasons dominated the military and para-military in Uganda. The second phase came in the wake of Obote's bid to regain power on 17 September 1972, which Amin repulsed with comparative ease. This programme of repression was more national in character but the tribal focal points were the Baganda, who had rejoiced at Obote's downfall, and the Ankole in the extreme south-west of the country, which had been a strong UPC area, who had cheerfully welcomed the guerrillas of Obote's 'People's Army'. For the sake of clarity and sequence it is necessary to separate these two phases of repression, for, although Amin's personal fear is a common denominator they arose for totally different reasons.

The killing in Uganda began simultaneously with the *coup*. Army Chief of Staff, Brigadier Hussein, who had headed the military counter-measures to Amin's assassination plot, is one of the first known to have been killed. He had escaped from the Parliament building with Oyite Ojok but was captured soon after by Amin's troops. The circumstances of his capture matter little, but the brutal means by which he was killed—which were known to Western embassies in Kampala—provided an important early warning of things to come.

At his first press conference on 26 January 1971, Amin sought to give the impression that the *coup* had been virtually bloodless and that only one soldier had been wounded. To some extent this is true, for in Colonel Tito Okello's 2nd Infantry Brigade there were certainly no casualties or resistance. The battalion at Moroto did fight, but it seems unlikely that at this point there had been any casualties.

But if the *coup* itself was virtually bloodless, it was certainly the signal for a massive bloodletting. Brigadier Hussein and Lieutenant-Colonel Oyok were dragged into the maximum security prison at Upper Luzira on the same day that Amin gave his press conference. A military spokesman announced Hussein had been captured in good health and would be allowed to return to his residence. But in the prison courtyard, in front of horrified warders, they were clubbed with rifle butts and kicked. Hussein's body was hideously mutilated before the end of the beating by soldiers whom warders insist were not Ugandans because of their tribal markings which were southern Sudanese. Amin was contacted and told of the condition of the two officers and he promised to have them taken to hospital. Almost an hour later, when no transport had arrived to remove the men, Amin was again contacted. A little later an armoured personnel carrier loaded with troops drove into Luzira. The two dying officers, in terrible agony, were thrown into the back and as the carrier drove out of the prison, warders could see that the beating with rifle butts had resumed.

Exactly how they finally died is not known. But a guard working at Amin's house, which became known as the 'Command Post', insists that Hussein's severed head was brought there in the carrier. The guard later fled into exile and according to his story the head was put on Amin's table, where he addressed it. Then it was kept in a fridge overnight.

Another example of what was occurring in Uganda's prisons

immediately after the *coup* was given to me in a vivid description
by Joshua Wakholi, who had been Minister of Public Service and
Cabinet Affairs for almost five years when Amin seized power
and who was killed in 1972. He fled immediately after the *coup*
to Kenya but returned to Uganda on 28 January when Amin
ordered all the former Ministers to report to him at the State
House in Entebbe. He handed in all the government property and
on 10 February quietly went back to live in his home village in the
Bugisu district. But on March 1st two men called at his house
looking for him. Wakholi was out and the men arrested his wife,
Alice, and two-month-old baby and took them to Mbale Police
Station where they were locked up.

Bugisu district was one of the UPC strongholds and a number
of important party conferences had been held in the area. Although it has been generally reported that in 1971 the Acholi
and Langi were the main victims of the reign of terror which
followed the *coup*, the Bagisu also suffered heavily. Wakholi
realised his wife and child were being held as hostages, so at 4.00
a.m. on 2 March he gave himself up and they were freed.

On the following day he was transferred to Makindye Prison
in Kampala, and within twenty-four hours his head had been
split open to the skull by a military policeman who hit him with a
stick. The most notorious cells at Makindye were named 'Singapore', after the Malaysian capital where Obote was when he was
overthrown, and 'Dar es Salaam', where he had gone into exile.
Wakholi was put in 'Singapore' cell with a number of other
prisoners and on the following day was joined by a police superintendent named Shekashshi. On 5 March the whole group were
transferred into the next door cell, which gave rise to the hope
that they were not condemned men as most of the inmates of
'Singapore' normally were.

The same night they learned why they had been transferred.
Soon after dark a group of thirty-six army officers and one
corporal were brought into the prison. Through a spyhole on
their door, the people in the adjoining cell watched the hideous
scene unfold. Some of the officers were crawling, crying out in
pain because their arms or legs had been broken. Military police

guards prodded them with bayonets and knives to hurry them up.

The thirty-seven were locked in until around 11.00 p.m. when one or more army personnel carriers arrived at Makindye. The prisoners were ordered out of 'Singapore' cell but refused because they realised they were to be killed.

'The prisoners started shouting and wailing and then the cell door was thrown open and we saw three or four soldiers move into it. They started shooting and when they stopped after a couple of minutes there was no sound except for the groans and screams from the wounded. Then they started dragging the bodies out and those who were still alive were killed with *pangas* (an African long knife like a machete) or shot. They did not seem able to kill one officer whom we thought was a military chaplain. He kept groaning and they kept on shooting and slashing him. The bodies were loaded into an armoured personnel carrier and as they drove away we could hear the man still shouting "Halle-lujah",' Wakholi said.

The next morning at 6.00 a.m. the prisoners in the adjoining cell were ordered out and given scrubbing brushes and pails of water. 'In "Singapore" cell the blood was a quarter of an inch deep on the floor. We scrubbed for six hours but it was very difficult to clean. There were pieces of skull, teeth, brain tissue and dozens of empty shell cases.'

I have two independent accounts of this incident. A Lieutenant Silver Tibihika, who was later to be an important witness in the matter of the killing of two Americans, was also detained in Makindye that night and his version of what he saw and heard totally corroborates Wakholi's story. Wakholi was killed in the September 1972 bid to overthrow Amin, and Tibihika is living in exile in Tanzania. The name of the third man, a civilian, cannot be given as he and his family are still in Uganda. But statements have been taken from all three on the Makindye Massacre of 5 March.

Wakholi was a man of considerable courage. He had fled and gone back. To free his wife and child he surrendered. After witnessing a number of other atrocities at Makindye he was finally released on 17 May 1971. Again he quietly went home spending much of his time hiding in a small house in the bush. He received a tip-off that he was to be killed when William Kalema, Minister of Commerce and Industry in the Obote government, disappeared. 'I realised then it was a matter of days before I also would be collected,' he told me when he reached Tanzania after fleeing early in March 1972. But he volunteered to join the September force although he had no military experience. He received a month's training but he was wounded during the retreat and died or was killed soon after being captured.

Another Makindye survivor, who again cannot yet be identified because he has relatives alive inside Uganda, gave this account of eleven days he spent inside the prison. 'I was arrested on 17 February and taken to Makindye. The first night I was there they killed forty soldiers in "Singapore" cell. They were a mixed group of Acholi and Langi officers and other ranks. Two armoured personnel carriers arrived from the Malire Mechanised Regiment after dark. The military police in charge of the prison had been told not to let any soldiers in but they were frightened. The soldiers went into "Singapore" and bayoneted the prisoners. Then they calmly drove away. Those who were not dead were taken to Luzira for treatment and the bodies were loaded into three-ton trucks and taken away.'

The Malire unit was located two and a half miles away on Mengo Hill in the former Kabaka's palace and for three consecutive nights the soldiers returned. 'More Acholi and Langi prisoners were being brought in every day from around the country. We always knew they were from these two tribes because they were kept separately. Each night they came back and killed all the people in the "Singapore" cell. They did not waste bullets. They used bayonets or knives, splitting people's stomachs open, cutting their throats or beheading them. After the first night they took the bodies away each time and made sure everybody was dead.'

For a week there was no more killing. But on 27 February a member of the General Service Department was brought in. He had a wound across his skull where a bullet had creased him. 'Some of those being detained at Makindye at this time were

Amin's soldiers who had got into trouble. They were allowed special privileges, roaming around in the prison, and they had *waragi* (Ugandan gin) brought in. They got hold of this young boy from the GSD and broke his jaw in several places. He was left for two days in agony and could not eat. Then these same soldiers forced him to eat by beating him. Finally they made him keep doing somersaults down a slope in the prison yard. He kept losing consciousness but they revived him. Finally he died.'

In another incident an Acholi officer who was detained went berserk, grabbed a gun and killed eleven guards before he was finally shot down. Another prisoner hit a guard on the head with a stone and despite a hail of fire clambered over two eight-foot-high fences before he was finally killed outside the prison.

After eleven days the witness to these events was transferred to the maximum security prison at Upper Luzira. There he spent four months in solitary confinement and at one point his only food was chicken mash. The prisons at Upper and Lower Luzira were run by civilian prison staff and there were fewer atrocities. But a few incidents are worth recalling. In July Radio Uganda broadcast that a Mr. Labeja, a traffic officer in the Railways Corporation, had been captured. It was claimed that he had brought a message from Obote saying that all Baganda, including his own children by a Muganda woman, should be killed. Mr. Labeja had heard the announcement while he was at Kitjumu burying his father. He had tried to flee but Kenyan police arrested him at the border, recognised his name and handed him over in handcuffs to the Ugandans. He was later killed at Mutukula.

On 7 March five officers were taken from Upper Luzira. They included Lieutenant-Colonel Oboma Ayumu, another half-colonel and three majors. Ayumu was the brother of Adoko Nekyon, a former Obote Minister. Witnesses at Makindye remember at the same time a number of senior army officers being removed from there. At 6.00 p.m. on 8 March Radio Uganda made the following announcement:

'A spokesman for the President's Office informs the public that there should be no cause for alarm as a result of an

explosion which was heard around Kampala near Rubiri
between 5.00 p.m. and 6.00 p.m. this evening. The explanation for that explosion is that the army was destroying a
damaged bomb. The spokesman informs the public that
there are still a few more damaged bombs to be destroyed.
Should the public hear such explosions from tomorrow
they should not panic unduly. This explanation is to counter-
act some rumours which might have already been spread as
a result of that explosion.'

The truth as to what had occurred was that thirty-two senior
Acholi and Langi officers had been herded into a room at Malire.
Explosives were packed around the room and detonated, killing
all of them. There were no more announcements about explosions
from 'damaged bombs'. That sort of method of murder was just
too public.

The soldiers on leave at Gulu did not definitely know until the
afternoon of 25 January that there had been a *coup*. They decided
to seize all the armaments at the Gulu Air Base but found there
were only enough rifles for a platoon and only enough ammunition to last five minutes. Neither was there any fuel for the planes.

After agreeing that there would be a meeting of officers and
NCOs on the following day the soldiers dispersed. At the meeting it was decided to oppose the *coup*. Major Obote, a cousin of
the deposed President, had been sent to Lira to check on the
situation there and he returned and reported to a second meeting
that day that there were an estimated 600 soldiers there, all on
leave, who were asking for arms. The commander of Entebbe
Air Base, Major Nyeko, who had been on leave at Kitgum when
the *coup* occurred, arrived at Gulu and personally accused Onama,
who was still there, of being involved in the *coup*.

The killing at Gulu began on 28 January. An infantry company,
supported by four armoured personnel carriers, attacked the
town where several hundred loyal troops were still uncertain
what to do. Houses and shops were ransacked and the house of
the army captain blown up with explosives killing seven people.
Most of the soldiers left the town for the bush and on 8 February,

323 officers and other ranks met and it was decided to send the captain to Tanzania to make contact with Obote. Eventually many of the others reached Tanzania, but almost every one of those who returned to his unit in answer to Amin's guarantee of safety was killed.

A private who was one of the group at Lira said that nearly 400 soldiers reported to the District Commissioner's office after Amin ordered everyone on leave to return to barracks. They came from units all over the country, but the first group who left were all taken towards Kampala, escorted by soldiers who supported Amin. The other 200 were told to report back the next day but less than fifty did so. The rest had heard what happened to their colleagues and had fled. A lorry had followed the first convoy and had seen one truck and a bus stop at Kartuma Falls. The soldiers had been ordered out, bayoneted and their bodies thrown into the Falls, which are on the Victoria Nile which links Lake Albert and Lake Kyoga. This was one of the first human meals fed to the scores of crocodiles in the river in the coming months.

Throughout February Amin's soldiers roamed through the Lango district hunting down soldiers who had not reported back to their units. Many, along with their relatives, were killed. Women were raped by groups of soldiers and shops and houses ransacked.

Little news came out about the killings in those early days and in Kampala Western diplomats—and in particular British and Israelis—openly ridiculed suggestions of mass killings. One of the first detailed accounts to appear was in the Tanzanian newspaper, the *Nationalist*, run by the ruling Tanganyika African National Union (TANU) party on 17 February. The paper reported that the police officer in charge of Jinja, Assistant Superintendent Oget had been shot by troops on 6 February and his body thrown in the Nile. At about the same time the headmaster of Busoga College at Mwiri had been clubbed unconscious by troops with rifle butts and hospitalised. A squad of five soldiers headed by a lieutenant had said they were taking him away and he would never be seen again, but courageously several hundred staff and students stood in front of the jeep and refused to allow the unconscious men to be removed. Two days later a Zambian journalist, Nebukadonezu Ocoo, reported in the same paper after leaving Uganda that he had seen troops being executed, a truckload of bodies and the rotting corpses of soldiers lying beside the Koch to Bodi road. On 14 March a British freelance journalist, Brian Tetley, based in Nairobi, writing in the *Observer* reported that nightly executions were being carried out at Kartuma Falls, where he had personally seen the blood-stained stonework, and the bodies were being fed to the crocodiles. Former UPC leaders and soldiers in hiding at this point decided to organise an escape route into the southern Sudan and the private from Lira was one of those sent to survey various routes.

Only a handful of people knew that Obote had slipped out of Dar es Salaam on or about 15 February after it had been agreed to set up a training camp about 100 miles west of the capital for those who reached Tanzania. He flew to Khartoum where the Sudanese government gave him a house and set about laying on training facilities in the southern Sudan for his plan to regain power. His Presidential emblem continued to fly at the masthead above Dar es Salaam's State House, convincing many people he was still in the Tanzanian capital.

Contact was made with soldiers in hiding in northern Uganda and with civilians willing to fight, and on 13 April several hundred people set out in trucks from Lira to join Obote. Four trucks headed north through Palabek with 217 people in them. The total number to cross into Sudan that night was supposed to have been 680 and finally other vehicles joined them at the rendezvous point bringing the number of people to 635. Guides met the group north-west of Palabek and they set out on foot, crossing the Aswa River into Sudan at 6.30 a.m. on 14 April.

Almost immediately they met a heavily armed band of Anyanya and they were marched five miles to a guerrilla camp just back across the frontier in Uganda. The refugees, realising they might be handed over to Amin's soldiers, made a mass break and seventeen of them got back to the Sudan. The rest were to be slaughtered. At dawn on 16 April five of the survivors went back to where they had last seen the rest of the group. Blood was scattered over a wide area but there were no bodies.

Both Anyanya camps had been evacuated, and the private from Lira, who was one of the five people who went back to find the remainder of the group, said in a statement:

'The track continued towards Palabek. We followed it up to a village. There we were told that our people had been escorted through the village by Anyanya and Amin's soldiers the previous evening. The five of us spent the night in the village.

'The next day, 17 April, the villagers told us that Amin had come by helicopter to Palabek, spoken to our men, praised the Anyanya and ordered the execution of all our men.'

One of the group, with part of his intestines hanging out, eventually reached the Sudan. All of the remaining 617 people had been slaughtered. On 29 April, Amin, in a protest note to the Sudan, said that Obote supporters had established a training camp at Owiny-ki-Bul inside the Sudan and the deposed President had been there two days earlier. Amin claimed Sudanese troops had crossed into Uganda and had been repulsed with loss of life and two days later the Sudanese Chargé d'affaires in Kampala, Mr. Ishag Muhammad Ibrahim, was given twenty-four hours to leave.

The murders continued unabated throughout the next few months. Sixty young Baganda, recruited as an honour guard for the funeral of the late Kabaka whose body was being brought back from Britain for a state funeral, were taken to a training site at Kabamba near Mubende and executed. Their crime apparently was that they had demonstrated by volunteering that they were too anxious to get military training and, Amin, despite the way the Baganda welcomed Obote's overthrow, knew that they still remembered him as the 'murderer of Mengo'.

On 1 February in Kampala troops surrounded a house where Lieutenant-Colonel Emmanuel Ogwal, who was loyal to Obote, was hiding. He held them off courageously for several hours until a recoilless rifle blasted a hole in the wall, killing him. The house belonged to a British-trained gynaecologist, Dr. George Ebine. He was dragged from the operating theatre and killed. The woman patient he was operating on also died. Professor Vincent Emiru, a brilliant eye specialist at Makerere University, was taken away by troops and murdered. Hundreds of others whose names are unknown except to their friends and relatives died as Amin's soldiers scoured the country. In May he passed a decree empowering his troops to shoot on sight anyone suspected of having, or being about to, commit a crime.

The first of the eighteen reasons given for the *coup* had been: 'The unwarranted detention without trial and for long periods of a large number of people, many of whom are totally innocent of any charges.' Immediately after the *coup* in a fanfare of publicity Amin released fifty-five political detainees, including the former Prime Minister, Benidicto Kiwanuka. By the standards of many African countries that was a comparatively small number. Then on 11 May, Amin himself issued a decree providing for detentions without trial. At that point about 1,000 people were in detention. They were almost all to die like many others who had been arrested. It is ironic that the eighteenth reason for the *coup* was to prevent bloodshed.

Massacres of Acholi and Langi who were still in the army began on a massive scale in late June. Lieutenant Tibihika, briefly detained after the *coup*, had been the intelligence officer at Mbarara Barracks, headquarters of the Simba (Swahili for lion) Battalion. The Acholi and Langi at Mbarara had not acted to support Obote five months earlier when the *coup* occurred. But on 22 June they were separated from other troops on the square. Then they were herded into lorries and driven to a nearby ranch where their throats were cut. According to Tibihika, who witnessed the slaughter, between 150 and 200 were killed. But other accounts put the number killed at Mbarara over that period as high as 500.

News of the slaughter filtered through to Kampala where it was picked up by thirty-three-year-old American freelance journalist, Nicholas Stroh, the son of a wealthy Detroit brewer.

He had left his job on the *Philadelphia Evening Bulletin* some months earlier to try his hand as a freelance in Africa and the news of the Mbarara Massacre provided him with the chance of the big breakthrough he needed. On 7 July, accompanied by another American, Robert L. Siedle, a lecturer in sociology at Makerere, he set out for Mbarara to investigate the rumours. For nine months there was no news of either man until Tibihika, who had just fled to Tanzania, was put into contact with me.

In retrospect, reading the story I wrote for the *Observer* at the time, I realise how circumspect I was about Tibihika's story. But at a subsequent inquiry it was to prove accurate in the main details. The Lieutenant said that on 7 July the two Americans arrived at the barracks asking to see the commanding officer, Lieutenant-Colonel Ali, who was away at a conference in Kampala. Instead Stroh later saw the second-in-command, Major Juma, who had been a taxi driver at the time of the *coup*. There was a heated argument and Stroh was arrested. Later that day Tibihika saw the Major driving the American's blue Volkswagen.

That night in the mess a group of officers promoted from the ranks after the *coup* were laughing about the Americans' deaths. 'They started talking about how the man had been proud and how they had killed him with his friend. They talked in the mess about how they had killed the Americans and one repeated Stroh's last words and laughed. He said these had been: "You may kill us but you will answer for this one day." '

Lieutenant-Colonel Ali returned to the barracks on the following day and, according to Tibihika, ordered his second-in-command to stop driving the American's car. Then a week later, after the American Embassy in Kampala began inquiries, the Lieutenant says he was called by Ali, sworn to secrecy and sent to dig up the bodies of the two Americans from a shallow grave ten and a half miles from the camp. The ribs of one of the men were protruding above the surface and Tibihika says that although they were badly decomposed the bodies were recognisable. They were put into sacks, taken to the barracks and burned near the mess. Then the remaining parts were dumped in a river. Next the car was burned and again according to the Lieutenant, dumped over a cliff on the Fort Portal road.

After two abortive military inquiries to ascertain what had happened to the men, Amin had been forced, as a result of American pressure, to appoint a judicial inquiry headed by a courageous British judge, Mr. Justice David Jefferys Jones. They were publicly making little progress until Tibihika's story. The Judge then headed for the Mountains of the Moon—the rugged Ruwenzori range—to search for the remains of the car and a day later when they had not been able to find it, I was telephoned from Fort Portal to get a more detailed description of the exact location from Tibihika. They found the wreck, soon after, in the remote Buranga Pass in the foothills of the Mountains of the Moon, 180 miles from Mbarara. Amin accused the Judge of going behind his back by finding it. Other details then began to come to light and finally Amin ordered the inquiry to wind up before a search could be instituted for possible remains of the bodies where Tibihika said they had been dumped.

The Jones report, which he described as 'mission impossible', identified those who might have been involved in the murders after Mr. John Wilkinson, a British Q.C., had flown to Tanzania to take a full statement from Tibihika. Mr. Justice Jones, in fact, completed his report and left Uganda amid rumours that both he and the Q.C. would disappear. No action was ever taken against any of the army officers implicated in the Judge's report which Amin dismissed as resulting from the Judge's 'prejudiced mind'.

Amin's response to mounting rumours of the massacre at Mbarara came on 3 July when he announced he had called off a planned state visit to Malawi because of the security situation on the border with Tanzania, where, he said, seventy officers and about 600 other ranks of the Ugandan army had been killed in fighting at the frontier. President Nyerere replied by inviting Colin Legum, Commonwealth Correspondent of the *Observer*, Miss Bridget Bloom, Africa Correspondent of the *Financial Times* and myself to visit the frontier to ascertain for ourselves if there was any fighting. At the dusty border town of Mutukula we walked to a frontier post accompanied by a Tanzanian army captain. A group of Ugandan soldiers, obviously viewing us with great suspicion, came to see what we were doing. We wanted to know if there had been any fighting at the frontier between the two armies. They insisted there had not. Soldiers of the Tanzanian and Ugandan armies were brothers, they said. Amin next closed the frontier and threatened military action against Tanzania, but it was clear the dead he referred to on 3 July were the victims of the Mbarara Massacre and killings elsewhere.

Then on 11 July Amin left for Tel Aviv to see the Israeli Prime Minister, Mrs. Golda Meir, and later for England to see Mr. Edward Heath and to have lunch with the Queen. The trip itself was bizarre enough. A former British army officer, Major Ian Walsworth-Bell, had drawn up a plan for the invasion of Tanzania for Amin, who planned to seize the north of the country across to the port of Tanga, to give himself an outlet to the Indian Ocean. In addition to his attempting to cover up the murders in the army by claiming that almost 700 army personnel had been killed in border clashes with Tanzania (he increased the figure to 1,000 a few days later), it was obvious that he was trying to create a more favourable atmosphere for his plans to purchase new sophisticated weapons in Britain.

In London, Amin demanded tanks and aircraft at a meeting with the Foreign Secretary, Sir Alec Douglas-Home. The initial reaction was to consider the request favourably if Amin could pay cash, which he certainly could not. Then Amin demanded the latest British vertical take-off Harrier jet-fighters—it is said as many as twenty-five—and Home questioned why he wanted such expensive equipment. 'To bomb Dar es Salaam,' the General is said to have blandly replied.

All he got in London was the promise of a military mission to examine training needs in Uganda. So Amin flew back to Israel. There he met Foreign Minister, Abba Eban, and Defence Minister, Moshe Dayan. Amin bemoaned the fact that Uganda did not have a port. He made it clear he wanted more military supplies and planned to seize Tanga, and as a result Israel stalled on new requests for military aid.

While these incredible meetings were taking place—Amin at

Buckingham Palace was referring to the Duke of Edinburgh as 'Mr. Philip'—renewed slaughter had begun in Uganda. The killings took place mainly at Jinja, Soroti and Moroto and once more the targets were Acholi and Langi soldiers.

The following is taken from a statement made by a private who was in the Jinja barracks on 11 July—the day Amin left for Britain and Israel and the day the killings started. The private says he was in his home on Mpumudde Housing Estate on 11 July, when a large number of Amin soldiers in civilian clothes arrived from Jinja. At 5.00 a.m. the next day he was dragged from his house and taken to the barracks where Acholi and Langi soldiers were lined up. One man was already lying dead and another escaped. The remainder were ordered to lie down in front of the quarter guard and a Land-Rover arrived loaded with bodies. All of the soldiers were then crammed into the building, and they finally managed to break into an adjoining room where they found one sterling machine-gun and 600 rounds of ammunition.

'It was agreed that the gun be used at night for a mass escape. However at about 1.00 p.m. they brought another captive in with his right eye plucked out. The door was opened and the man was pushed in to us. At this point one of us who appeared to have been seriously affected by our captivity and who was nearest the door when the latest captive was brought, tried to prevent the guards from closing the door while at the same shouting that we use the gun against the guards. The shouting was in Luo but at least one guard understood what it meant for them. A guard came to the door and began shooting inside, killing several before he was killed. Corporal Owiny who had our sterling was wounded slightly but he moved to the door and shot dead several guards. We closed the door. There were very many guards all around the building. Shooting from the guards and from us continued through the windows. At about 2.00 p.m., using our sterling we shot at the door of the second room. In this room we found one light machine-gun and sixty rounds. At 3.00 p.m. the captors hit the front wall of the building twice with 106 mm shells. There was some damage to the building but it did not fall and we were lucky that the door was not hit.

'Two armoured personnel carriers then came and they were used to pull down the house or break the walls. One part of the wall facing towards the Rubaga Catholic Mission fell. The majority of the captives got out of the building through that opening and many were killed but some escaped. The remainder of us, numbering about twenty, moved inside into one room between 6.00 p.m. and 7.00 p.m.

'That evening under cover of darkness our leader, Sergeant-Major Ojok, who was surveying the best side of the building for our escape, was shot dead. We continued to shoot at the guards throughout the night but used our limited stock of ammunition sparingly. We had some advantage in the exchanges. We could see the guards but they could not see us.

'On Tuesday 13 July, at about 10.00 a.m. I was near the door and I had the sterling. The guards were throwing grenades at us. An officer came and ordered them to use the 106 mm and APC against us. One sergeant answered that "The bastards had killed the crew". The officer ordered the guards to keep on shooting at us. They were talking and shouting in Swahili and I guessed that the officer gave his orders to Sergeant Bindeba who came from Kigezi.

'When darkness came we had only one full magazine for the sterling. We resolved to get out, and Corporal Owiny, who was suffering greatly because of his wound, offered to give cover to the rest of us. The guards were very active that night. We waited until dawn on 14 July to get out. I was in the first party which jumped over part of the wall broken by the APC and we headed towards the sergeants' mess where we found an APC facing the officers' mess. It began to fire at us but none of us were hit. We jumped over the fence, regrouped and then agreed to disperse. I went into the grass and remained there until about 2.00 p.m.

when I moved to another area near by. There I found two of
the men who had escaped on Monday. They told me the
area was surrounded by our tormentors and other escapees
were near by.'

In all the private said there were seventeen escapees in his area.
Amin's troops were ineffectually shooting into the area at random
and during that night and on the following day he made his way
to the home of a man he knew was a staunch UPC member. But
he found the house, and several others in the area, riddled with
shell holes. At another house he was hidden and his wounds
from splinters from a grenade were treated. After resting for
some days he reached Kenya on 22 July and made contact with
Obote's UPC underground who were ferrying escapees in early
August to a training camp near Tabora in north-west Tanzania.
A Uganda press release announced that the shooting around
Jinja was simply 'manœuvres'.

Another soldier who escaped from Jinja said he was recaptured
almost immediately and with 270 others was taken to a police
station at Kamuli fifty miles from Jinja, where one of Amin's
soldiers, who had been a close personal friend before the *coup*,
helped him to escape. The others all had their throats slit according to the private and police sources who saw the mass executions.

The killings, but on a smaller scale, continued through 1971.
In August the body of Martin Okello, a former Member of
Parliament was found in a shallow grave. During the last quarter
of 1971 the killing came under more specialised control. Four
units—military intelligence, the State Research Office, military
police and what was called ironically the Public Safety Unit
headed by a Nubian police superintendent, Ali Towilli—spearheaded the selective killings. The BMWs, Peugeot 504s and 404s
of these squads, made up mainly of Nubians and Amin's Kakwa
tribesmen, became a dreaded sight wherever they stopped in the
coming months. Michael Kagwa, President of the Industrial
Court, was found dead, his hands and legs tied to the wheel of
his burned-out sports car which had its doors locked on the
outside.

Twice in the latter part of the year Tanzanian and Ugandan troops clashed at the frontier. The cause of the first clash appears to have been that Tanzania arrested four Ugandan soldiers who had crossed the frontier. Uganda had already arrested nineteen Tanzanian civilians in the border area and it seems probable the Tanzanians contemplated an exchange. The result, however, was a brisk battle in which Tanzanian artillery mauled Ugandan armour, knocking out four tanks. The second clash came in October at a time when Amin was demanding the annexation of about 100 square miles of northern Tanzania bounded by the Kagera River, Lake Victoria and the Uganda border.

One typically bizarre claim by Amin marked the first incident. On Radio Uganda he claimed a Chinese colonel fighting with the Tanzanians had been shot dead during the clash. Amin put his body first on display on the table at a transporters' conference and then at a stadium at Nakivubo, while Radio Uganda claimed the man before he died 'begged for mercy saying he was only a Chinese sent by Nyerere'. In fact the man was Hans Poppe, the police commander in the border area, who was of mixed German and African parentage. The Tanzanians could have swiftly quashed Amin's wild claim as Poppe had a large mole on the right side of his face, near his nose. But the photograph the Tanzanians released of the missing policeman, who had been shot when he drove to the frontier, was taken from the other side and barely showed the distinctive mole. Poppe's driver said he had been shot in the stomach. But when the body was on display, people saw a bullet wound just behind the ear.

All these killings had been taking place in the last eleven months of 1971. But generally they were given little credence, for they were coming largely from Ugandan exiles and their version of events was regarded as highly dubious. The human sacrifices at Karuma Falls had been written about and it was known there had been killing in the army in July. Stroh and Siedle were missing but there was no clue what had happened to them. Many officers had disappeared after the *coup* but little heed was paid to this and they were generally written off as victims of the fight between troops loyal to Amin and those loyal to Obote.

Despite having lived in Tanzania through those months, where the press published more about the killings than anywhere else, I was still not prepared for a phone call at 6.00 p.m. on 1 January 1972. The caller was Adoko Nekyon, a second cousin of Obote, who had been a Cabinet Minister until he resigned in 1968. Nekyon was almost hysterical and in retrospect, given the fact that the exiles had said nothing publicly since Obote's first press conference, I should have realised that Nekyon ringing me with a prepared statement was highly unusual.

He said that at least 300 detainees had been moved from Luzira Prison in Kampala three days earlier and taken to a remote part of Uganda—possibly the prison at Mutukula on the frontier with Tanzania. They were assured, Nekyon said, that they were being taken to be court-martialled, which conformed with an announcement made a few days earlier by Amin. Nekyon said they were almost all soldiers or members of the disbanded General Service Department, but the group also included Assistant Commissioner of Police, Muhammad Hassan, who was head of CID, his deputy, Mr. Festus Wauyo, and the third-in-command of the CID, Mr. Ochungi. Although I did not realise it at the time, I later learned these were the three most senior police officers who had handled the Okoya murder case.

Nekyon's statement read: 'We think the whole world should be concerned about this move because about a month ago we received reports that about 1,000 soldiers and GSD officers who were in detention were to be moved to Mutukula under the pretext that they were to be court-martialled there. But after some time an announcement was to be made to the effect that before their trial Tanzanian troops attacked the prison and killed all of them. Now the transfer has been made we are sure that within the next few days we will hear the announcement.'

He went on to argue that there was no reason why they should be court-martialled for they had been arrested for doing their legitimate duty in resisting the *coup*. 'The three police officers are alleged to have tried to implicate General Amin in the murder of Brigadier Okoya. This is an alleged crime which cannot be brought before a military court-martial.' Nekyon attacked Britain, Israel, Amnesty International and the Red Cross for turning a deaf ear to the killings in Uganda. I did not realise how seriously Obote was taking the story although I found out later than one of his former Ministers, Shafiq Arain, in exile in London, was trying to make contact with the British government. An envoy had been sent to see President Kaunda and the Pope had been cabled. All had been asked to intervene.

I had grave doubts about Nekyon's claim but the next morning the *Guardian* carried a brief story. A month later, in a ramshackle refugee camp at Pangale, twenty miles from Tabora, I interviewed nineteen of the only twenty-three survivors of the 560 soldiers who had been taken to Mutukula. The other four were in Tanzanian hospitals being treated for bullet wounds.

On 28 December, 642 prisoners had been transferred from the maximum security prison at Upper Luzira and from Lower Luzira in Kampala. There were a handful of police officers and civilians, over eighty members of the General Service Department and the remainder were Acholi and Langi soldiers.

The detainees at Luzira were told to hand in all government property, including prison uniforms, and change back into the clothes they had been arrested in. Then at about 5.00 p.m. their hands were tied together with rope and they were transported in a convoy of buses and lorries under heavy escort to Makindye Prison. At 8.30 p.m. the buses set out in convoy on the three-hour, 138-mile drive to Mutukula. The prisoners who survived say that they believed they were being taken to be court-martialled and this view appeared to be confirmed when a few days later a group of NCOs from military intelligence arrived to question them. The prisoners were asked to give their names, units, when and where they were arrested, by whom and why.

The questioning took ten days and in early January 1972 around twenty Acholi and Langi bandsmen were taken away. The other prisoners were told the musicians were to be released and they were to practice for celebrations to mark the first anniversary of the *coup* on 25 January. The bandsmen, it was said, were to be credited with their full service while imprisoned, paid a bonus and given leave pay. The other prisoners were told

Amin only intended to court-martial a few of the officers and the remainder of them would be released on 25 January. Amin, in fact, on 25 January announced a general amnesty for all detainees, who he said would be released immediately with the exception of fifteen who would be held pending further investigation. But on 12 January a number of the forty-five officers held at Mutukula were taken away and the prisoners were told they were to be court-martialled.

On the same day the General Service prisoners, who were being held separately from the soldiers, were taken out to dig a series of trenches. They were told these were waste pits and as there was a pail system in the prison the explanation at that point sounded plausible. But after a week of digging trenches every day they realised they were graves. Most of those killed were buried between 500 yards and a mile to the north of the prison, away from the Tanzanian border, although one lot of bodies was transported as far as Masaka.

The soldiers were being held in two small cell blocks surrounded by barbed-wire and the GSD officers assigned to clean the blocks and take away the pails passed on the view of the 'grave detail', that people who were being taken away were being killed.

One of the twenty-three who reached Tanzania recalled: 'We heard from the GSD that those who were being taken were killed. The first group taken were all officers and included Major Oyet, Captain Agana, Flight-Captain Atyang, and Flight-Lieutenants Okello, Chalo and Ororo. They were taken with their hands tied behind their backs and our windows were closed so we could not see anything.' The brutality of the past year had bypassed most of the prisoners but the news of the mass graves brought a new air of desperation. A few days later three of a group being taken away tried to escape. Two were shot before they had gone a few yards and the other killed just short of safety on the Tanzanian border. This was the first killing the prisoners had actually witnessed at Mutukula.

Then on about 24 January a captain from the Mubende Barracks wearing a yellow lanyard arrived at Mutukula. Eleven prisoners were taken out. Those who survived remember the names of seven: Corporals Aldo, Pius, Loto and Santo and Privates Odongo Black, Odong and Omara. The men's hands were tied behind their backs and in view of the other soldiers they were shot dead. By 25 January all the forty-five officers had been killed and many of the 250 NCOs. Some of the NCOs were old men recalled in 1964 after Moise Tshombe's planes bombed Uganda. One had joined the army in 1946 with General Amin.

The same officer returned about a week later while the prisoners were eating and told them: 'Tomorrow you will eat good meat.' They understood this to mean human flesh. Mr. Hassan and four soldiers were ordered out but they refused realising they were to be killed. At 6.00 p.m. people were ordered out of the other room. Again everyone refused to move. An hour later they returned and called nine people and a Private Okot who was nearest the door in the other cell was dragged out. They were gunned down ten yards from the cell block.

For the next two days the prisoners were kept without food. 'We thought they were coming to kill all of us but they stayed away. They told us we would get no food or water and that we should eat excrement and drink our urine.' The stalemate continued during 3 and 4 February. Then one of the guards was overheard saying that government food would no longer be wasted on the prisoners and they were all to die.

The mood in the GSD block was somewhat different. Acholi and Langi officers had been taken away and it was presumed they had been killed. But the remaining sixty-four in the block were from other tribes and they continued to believe, correctly as it proved, that they would be released. But as far as the soldiers were concerned there was no longer any pretence about being released or court-martialled. They had seen colleagues killed and had been ordered to wash the blood from the trucks, which had taken groups of prisoners away each day, when they returned to the prison. 'We knew also that their favourite methods of killing were to behead or bayonet the prisoners,' survivors said.

'We decided it would be much quicker to die from a bullet so we decided to break out.' Throughout 4 February, using a spoon, the prisoners dug around the bricks inside their cell. As long as the stalemate continued they knew none of the guards was likely to come in so they were safe from discovery. Then on 5 February at 1.00 a.m. they pushed the last bricks away and one man crawled through. He opened the bolts on the outside of the main door but a guard spotted him and fired two shots sounding the alarm. 'After that it was just a matter of plucking up the courage to run. Many were killed in the doorway but their bodies acted as sandbags and helped many others escape.'

The escapees had to scramble through a ring of barbed-wire around their cells and another surrounding the prison and many died there. Mr. Hassan, a chronic diabetic, weakened by two days without food, was one of those who did not try to run. Only twenty-three reached the Tanzanian border a quarter of a mile away. Among the dead in the Mutukula Massacre was Michael Egena, a younger brother of Obote and formerly a security officer in the Ministry of Home Affairs.

None of the GSD officers had tried to take part in the breakout. They were released on the following day and have verified and completed the soldiers' account of what occurred at Mutukula.

'The shooting continued almost until dawn on 5 February by which time there was nobody moving outside the two prison blocks,' one of them told me months later. 'Then the guards brought in dynamite, began digging around the blocks and blew both of them up.' Dawn revealed the full carnage. Bodies hung on barbed-wire and others were scattered around the yard where they had been felled by a cross fire from four machine-guns. Those who were still alive were shot.

The GSD officers were ordered to collect the bodies for burial and they counted 117. 'Then to everyone's amazement, Mr Hassan crawled from one of the blown-up buildings. He was soaked in blood but did not appear to be injured. He walked across to where we were piling up the bodies and the soldiers began muttering that he was bewitched and had a curse on him.' One of the soldiers suggested burying him alive with the bodies and they started to tie his hands and feet together. 'Hassan knew he was going to be killed and he took off his watch and gave it to one of the soldiers. Then he took a gold chain from around his neck and handed it to the same soldier saying "this was a gift from my wife".'

The soldier angrily picked up a piece of wood and hit Mr. Hassan across the head. 'He fell to the ground and then they tried to cut his throat but he was already dead,' said one of the GSD officers. At about 9.00 a.m. the bodies were taken to a mass grave 600 yards on the Uganda side of the prison. The guards insisted Hassan's body should be put in first and the others piled on top. Then at about 3.00 p.m. the officer in command of the Mutukula guards, Lieutenant Marella, a brother of Lieutenant-Colonel Marella, head of the military police, said he had spoken to Amin on the phone and had been ordered to bring Hassan's body to Kampala. The mass grave was dug up again and the policeman's body removed.

Then Amin made an incredible statement which was to be largely responsible for so much of the story coming out immediately. On 6 February, at Entebbe Airport before departing for a week's visit to West Germany he made the following statement which was broadcast on Radio Uganda in English at 18.00 (GMT):

'President Amin disclosed that there was a minor incident at Mutukula Prison two days ago. The fifteen remaining detainees, who consisted of former army personnel and former members of the General Service Department who are detained there pending court-martial, he said, overpowered a guard, and there was an exchange of fire during which some of them managed to escape after wounding the guard. They fled to Tanzania where they were arrested by the Tanzanian security forces and handed back to the Uganda armed forces at Mutukula. Among those who were handed over was Muhammad Hassan, the former head of the CID. General Amin expressed his personal and government's gratitude to the Tanzanian security forces at the border for their prompt and friendly action in comprehending [sic] the escapees.'

The Tanzanians were infuriated by the claim and on the following day issued a statement refuting it. Twenty-three soldiers, four of whom were wounded and in hospital, had escaped and they were in 'protective custody' and would not be handed over. By this point Amin had left Uganda, and on 8 February the Luganda vernacular daily newspaper *Taifa Empya* ('New Nation') printed an interview with the Acting President, Mr. Charles Oboth Ofumbi. He said there had been a mass breakout, in which a number of detainees, including Hassan, had been killed. There the matter rested until Amin's return on 12 February when he denied that a massacre had taken place and claimed that the nineteen at Tabora were guerrilla supporters of Obote.

Adoko Nekyon's bizarre claim had proved all too tragically accurate. I have no doubt about the stories of the nineteen at Pangali. Several of them had bone-deep gashes clearly caused by barbed-wire as they ran in panic. For me the Mutukula Massacre, sanctioned by Amin, was a very rude awakening.

The decimation of the army can be further seen from the fact that of the twenty-three officers of the rank of lieutenant-colonel or above at the time of the *coup* only four are still in the service including Amin, the Paymaster and Chief Medical Officer. Thirteen others have been murdered. Two escaped into exile in Tanzania. One is a Minister and of the remaining four who were dismissed there is some doubt whether two of them are alive. Here is the list of the thirteen dead and how they were killed:

Brigadier Suleiman Hussein, Army Chief of Staff. Captured in Kampala on 29 January 1971 and beaten to death at Luzira Prison in front of warders. Then decapitated and his head taken to Amin who addressed it and kept the head in the fridge overnight.

Colonel Meseura Arach, Commander, 1st Infantry Brigade. Arrested at Jinja and subsequently tortured and beaten to death. His penis was severed and pushed in his mouth. Then his body was taken to Amin in a Land-Rover, which was seen by a British correspondent.

Colonel Albertino Langoya, Commandant, School of Infantry, Jinja. Arrested with Arach and died with his stomach split open with a machete. His body was also taken to Amin.

Lieutenant-Colonel Akwango, Commanding Officer, Malire Mechanised Regiment. Arrested and beaten by troops when the *coup* began and finally beaten to death on the following day.

Lieutenant-Colonel Ojok, Commander, Burma Battalion, Jinja. Went into hiding after *coup* but telephoned his wife asking her to bring his briefcase with personal papers to the Silver Springs Hotel in Kampala. The call went through his unit's exchange and was overheard and he was arrested at the hotel. He was severely beaten at Luzira with Brigadier Hussein but it is not known if he died then or was one of the thirty-two officers blown up at Makindye on 5 March.

Lieutenant-Colonel Tom Loyira, Commanding Officer, Moroto Battalion. He was on leave at Kitgum on the night of the *coup* and went into hiding. He answered Amin's call to all troops to report back, promising they would not be victimised. Both Okello and Obote, from Dar es Salaam, urged him to get out but a few days later he was arrested and was one of the thirty-two blown up.

Lieutenant-Colonel Abwala, Commander, 'Tiger' Battalion, Mubende. Wanted to fight after the *coup* and made contact with Lieutenant-Colonel Oyite Ojok who was in hiding in Kampala. But his unit was poorly armed and in early February he decided to flee to Tanzania. He went home to collect his family and told the local bishop his plans. The bishop was convinced he would not be harmed and persuaded Abwala to go with him to Kampala where he 'surrendered' to the Inspector-General of Police, Oryema. The police officer phoned Amin and was told to bring Abwala to the 'Command Post' but as Oryema drove out of the 'Command Post' shots were heard and Abwala was never seen again.

Lieutenant-Colonel Oboma Ayumu, Commander, Border Guard, based at Fort Portal. Arrested in hiding at the home of his brother-in-law and taken to Luzira. Was one of thirty-two officers blown up on 5 March.

Lieutenant-Colonel Ekiring, Staff Officer, Army Head-quarters. Taken from his office by a sergeant and six privates. Ekiring's body was found floating in Lake Victoria the next day and the sergeant's and privates' bodies were found near by.

Lieutenant-Colonel John Ebitu, Commanding Officer, Ordnance Depot, Magamaga. Arrested the night of the *coup* and blown up on 5 March. He had reported the missing guns from the Magamaga armoury just before the *coup*.

Lieutenant-Colonel Pirimo Obol, Staff Officer, Army Headquarters. He refused to give Ekiring a private burial as Amin ordered. A few days later he was poisoned at the Rock Hotel at Tororo. Poison is thought to have been put in a bottle of liquor in his room while he was at lunch. Amin refused to allow an inquest and the hotel manager, who was believed to have known what occurred was subsequently murdered by troops.

Lieutenant-Colonel Emmanuel Ogwal, Commanding Officer, Artillery Unit, Masindi. Went into hiding after the *coup* and was in contact with Ojok and Abwola. His cousin, Felix Onama, refused to give him sanctuary and he went to the home of another cousin, Dr. George Ebine. A European friendly with Onama and linked with Amin is believed to have given him away. Ogwal fought a battle lasting several hours in the heart of Kampala but was finally killed when a recoilless rifle blasted the side of the house in. Ebine was dragged from the operating theatre and bayoneted to death and his patient also died.

Lieutenant-Colonel Kakuhikire, who was a staff officer working on the history of the Ugandan army, was killed during 1973. He had narrowly escaped death in December 1972 when he was in detention but Amin was forced to release him after a story appeared in the *Observer* listing him as missing.

During January 1972 William Kalema, Obote's Minister of Commerce and Industry became a new victim. He had been in

Dar es Salaam in the first days after the *coup* with the deposed President but decided to return. He was arrested near Lugogo. A Public Safety Unit BMW car followed him and near Lugogo Stadium it drove across the front of his car forcing him to stop. Kalema was ordered to get into the BMW, his own car abandoned by the road, and he disappeared.

9 Amin, Israel and Britain

Two countries more than any other stood to gain by the over-throw of Obote and initially by the advent of power of Amin: Britain and Israel. Whether or not, as Obote implied they were actively involved in organising the *coup* is questionable, but certainly once it had occurred they celebrated with abandon.

Israel's reasons were entirely political and were an extension of her Middle East conflict with the Arab world. Obote as Prime Minister had visited Israel on the eve of Ugandan independence in 1962. The importance Israel attached to Uganda can be seen from the flow of leading Israelis to Kampala over the next few years. Mrs. Golda Meir, as Foreign Minister, was in Uganda for four days early in 1963 when she signed a technical co-operation agreement. In 1966 Israeli Prime Minister, Levi Eshkol, also spent four days visiting Uganda and Foreign Minister, Abba Eban, was there in 1969. During 1968 Amin visited Israel to observe the independence parade in Jerusalem. This was the parade where Israel put on display armaments captured in the Six Day War. Subsequently some of these captured weapons were sent to Uganda, and Arab tanks supplied by Israel were used in the *coup* which brought Amin to power.

With the Arabs a vocal force in the Organisation of African Unity, the Israelis had decided to establish embassies in every possible black African country and, in the context of Israel's own financial strictures, to pump in considerable quantities of assistance. But the interest in Uganda was geopolitical, for the country bordered on the southern Sudan where black guerrillas had been fighting for years for independence from the predominantly Arab north.

Israel did not back the southern Sudanese on moral or ideological grounds. It was simply a means of stabbing the Arabs in the back. The full extent of Jerusalem's political cynicism can be gauged by her position in neighbouring Ethiopia where Israeli officers carried out training in counter-insurgency tactics for troops fighting Eritrean seccessionists in northern Ethiopia until Emperor Haile Selassie broke relations in October 1973.

For Israel, Uganda was the base for material aid to the southern Sudanese guerrillas and perpetuation of the war. Obote had visited the Sudan early in 1963. From 1965 to 1969 Ugandan troops had co-operated in border exercises with the Sudan army against the Anyanya. Before Nimeri came to power in 1969, Obote had played a leading part in a number of reconciliation attempts and although the southern Sudan war was an emotive issue for black African leaders in the early 1960s, relations between Khartoum and Kampala improved considerably.

By backing the Anyanya and thereby tying down a large section of Sudan's army, Israel was able to neutralise effectively the possibility of Sudanese military involvement in the Middle East zone. On at least two occasions Israeli officers were seen inside the southern Sudan with Anyanya and air drops of equipment were made regularly by Israeli planes flying into the guerrilla areas across Ethiopia and Uganda.

The arrival in power in Khartoum on 25 May 1969 of General Nimeri subtly altered the delicate political balance in the area. Like Sudan leaders before him he committed himself to ending the southern war, but on this occasion the pledge had a truer ring. In part the young soldier's identification with the progressive African bloc was an important aspect of this credibility, and so when in late 1969 the Israeli chief of the Central Intelligence Organisation, General Zamir, sought refuelling rights in Uganda for their arms ferry to the guerrillas, he received a blunt refusal from Obote. Obote's cousin, Akena Adoko, head of the General Service Department was approached and he said he could do nothing. Next the Israelis went to Amin and there are strong indications that the General, with his close tribal ties with the southern Sudan, responded more positively. Certainly he was subsequently in the southern Sudan with Israeli officers.

Whether or not the destruction of growing links between Khartoum and Kampala was enough to involve Israel in the *coup* is in dispute. But the behaviour of the head of the Israeli mission in Uganda, Colonel Bar-Lev, immediately prior to the *coup* suggests he had wind of something. Twice, in the forty-eight hours before Amin seized power he warned Lieutenant-Colonel David Oyite Ojok to be careful. When the head of the police, Mr. Oryema, went to Bar-Lev after the *coup* and asked his advice as to whether he should use force to turn the tide, which he was probably not in a position to anyway, given the limited armaments of the police force, Bar-Lev is said to have advised him to surrender rather than go into hiding and to have written a short speech for the policeman which he subsequently read on Radio Uganda agreeing to serve under Amin.

Given the degree of the Israeli involvement with the Anyanya it seems highly improbable that they did not know that for months Amin had been recruiting guerrillas for his *coup* bid. Nor could Bar-Lev and his colleagues have escaped noticing Amin posting a number of officers he could rely on to the critical Malire Mechanised Battalion or sending many others off on leave as soon as Obote left for Singapore. Amin was in deep trouble at this time and anything unusual would have been noticed by the trained observer on the inside of the military establishment.

On 5 April 1971 a thirty-minute television documentary was shown on ITV in Britain. It was entitled 'The Man who Stole Uganda' and had been filmed by a 'World in Action' team in February and March. The programme said categorically that there was evidence that Israeli military advisers helped Amin carry out the *coup*. Israelis, it said, had been seen by eye-witnesses driving tanks in the initial hours and flying planes in the victory parade. 'The Israelis had to fly the planes because most of the Ugandan pilots had either been executed or detained.' A Briton, Bob Astles, who was close to both Amin and Onama was quoted on the programme and described as an intelligence adviser. 'The Israelis are very tough people,' he said. 'They're surviving. And they like Amin. They like him very much. And I am sure you would not be able to hold them back.'

Exactly what Astles meant was not made clear, but in addition to Obote's growing links with Khartoum and the problems they imposed, there were several other reasons why Jerusalem would have been glad to see him removed. Early in 1970 questions had begun to be asked in the Ugandan Cabinet security committee about the activities of Colonel Bar-Lev. It was decided that all foreign military advisers should be told to leave Uganda before the end of the year, but despite this and without the knowledge of the committee, Onama, as Defence Minister, concluded a new three-year air force training agreement with Israel. The Israeli Ambassador, Mr Ofri, complained at the decision of the committee as well as the fact that it had been indicated Israeli training of the police special force would also be terminated in 1970. Ofri also complained about Uganda sending her Cairo Ambassador to the United Nations where he had voted for what Israel regarded as a pro-Arab resolution. Two scholarships offered to the Ministry of Agriculture and Forestry had also not been taken up and he further objected to the Minister not having visited a fruit farm being set up by Israel. The arrest of Steiner and the decision to hand him over to Khartoum was clearly embarrassing for Jerusalem, and one secretary in Amin's office on the morning of the *coup* insists Bar-Lev was active in choosing the new Cabinet.

On 25 January, the day of the *coup*, while most Kampala residents elected to stay safely at home until it was known what was happening, Israeli diplomats moved freely about the city. Other people in Kampala on that first day insist Israelis were driving some of the armoured vehicles which played a prominent part in the *coup* and were manning the radio when news of the take-over was announced. The Israelis denied any involvement but there was no denying their obvious delight at Obote's downfall.

But they had not counted on Amin's unpredictability. He visited Israel twice in July 1971 seeking armaments for his plan to invade Tanzania and seize the north of the country across to the Indian Ocean port of Tanga to give him an outlet to the sea; he requested Phantom jet-fighters, armed boats to carry his forces across Lake Victoria into Tanzania, helicopters and a £10,000,000 grant. As Amin left the meeting in Jerusalem, Defence Minister Moshe Dayan is said to have turned to Foreign Minister Abba

Eban and said words to the effect: 'This is a dangerous fellow with whom we should have no serious dealings.' Israel supplied Amin with the executive jet he had asked for and a small quantity of arms in the pipeline, but that was all.

Amin by this time realised that he was not going to get the armaments he wanted in the West unless he paid cash—and he was not in a position to do that. The Chinese, who had had considerable reservations about Obote, were even cooler towards Amin. The Soviets were initially cautious and so Amin approached the Egyptians. They were not in a position to help but it was suggested he should try Libya's erratic leader, Colonel Qadhafi.

Throughout 1971 Amin had been publicly thanking the Israelis for their assistance, continuously asking for more and promising he would open an embassy in Jerusalem. Partly as a result of military over-spending he was running into debt-servicing problems by the end of the year, but the Israelis indicated that they were willing to renegotiate these.

Then on 13 February 1972, Amin visited Tripoli and in a joint communiqué with Qadhafi, began an amazing volte-face. He arrived there from Munich after another abortive attempt to get arms without paying cash from West Germany. The joint Amin-Qadhafi communiqué at the end of the brief visit spelled out Israel's changing fortunes in Uganda. It read: 'Regarding the Middle East situation the two Presidents affirmed their support for the Arab people's rights and just struggle against Zionism and Imperialism to liberate their occupied territory and also the Palestinian people's right to return to their land and homes by any means. The two Presidents agreed that religion and national-ism created history and motivated the march of nations and people towards progress and revolution. Islam provided a good example.'

Two points arise from this section of the communiqué. In the first place it was the beginning of the end for Israel in Uganda and secondly it was the beginning of Amin's commitment to turn Uganda into a black Muslim state.

Within ten days a Libyan delegation was in Kampala discussing economic and military co-operation. Amin said Libya had agreed to give 'tremendous' financial help but he did not disclose the amount although this was put at £10,000,000. The leader of the Libyan delegation to Uganda, Major Elhameidy, promised economic aid to the country as well as assistance for Muslim institutions, the construction of mosques and schools. The day after the Libyan visit ended Amin accused Israel of subversive activities and threatened to close her Embassy.

The Israeli newspaper *Davar* on 19 March unwittingly provided Amin with the excuse he was looking for to break with Jerusalem. A correspondent, Dan Bein, wrote that Amin had called off a visit to Cairo because of anxiety over the security situation in Uganda. Amin angrily responded by saying that as a result of the report he would not renew military training agreements with Israel. The next day he ordered out all Israeli military instructors. A day later he said he was cancelling military orders and stopping Israeli civilian construction projects.

On 27 March he ordered all Israeli personnel to leave the country and three days later, after accusing Israel of having a 700-strong hidden army in Uganda, broke off relations. Israel responded by saying that there were 149 people working in the country—plus 321 dependents—but even so they had all gone by 9 April.

All of Amin's accusations in those few days were of course a total cover. In Tripoli, Qadhafi had bought him over and the deal quite simply was that, in return for Amin breaking with Israel, Qadhafi, from his ample oil-filled coffers, would assist him. It is noteworthy that the amount Qadhafi is believed to have promised Amin is the same amount he had asked for as a grant in Israel seven months earlier. In fact Qadhafi came across with little of what the Ugandan General expected. Many Ugandans say that in the ensuing months Christians were paid to convert to Islam with Libya and Saudi Arabia supplying the money. The price was from shs 100 upwards depending upon how important you were. Qadhafi was ignorant of the Muslim content of Uganda's population which was put at 5·6 per cent in the last census. In November 1972 Qadhafi charged that Britain had rigged the census statistics in Uganda where in fact he claimed 70 per cent of the population were Muslims. Qadhafi went on to further indicate his ignorance of Eastern Africa by claiming that all the Muslims on Zanzibar had been annihilated in the past decade, whereas in fact today about 97 per cent of the population is Muslim.

Israel Foreign Minister, Abba Eban, addressing the Knesset put the financial loss to his country of being ejected from Uganda at between $15,000,000 and $20,000,000. In agriculture, administration, police, education, health, defence and other economic areas they had done much in a decade. After Amin came to power Israel was allotted a contract to develop a 7,500,000-acre area (larger than Israel itself) in the northern Karamojo area, where ironically seventy years earlier Britain had proposed creating a Jewish homeland. Once the Israelis had gone, Amin's accusations became increasingly wild. He said they had planned to poison the Nile, which has its source in Uganda, to kill all the Arabs in Sudan and Egypt. He told the Beirut magazine *Arab Week* he would lead the Arab armies to conquer Israel where he falsely claimed he had spent five years training. The presidents of Egypt, Libya and Syria were meeting as the Presidential Council of their three states when Amin jetted in to take part in their talks and, as if to rub it in, he gave the Israeli Ambassador's residence in Kampala to the Palestinian Liberation Organisation.

There is as little reason to view with sympathy the outcome in Uganda for Israel as there is for Britain. With indecent haste, Britain had recognised Amin within ten days of his seizing power. Throughout the remainder of 1971 both countries had considerable influence in Uganda, yet they turned a totally blind eye to the killings of hundreds of Ugandans when some pressure might have checked the slaughter. The interests of Britain and Israel, it seems, were limited to their own economic-political interests and to their nationals.

Similarities are to be found in the ultimate fates in Uganda of both these countries. Amin's two visits to Israel and one to Britain in July 1971 were to prove the crucial factors for deteriorating relations with Whitehall and Jerusalem. It seems Britain would have had little compunction about selling Amin sophisticated military equipment—but not Harrier jets—if he had had the money to pay. That there was a strong likelihood he might use them against one or more of his neighbours seemed to be of little concern in London. Israel, it appears, took a somewhat more cautious view. The outcome was that Amin was forced in pique to shop elsewhere. The break with Israel was a direct result of his visit to Tripoli, and there is reason to believe that it also triggered the expulsion of 40,000 non-citizen Asians from Uganda seven months later. In July 1970 Qadhafi had expelled 19,000 Italians and seized—without compensation—property valued at £40,000,000. Sources in Kampala say that the Libyans pointed out the parallel to Amin between the Italians and Asians, both of whom were described as 'exploiters'.

Some early indicators of the coming harassment of Uganda's Asian community came during 1971. Amin ordered an Asian head count in June that year and in December he verbally lashed out, accusing Asians of currency racketeering, smuggling, undercutting African businessmen and of refusing to allow their daughters to marry Africans. Two months later he was praising the Asians for their contribution to the economy. And the Aga Khan, spiritual leader of the Ismaili community, about 6,000 of whom had taken Ugandan citizenship but were expelled anyway, noted in a speech in Kampala in front of the unpredictable General: 'We are confident that in due course we shall succeed in being accepted as full and true citizens of Uganda in every sense of those words. That is what we understand integration to mean.' Late in 1971 Amin announced that 12,000 Asian citizenship applications would not be considered and in January 1972 he warned that any Asians holding political meetings would be summarily shot.

Then on 5 August 1972, Amin dropped his bombshell. The British government was to be asked to assume responsibility for its nationals of Asian origin in Uganda who were sabotaging the economy, Amin told troops at Tororo. He wanted to see the economy in the hands of 'black Ugandans' he added. His speech took his own government as well as the British by surprise. The next day he said that the 80,000 Ugandans had ninety days to leave. In London his Foreign Minister, Kibedi, protesting that the decision was not racial, said: 'If they still remain they will soon see what happens to them.'

Next, Amin bizarrely explained the reason for his decision. He was quoted as telling a group of traders 'that in whatever he does for the people of Uganda, God has always guided him through the right path'. Early in the month he had spent the night at Moroto. 'That same night a dream came to me that the Asian problem was becoming extremely explosive and that God was directing me to act immediately to save the situation and win. The economic war which is going to be embarked on is definitely a problem. In that dream the same night I was advised never to look for courage or any other assistance from brave people but to have confidence in God and it was only through God that I was able to succeed in this particular problem.'

That of course was all arrant nonsense. The truth was that by August 1972 Amin was in deep trouble inside Uganda. The economy was increasingly under pressure because of excessive military expenditure. His claims that the hundreds of people who had disappeared had been murdered or spirited away by Zionists, Imperialists, pro-Obote guerrillas and *kondos* were no longer believed. Only a few weeks earlier he had been forced to fly home from the OAU summit in Rabat as a result of fighting in the army. After the *coup* he had recruited indiscriminately from West Nile tribes. But the largest element had come from the Lugbara and not his own Kakwa tribe and the Lugbara had begun a series of plots to remove Amin which went on throughout the next year. The General needed a diversion. In 1971 Tanzania had provided the external enemy with which to try to forge national unity behind him. In 1972 the enemies were the Israelis and Asians.

By his decision to expel the Asians Amin bought time. In part his charges against them were true. They had not integrated and had taken little interest in the political affairs of the countries in East Africa they had adopted. Their dominance in the wholesale and retail trades—at independence, Asians ran four out of every five businesses—and as landlords, made them conspicuous and the charges of foreign exchange racketeering, income tax evasion and overcharging, while more appropriately levelled against a minority, had come to be levelled at all Asians.

The British at first seemed to doubt that the blustering General was serious. 'We always thought that Amin was a decent chap. After all, he served in the British army for fifteen years, and our relations with Uganda seemed to be going along quite well', a Foreign Office official was quoted as saying in London. Conservative newspapers and politicians in Britain accused Amin of racialism and argued that 'brown Britons' should be kept out. Britain was in no position to accuse Amin of racialism. Despite the fact that, in law, those Asians were British citizens, the Labour government had created a quota system to phase their entry into Britain, and at the time of Amin's decision only 3,500 heads of families around the world annually were allocated vouchers and Uganda got less than 100. As Britain had accepted their right to citizenship there was a clear legal and moral obligation and legislation denying them entry was itself blatant racialism.

Britain protested that it would be logistically impossible to move 50,000 within Amin's ninety-day deadline but in the final analysis less than 30,000 moved to Britain beating the deadline with comparative ease, while many others elected to go to America, Canada, India and Pakistan. The ease with which Britain absorbed the Uganda Asians and lack of racial incidents made a mockery of the whole quota system.

While Britain had no right to accuse Amin of racialism Africa's own credibility was deeply impaired by his decision. A cornerstone of the policy of the OAU is opposition to racialism in southern Africa and only two African leaders had the courage to speak out. The position was complicated by the fact that despite the obvious racial overtones of Amin's decision there was little that could be said when those affected were British citizens. But when he extended it to include Asians who by birth or registration had become Uganda citizens both President Nyerere and President Kaunda publicly condemned the General.

Nyerere referred to Amin as a racialist and likened racialists to primitive animals. Kaunda said: 'What is happening in Uganda is terrible, horrible and abominable and a shame to the whole human race.' But other African leaders consistently so outspoken about white racialism in southern Africa, remained silent. Some Arab states, notably Egypt and Libya, publicly supported Amin. In part it might be argued that the decisions of Nyerere and Kaunda to speak out arose from the need to speak to racialists in their own countries where they have sizable Asian communities, and to make it clear they did not intend to emulate Amin. Even so it is clear that both leaders were as concerned with the credibility of Africa as their domestic audiences.

The Asians were treated brutally as they left Uganda. Some were killed by Amin's marauding troops. And at airports, border posts, railway stations and road blocks they were harassed, manhandled, robbed and a few raped. They were forced to leave all their property behind with their businesses, which were being allocated to Africans, mainly from West Nile. Utter chaos followed. Machinery in factories broke down and there was nobody to repair it. Large numbers of troops moved out of their barracks into the Asian houses they had been awarded as the spoils of Amin's economic war. Africans, with no retail experience, fixed the prices of expensive imported shirts in Kampala shops according to the collar size thinking that was the price tag. Shortages of essential items became common and prices spiralled. The populist reaction to the Asian exodus was only to bring Amin temporary respite.

The countdown through the Asian exodus read something like a comic opera as far as the exchanges between London and Kampala were concerned. Britain followed up the announcement of the Asian expulsion by suspending financial and technical assistance. Amin responded by accusing the British of planning to assassinate him, expelling the British military team and warning the British community against subversion. High Commissioner Richard Slater was summoned to Makindye Prison where Amin showed him a number of biscuit tins holding Uganda currency which the General said an Asian was planning to smuggle out. As Slater moved closer to look at them, photographers appeared.

Britain formally protested at what it regarded as a trick to get pictures of Slater handling the money. Once more Amin responded by demanding Slater should be recalled and Whitehall did just that and terminated all forms of financial aid to Uganda. And finally Amin added his own tragic postscript: 'Though the British hate me I love them and respect the Queen.'

10 The September Invasion

On 17 September 1972, three days after Britain's military mission to Uganda was expelled and less than twenty-four hours before the first plane-load of Asians was scheduled to fly out of Entebbe for London, a force of 1,000 men smashed across the frontier from Tanzania wiping out the light border defences and swiftly moving north in open trucks in a bid to oust Amin.

The 'People's Army' as it was called, consisted mainly of soldiers who had fled after the Uganda *coup* to Tanzania and Sudan to join the deposed President in exile and train in guerrilla camps to go back into Uganda to overthrow the General. The bulk of Obote's guerrilla force came from the Acholi tribe with the second largest group from his own Langi tribe.

When the initial joint plan by Somalia and Tanzania in February 1971, a few days after the *coup* was called off, largely because of fears of British and Israeli military intervention to keep Amin in power, Obote began laying plans. Messengers were sent into Uganda to recruit soldiers and UPC supporters to move out to Tanzania and Sudan for training. It had been anticipated that more Obote supporters would reach Tanzania, but early in April there were two severe setbacks. In the first few days of the month, Amin had announced the capture of one General Service Department officer on his way to Tanzania and that thirteen others training abroad had gone to Tanzania instead of returning to Uganda. Then on 15 April Amin paraded eighty recruits, intercepted by security forces on their way to Tanzania. He castigated them and said they would be sent home to Lira but all of them were killed. Two days later another 617, who on 14 April had been captured by the Anyanya after crossing the Aswa river into Sudan and handed over to Amin's troops, were slaughtered near Palabek.

Thus in the space of a few days 697 recruits had been killed and the publicity given to this including pictures of the bodies of those killed in the north, must have acted as a deterrent to many. Although there are only a few points at which the Aswa river can be crossed on foot into the Sudan this became an easier exit-point than the shorter frontier with Tanzania to which there were only two routes for large groups of recruits.

Nyerere had agreed to let Obote set up a training camp at Kingolwira about 120 miles west of Dar es Salaam near the town of Morogoro and with this safely arranged the deposed President slipped quietly out of Dar es Salaam in the second half of February and flew to the Sudan capital, Khartoum, where President Nimeri gave him a house.

Obote left his Foreign Minister, Odaka, as his representative in Dar es Salaam in charge of administering the movement in Tanzania, dealing with the men in the guerrilla camps and acting as the contact with the Tanzanian government. It was a role Odaka clearly did not enjoy, for, on Obote's return from Khartoum sixteen months later, he promptly resigned, and although this was not formally accepted, his contact with the former President diminished thereafter as Odaka's business interests simultaneously expanded. In Sudan in early 1971 Obote began preparations for his second training camp. This was established at Owiny-Ki-Bul, a former Anyanya administrative centre which had been captured by Sudanese troops and turned into a garrison camp. This was located about ten miles inside Sudan from the Ugandan border near Issore and the grass hut encampment was set in a shallow depression, surrounded by hills. Over 200 Sudanese soldiers provided a perimeter guard for the Obote supporters who reached the camp and in the coming months this was to prove fortunate. Twice in January 1972 Anyanya guerrillas, possibly supported by Amin's troops, attacked; the first fighting came a few days after the New Year when at 10.00 p.m. the camp was attacked by a group using mortars, light machine-guns and rifles. No one was injured in this attack nor the second about a fortnight later when the attackers were sighted as they moved in and the Sudanese troops returned fire instantly. Another not-able incident at the camp had occurred in late August 1971 when a Ugandan reconnaissance plane flew low overhead; it was believed to have been piloted by an Israeli officer with Amin as a passenger. The plane, whose radio was monitored at the camp, had to take hurried evasive action because of heavy ground-fire.

In the initial weeks the recruits at the camp had precious few arms; possibly only about 200 old rifles. But in July 1971 in Khartoum in the space of four days Nimeri was overthrown in a communist *coup* and regained power largely as a result of the 2nd Tank Brigade whose headquarters were at Shajarah camp on the outskirts of Khartoum.

The first Obote and his aides in their Khartoum house knew about the *coup* was on the afternoon of 19 July when they noticed their Sudanese security guards paying an unusual amount of attention to the television where a young officer was speaking in Arabic. The next morning just before 7.00 a.m. an aide went to Obote and told him: 'There are some men downstairs who want to see you and one of them looks like the man on television last night.' The aide was correct. The man was Major Hashim al-Ata, leader of the *coup* and a hard-line communist.

Obote's first reaction was that this meant the end of his plans from Sudan and the possibility they would be handed over to Amin. For some time his intelligence reports from Uganda had indicated that Amin was becoming friendlier with the Russians and now the Sudan Communist party, which was strongly aligned to Moscow, had taken over. He called two aides to his room and handed them a set of documents, which if they reached Amin would mean the death of many Ugandans Obote was in contact with at home, as well as a brief-case stuffed with other documents. The aides were told to lock themselves in the room and admit no one. If they heard shots or shouting downstairs they were immediately to begin burning the documents.

Then Obote went downstairs. The reception was quite different to what he had expected. Major al-Ata snapped to attention and saluted Obote. He had been told, he said, by his colleagues to assure Obote that he could stay in the Sudan as long as he liked. His safety would be guaranteed and they would help him achieve his objectives. Obote's political blueprint for Uganda, 'The

Common Man's Charter', was in the process of being trans-
lated into Arabic the Major added, as if to imply ideological
affinity.

After briefing the security guards in Arabic the Major left. If
Obote was surprised by the reception he was certainly less happy
when he learned that Colonel Babikr al-Nur, a former Assistant
Premier for Economy and Planning, was flying back from exile
in London to become chairman of the new Sudanese Revolution
Command. Before Nimeri came to power, when al-Nur was a
military attaché in the Sudanese Embassy in Kampala, Obote had
asked the Sudan govenment to recall him because of his activities
in Uganda. The Colonel, however, was not destined to reach
Khartoum as he had expected. As a BOAC plane flew over the
Mediterranean, Colonel Qadhafi sent up jet fighters and ordered
it to land. Faced with the threat of being shot down the pilot had
no alternative but to land at Tripoli. Colonel al-Nur and Major
Farouk Osman Hamadallah, a former Interior Minister linked
with the anti-Nimeri Iraq Baathists, who had also been living in
London, were removed at gunpoint from the plane. The Colonel
had made the fatal mistake of saying in a BBC African Service
interview how he was travelling home, so Qadhafi knew which
plane to intercept. Both al-Nur and Hamadallah were sent back
to Khartoum when Nimeri regained power a few hours after the
plane was intercepted and there, with a number of other leading
communists, they were executed.

Nimeri had visited Moscow only two months before the *coup*,
but in the wake of his regaining power, relations with the Soviet
Union deteriorated sharply and there are strong indications that
he began to view with more concern the growing Soviet ties
with Amin. Obote, greatly relieved that Nimeri had survived,
swiftly reported his meeting with Major al-Ata to the Sudanese
Vice-President and almost immediately supplies of arms to the
Ugandan camp at Owiny-Ki-Bul increased considerably.

With access to the arms and ammunition he had hitherto
lacked Obote's plans now began to move at a more rapid pace.
The support weapons which the group at Kingolwira had been
training on were part of a consignment ordered before the

Uganda *coup* by Obote's government and intercepted in transit for him by the Tanzanians. At Owiny-Ki-Bul, where there were now just under 1,000 men, there was growing impatience and the indications are that Obote's first attack with his Ugandan supporters was scheduled for August 1971.

The timing of this plan is important for its chances of success were probably much greater than the abortive invasion thirteen months later. At this point in 1971 Nimeri was willing to give Obote all the backing he needed, for like Nyerere he correctly realised that Amin posed an enormous threat to the security of his country. Amin had just been to Britain and Israel seeking fighter planes, patrol boats and other military equipment to attack and seize northern Tanzania and there can be no doubt that Nyerere's fears were well founded. In addition the attack would have followed the massive slaughter in July in the Ugandan army after which morale in the barracks among the troops, with the exception of the Nubian and West Nile groups, had fallen to its lowest ebb. The trained officer corps at the time of the *coup* had been decimated and the raw recruits, largely from West Nile, while highly effective murderers of unarmed prisoners, could be expected to break under fire. Amin could not count on any support in Africa and his troops were an ill-disciplined, untrained rabble.

Obote's plan in August 1971 appears to have been fairly similar to the one in September 1972. The 1971 plan consisted of a three-pronged, simultaneous attack. The 1,000 men at Owiny-Ki-Bul would cross from the north and as they were largely Acholi and Langi they could count on considerable support, moving initially into their home areas. The 294 men at Kingolwira had been moved secretly across Tanzania by train leaving Morogoro on 3 August to a disused Tanzanian National Service camp at Kigwa a few miles from the town of Tabora. This group, which included many more people from western Uganda, were to attack from the south. The third prong was an airborne attack. A guerrilla force was to be air-lifted at night into Entebbe Airport and then to head into Kampala. What plane or planes were to be used is not known but it seems likely that it was a Sudan Airways

Comet which would attract less attention than a military aircraft when it landed at Entebbe.

Several reasons are advanced as to why the attack did not go ahead. In the first place the threat of British and Israeli intervention to support Amin, which had made Nyerere stay his hand seven months earlier, was still seen as very real. The plan was considered to have a fifty-fifty chance of success by Obote's commanders, but senior Tanzanian military officers regarded the odds at worse than that and vetoed it. Another argument put forward by Obote opponents linked with the guerrilla group, the Front for National Salvation, is that tribal disagreements had broken out at Owiny-Ki-Bul between the Acholi and Langi and the Sudanese army had been forced to disarm the Ugandans. But given the fact that arms supplies to the camp had increased after Nimeri regained power this is improbable.

There was however one considerable point of difficulty between the Ugandans and Sudanese. Inevitably, as always occurs among exiles, personal differences which existed previously were exacerbated. At Owiny-Ki-Bul a Western Acholi police officer named Odonkara attempted to play upon tribal differences between the Acholi and Langi urging the guerrilla force to go into Uganda without the knowledge of either Obote or the Sudanese after arms supplies had been stepped up. Odonkara had been an Assistant Commissioner in charge of police at Mbale at the time of the *coup* and deeply resented being moved there from his former job as head of the Police Special Force. His brother had been defeated in party elections by Alex Ojera and he particularly resented the Minister who was one of Obote's most loyal supporters.

Matters came to a head in Khartoum when one of Obote's aides saw Odonkara slip a letter to a medical assistant at a military clinic. The aide immediately reported to Sudanese special branch who seized the letter. It was written in English to an Ambassador in Khartoum—there is reason to believe it was the British envoy —and gave details of Obote's residence and staff, plans and the guerrilla force at Owiny-Ki-Bul. The letter said that if more information was required the Embassy should park a car at certain times of the day in the road beside a tennis court at the house Obote was living in. A tennis ball would be hit out into the road and under the pretext of retrieving it, Odonkara could pass and receive notes.

Not surprisingly the Sudanese were infuriated and wanted to detain Odonkara, a prison officer named Nokrach, a Lieutenant Ociti, who had taken part in planning sessions with the Sudanese and the former second in command of the General Service Department, Opira. Obote persuaded them not to, but they were moved to another house under virtual house arrest and three days after Obote arrived back in Dar es Salaam on 30 June they were detained by the Tanzanians.

Whatever the full reasons for the August 1971 attack being called off, a crucial opportunity had once again been lost. Part of the reason for Nimeri's support of Obote was because Amin was supporting the Anyanya guerrillas fighting in southern Sudan for independence from the north. The sixteen-year war was estimated to have cost 500,000 lives and for years attempts had been going on behind the scenes to end hostilities. These contacts bore fruit a year after the Ugandan *coup* and in February 1972 representatives of the Khartoum government and various southern movements met secretly in the Addis Ababa Hilton Hotel with observers from the World Council of Churches and African Churches.

With surprisingly little difficulty agreement was reached. The Anyanya, who a year earlier had backed Amin to oust Obote because he was threatening their supplies, now no longer needed a sympathetic figure in Kampala but none the less they had much to be grateful for to Amin. In turn the settlement imposed new pressures on Nimeri. He needed the co-operation of the Anyanya guerrillas and their leaders to seal the peace. They knew about Obote's men at Owiny-Ki-Bul and certainly once the settlement was ratified in April the Anyanya would not tolerate the southern Sudan being used as a springboard to overthrow their friend in Kampala. Obote was warned in December 1971 by the Sudanese that preliminary contacts were taking place to reach a settlement and it was made clear that if these succeeded he would have to move before agreement was reached. But the odds were assessed as being no better than they were in August and again an opportunity was lost.

Obote's force at Owiny-Ki-Bul were moved out in March 1972. The journey from their camp to the White Nile town of Mongalla north of the southern capital, Juba, took about twelve hours through the bush. They headed by steamer to the town of Kodok near Malakal, where they remained until June, when they continued their journey up the Nile and then overland to Port Sudan before sailing down the Red Sea, through the Gulf of Aden and then on to Tanzania.

There was only one place the deposed President could go to continue his plans and that was back to Tanzania. His return followed a meeting between President Kaunda and President Nyerere who then secretly sent his Foreign Minister, John Malecela, to Khartoum to invite Obote back. After a sixteen-month absence, when only a handful of people knew where he was, Obote quietly slipped into Dar es Salaam at night on 30 June 1972, leaving Khartoum a day after his guerrillas sailed from Port Sudan. Nimeri arrived in Dar es Salaam a few days later on a state visit. Then in early July the 1,000 guerrillas arrived at the northern Tanzania port of Tanga, aboard the Sudanese shipping-line vessel, *Kordofan*, built in Yugoslavia.

Any possibility of keeping their arrival secret immediately disappeared. The port of Tanga had two British harbour pilots and only one alongside-berth. Regulations laid down that ships could not be brought in at night and a British harbour pilot on duty refused to bring it in under cover of darkness for safety reasons, after it had lain offshore for thirty-three hours. There was some considerable argument before a compromise was reached and the ship was finally brought in at dusk. The result was that unnecessary attention was drawn to the ship and within twenty-four hours tongues were wagging on Dar es Salaam's garrulous diplomatic circuit. The first thing I heard about the mystery ship was exactly twenty-four hours after it berthed, at a party given by the Tanzanian Foreign Minister to introduce Tanzania's ambassadors, who had been recalled for a conference, to meet their counterpart heads of missions in Dar es Salaam.

During the party one Western diplomat approached me and asked if I had heard that the Tanzanians had seized a Yugoslav ship at Tanga and that 1,000 armed Yugoslavs were being held under battened-down hatches. The story was obviously idiotic. The next day an American asked if I knew about a Yugoslav ship at Tanga which had brought 1,000 southern Sudanese prisoners of war who were being repatriated after the peace settlement.

One foreign mission in Dar es Salaam I feel must have known the truth. Whether or not the Tanzanians—and other former British-controlled territories—know it, the British created a substantial information-gathering network throughout these countries at independence. In each major urban centre there is what is known as a British representative or 'correspondent'. They are not spies in the usual sense of the word, but their task is to keep an eye on matters of British interest and to report these to the British High Commission. British interests are, of course, wide-ranging going well beyond such matters as Britons in trouble. At the southern Tanzanian port of Mtwara some years ago, the British representative was the harbour master. As this is a security zone close to the frontier with the Portuguese colony of Mozambique, where guerrillas assisted by Tanzania are fighting a liberation war, diplomats and other unauthorised people are barred from the area. But the harbour master was able to keep a weather eye on arrivals of armaments for the guerrillas and as Portugal is Britain's oldest ally this was certainly of interest to Whitehall.

The arrival of a mysterious ship, of Yugoslav origin, registered in the Sudan, with 1,000 Africans in the hold, and the clumsy attempt to land them secretly could not have escaped the attention of the British representative at Tanga.

For the guerrilla force the journey from Port Sudan had been a very difficult one. Few had ever been aboard a ship before and the majority suffered from sea sickness. To add to their discomfort, meningitis—a very common disease in the Kodok area—attacked a number of them and one man died during the voyage. From Tanga, in an assortment of vehicles, the group was immediately moved just over 100 miles inland to a disused

National Service camp near Handeni town and Obote's September invasion plans moved into top gear. The men were given two weeks' rest before training commenced and later support weapons, including 75-mm anti-tank recoilless rifles and 82-mm mortars, were issued.

Several reasons must have influenced Nyerere's decision at this point to let the attack go ahead. There was the return to Tanzania of Obote and with Nyerere still recognising him as the legal President of Uganda this inevitably created pressure. All the indications are that whereas the vetoed invasion plan in the previous year had received fairly wide scrutiny in the Tanzanian government, the planned attack in September 1972 was known only to a handful of Tanzanians and Obote's closest and most trusted associates.

The Tanzanians who must definitely have known were Nyerere; his Prime Minister, Rashidi Kawawa; Defence Minister, Edward Sokoine; and the then Director of National Service, Mr. Lawrence Gama, who is Nyerere's brother-in-law, who was the Tanzanian co-ordinator in planning sessions and who became Director of Intelligence a few months later. But it is questionable whether any of the senior officers knew anything about the plan until a day or so before the attack began. Obote called in his senior military officer, Colonel Tito Okello, told him in broad terms of the plan and ordered him to appoint a team of staff officers to finalise details. These were Lieutenant-Colonel Oyite Ojok, a thirty-eight-year-old Sandhurst graduate, plus an Acholi captain and a Langi lieutenant. In addition a young Ankole air force officer called Paul carried out reconnaissance inside Uganda. But his ex-Ministers and cousin, Akena Adoko, who had headed the General Service Department were kept in the dark until four hours after the attack began. However they must have wondered why some of their number, including former Ministers of Information, Broadcasting and Tourism, Alex Ojera, and Public Service and Cabinet Affairs, Joshua Wakholi, suddenly left Dar es Salaam a month earlier.

Apart from the pressure created by Obote's return on Nyerere, and the arrival of the Sudan group, Amin was also creating pressure for the Tanzanian. Before the first border clash a year earlier, Tanzania had captured—and was still holding—four Ugandan soldiers who had crossed the frontier. In August 1972 Amin first threatened to invade Tanzania to seize 400 prisoners to hold as hostages against the return of the four Ugandans. He followed this up with a more serious threat saying that he would invade Tanzania and seize the 100-square-mile triangle of the country in the extreme north-west bounded by the Uganda border, the Kagera river and Lake Victoria. Amin claimed that this should be part of Uganda and if Tanzania would not give it up he would take it by force. The Tanzanians took this threat seriously for they moved up to near the frontier the infantry battalion from Tabora and the heavy mortar and artillery support unit from Musoma.

The Kagera River triangle has continued to be a vexed question with Amin threatening to seize it—or even to invade Tanzania well beyond it—and Tanzania in turn being forced repeatedly to take new security precautions in case the rhetoric proved to be more than the accustomed bombast.

In 1972 Amin's military capacity to support his threats was limited. After the refusal in 1971 by Britain and Israel to supply him with military equipment to invade Tanzania he had turned to the Arabs. But the Arab world, confronted by the continuous prospect of renewed hostilities in the Middle East, had no hardware to spare. And in that phase the decimation of the officer corps of the Ugandan Army left a doubt as to its effectiveness: a feeling that was to be reinforced (despite its ultimate failure) by the way in which a comparatively small and ill-equipped force of supporters of Obote smashed north into Uganda, even though Amin knew in advance they were coming.

Since then the General has become deeply involved with the Soviet Union. They have supplied him with Mig21 jet fighters, T54 tanks, amphibious vehicles and have trained a substantial technical section of his army. Why the Soviets have done this, arming one African to threaten another, is a matter of speculation. By early 1975 Soviet officials were privately admitting that possibly the Kremlin was guilty of a severe miscalculation. Possibly China's substantial presence in Tanzania was a major cause of Soviet interest in Amin, despite his well proven unpredictability. But even more likely was the realisation that Amin could not survive indefinitely and that, by training key elements within the military, they were buying a future position of influence after his demise.

These were to be factors which in the future would not only alarm Tanzania, but also Kenya, which had initially provided ready access for Amin's military build up. But in 1972, on the eve of the attempt by Obote's guerrillas to topple Amin, one seemingly inexplicable event occurred. On 15 September, only two days before the invasion (but 15 days before it was originally scheduled to have taken place) a story appeared in the *Daily Express* quoting a Major Ian Walsworth-Bell, a former British army officer. He said that in 1971 he had gone to work for a company in Uganda and had been approached by Amin to carry out reconnaissance in northern Tanzania. Walsworth-Bell, a former British intelligence staff officer, who had been sacked by Whitehall for allegedly taking sides with the federal forces during the Nigerian war, said he had drawn up a plan for Amin's troops to seize northern Tanzania. This had been done in advance of Amin's visits to Britain and Israel in mid 1971 to ask for planes and equipment to carry it out. By late 1972 Tanzanian security were receiving intelligence reports linking certain prominent Tanzanian exiles with Amin and suggesting exiles were also active in Mozambique to the south where Tanzania was supporting Frelimo guerrillas. Walsworth-Bell's plan allowed for simultaneous attacks from Uganda and Mozambique, and not surprisingly some Tanzanians began to believe that the long threatened invasion was really in the offing. Intriguingly the *Daily Express* withdrew the story after its first edition.

Two quite isolated incidents influenced Nyerere at this point. The first occurred just before Obote flew back to Dar es Salaam from the Sudan. A group inside Uganda of considerable import who were planning a counter-coup sent messages out to Nyerere, to Obote and to Akena Adoko. Their action in contacting Nyerere and Obote came in the wake of the attempt in May by a group of young Lugbara officers to seize power while Amin was in Rabat attending the OAU summit. The plot backfired and one of the ring leaders was murdered. Amin hurried home and put the Nubians in charge of all the armouries before leaving on a Middle East tour. Why he went away again is unclear but it could have been because he underestimated the strength at the time of those planning his downfall or because he realised their strength at that juncture could not be challenged and that it would be safer to be away while events ran their course.

From Nyerere the plotters wanted a commitment of military support and from Obote they wanted a guarantee of support by his guerrillas if they were needed and in addition that he would back them so that the recognition which had initially been denied Amin would not be denied whoever took over. Nyerere had been moving arms on a small scale into Uganda for some time for a guerilla group calling itself the Front for National Salvation (Fronasa) which at this point few people had even heard of. The Front's leader was a young former Dar es Salaam student, Yoweri Museveni, who at this point was privately claiming to have training camps inside Uganda and a considerable number of armed men. Nyerere apparently accepted Museveni's claims as true although Obote, when he heard about them on his return from the Sudan, was extremely dubious.

Initially the attack was scheduled for the end of September. Museveni had claimed his guerrillas could capture Mbarara, Fort Portal, Mubende, Gulu and Mbale and he said he had smaller units in Jinja and Kampala. Obote's ground forces were to thrust north through Masaka, either on to the capital if they were not blocked by Amin's armour, or if that occurred, into the north of the country to open a new front. Obote was anxious not to attack until the end of September as he wanted to send men in to ascertain the truth of Museveni's claim. Obote's men were sent in to make contact with his supporters and check Fronasa's strength and Museveni was also sent in to alert his guerrillas that the attack was set for the end of the month.

On 5 September, the sixteen-nation East and Central African summit meeting began in Dar es Salaam. At this time the Tanzanians are believed to have received information from the Kenyans that Britain was preparing to fly troops into Uganda on the weekend of 17–18 September. The first Asians were scheduled to fly out on 19 September and the pretext for such an invasion by Britain would obviously be to 'protect British lives and property' which were certainly in some jeopardy.

It seems quite possible that Britain had such a plan and Nyerere's reaction was immediately to advance his to preclude British intervention. The Ugandan exiles were informed the planned invasion had been advanced to 15 September and the probable reason for this particular date is that it was the first one before the crucial weekend when an East African Airways DC-9 would be on the tarmac overnight at Dar es Salaam to be 'borrowed' to fly part of Obote's force in. A series of coded messages were to be put out on an East African radio station giving a countdown to supporters inside Uganda. The first would indicate the attack was set for three days. The next that it was two days off. And the final one that it would take place that night. Support weapons were taken to the Handeni camp but the guerrillas here had no time to practice with them as they arrived only hours before they were to move out. Inside Uganda contacts had been made with some army units but all that had been agreed was that they would support the attacking force when they neared their respective barracks but not before.

The first public indicator of what was happening occurred at Dar es Salaam Airport early on 15 September. An East African Airways crew went to the airport to set out on a scheduled flight in a DC-9 which had been parked there at 11.00 p.m. the previous night by another crew at the termination of their flight. To the astonishment of the crew the plane had disappeared. Several hours later it was found at Kilimanjaro Airport in northern Tanzania, facing across the runway with its tyres burst.

Apparently soon after midnight at Dar es Salaam Airport, police and security officers in civilian clothes had taken over the terminal at gunpoint. Amin claimed later Tanzania's Prime

Minister, Rashidi Kawawa, supervised the operation. Phones to town were cut and no one was allowed to leave the building. Then two Africans boarded the EAA DC-9 and took off. The next day the Tanzanians expressed utter bewilderment at the incident and promised there would be a full inquiry. But it was immediately noticeable that they did nothing to tighten up airport security. There was no need. The plane had been borrowed and not hijacked.

The pilot of the missing plane was a Ugandan, working for EAA who had recently been on a conversion course in the United States with Eastern Airlines on DC-9s which EAA had just acquired. In the month prior to the hijack he had been riding as an observer on the intercapital flight from Nairobi through Dar es Salaam to Lusaka. Generally he got off in Dar es Salaam and rejoined the flight on the way back and it was clear that he paid far too little attention to his cockpit drill in this period.

According to East African Airways pilots, who pieced together what happened, the pilot did just about everything wrong and he was very lucky not to kill himself and write off the plane. There is a cockpit check-list which the pilot must go through before take-off and the pilot missed at least two critical checks. The first, which was to prove his undoing, was that there is an anti-skid switch located on the cockpit ceiling which is left in the off position when the plane is parked. During checks three red lights show on the panel indicating that it is still off. But once a DC-9 takes off these automatically go out, so if the check has been missed he would not be warned that the switch is in the wrong position. The second check the pilot missed was that in Dar es Salaam, when the plane is parked, pressurisation is set at sea level. The result of this was that as he climbed out of Dar es Salaam that night a large red warning light came on in the cockpit. Looking for the problem, the indications are that the pilot then hit circuit breakers which brought the flight recorder on at 13,000 feet and recorded the rest of his journey in the 'black box'. Between 11,000 and 15,000 feet the yellow oxygen mask dropped down through the empty fuselage because he had not set the pressurisation. Between Dar es Salaam and Kilimanjaro he had two further problems which cannot be readily explained. The flight took about 50 per cent longer than it should have done and this may have been due to navigational errors. It is in fact said he overshot and reached Nairobi. Secondly he did not retract his undercarriage and pilots are at a loss to explain this. The result was that as he swung into Kilimanjaro Airport, at the base of Africa's highest mountain, his undercarriage was still firmly down and the anti-skid switch in the off position. He landed much too fast, possibly over 150 knots, when with an empty plane he should have touched down at 110 knots. When he braked, as he hurtled down the runway, he got maximum braking because of not turning on the anti-skid switch. The tyres blew and the plane gorged a deep line down the tarmac before swinging across it at 90 degrees to face the terminal.

It was a deeply embarrassing incident for the Tanzanians who found themselves under attack by Ugandan Members of the East African Assembly, which is the legislative wing of the East African Community.

The pilot promptly disappeared, leaving his EAA job without notice. Reports that he was killed for his failure are untrue for over a year later he was still living in Dar es Salaam.

The significance of the DC-9 hijack, although not realised for several days, was that it was to ferry two companies, with ninety-six men in each, of Obote's force to Entebbe Airport. They were part of the Sudan trained group who were moved up to near the airport from Tanga on the eve of the hijack. The DC-9 was to fly 'G' Company in first and their job was to seize Entebbe Airport and then head towards Kampala. A convoy of trucks supplied by an Obote supporter had been hidden on the road between the airport and Kampala to await the force. The overall DC-9 operation was to have been commanded by Lieutenant-Colonel Oyite Ojok. The DC-9 was to fly back to Kilimanjaro but, with its tyres burst, this first phase of the operation had to be called off.

To this day why Nyerere and Obote still decided to go ahead is a mystery. The wise course would have been to find some means of covering up the DC-9 hijack and wait for another day.

A hurried conference was held and it was decided that the DC-9 fiasco had not given the plan away and there was still a reasonable chance of success. And lurking in the background was the belief of Nyerere and Obote that if they did not move the British would. At a press conference for a visiting group of Scandinavian journalists five days later Nyerere bluntly told them in a reference to the American–Belgium operation into the Congo in 1965 to rescue nationals, that Africa would not tolerate another Stanley-ville. If Britain sent troops into Uganda, Tanzania, despite her feelings about the General would support Amin. At the time the remarks seemed inexplicable but it indicates that Nyerere seri-ously believed at that point that Britain intended to put troops into Uganda.

The excessive optimism of the operation doomed it to failure. The Entebbe group, apart from seizing the airport, were under orders to take the small air force armoury and a contingent were to head at speed into Kampala to seize the radio station. It is believed that Obote had prerecorded a message to the nation which the attackers were to play. What this tape recording con-tained is not known but it would have had a vital psychological impact for it would have given the impression in the early hours of 15 September that it was Obote himself broadcasting from the radio station in Kampala.

Once the DC-9 operation failed, Obote, under pressure from the Tanzanians, altered his plans. The original attack had not envisaged a force being sent to Mbarara and if it had it seems certain Obote would have sent a group from his better-trained Sudan guerrillas rather than those from Kigwa, some of whom had never handled guns, and others who had not for thirteen months.

But the fear was that if the single ground attack from Mutukula through Masaka to Kampala was now made, Amin's battalions at Mubende and Mbarara would move in behind Obote's guer-rillas cutting them off between Masaka and Kampala. So the group from Kigwa Camp on the Saturday morning only hours before the attack was due to begin were assigned to seize the armoury at Mbarara Barracks and turn the guns and ammunition over to the civilian population before heading north east to join the main force.

The story of the lack of co-ordination at Kigwa is even worse than what occurred at Handeni. A large number of untrained civilians had moved to the camp to join the 294 men who had been there for thirteen months. Then at about 4.00 p.m. on 14 September the Tabora Regional Commissioner, Mr. Philemon Mgaya, a senior police officer and former ADC to Nyerere, arrived at the camp. First he spent several hours with the commanders and late that night he briefed the whole group. Trucks would be arriving just before midnight when they would move out to the holding area south of Bukoba where they would link up with the main force and go into Uganda. But the trucks did not arrive until about 10.00 a.m. the next morning. No explanation was offered and the group was delayed for hours. Again it was in a sense fortunate the DC-9 operation failed. Mgaya told the whole group the decision to go into Uganda had been taken in Dar es Salaam by Obote. They were warned not to say anything to anyone outside the camp and told arms would be issued near the border.

Soon after 10.00 a.m. on 15 September, when the open civilian Bedford trucks used by the Tanzanian National Service finally arrived, they moved out of Kigwa. Almost immediately the secrecy of the operation was undermined for the loaded trucks drove into the heart of Tabora stopping at a petrol station for fuel. They had been told not to talk to the town people who gathered around, but even so the blacker-skinned Ugandans stood out prominently.

From Tabora the convoy headed north over murram roads through Nzega and then westwards through Kahama to Nyakanazi and north again to the rendezvous point twenty miles south of the town of Bukoba and eighty miles from the frontier. The Kigwa contingent, were tired, dirty and hungry after riding in open trucks on the dusty roads in the tropical sun, and near Nshamba they found almost 600 more men in six companies from the Sudan group.

The logistics of moving 800 men right across Tanzania secretly by truck to link up with the Kigwa force posed obvious difficulties and the plan was timed carefully. On 12 September, around 7.00 p.m. Obote accompanied by aides arrived from Dar es Salaam by car at the Handeni camp to brief his commanders and the political leaders of the group. His arrival at the camp was difficult itself for it had rained heavily and the dirt road leading to Handeni had been turned into a quagmire.

First of all that night he briefed his military commanders and later the political organisers who were to go in with the force. The full extent of the latter's role is in doubt but it appears to have been twofold. As the guerrillas pushed north into Uganda some of the political organisers were to remain behind to mobilise the civilian population while others would head north as fast as possible to organise in areas where there was no fighting. The men were briefed last and the carefully timed schedule had planned that they would all move out on trucks at 4.00 a.m. Obote went to each truck wishing the men good luck as they boarded. But then came the first of a series of incredible blunders by the Tanzanians. The trucks had not been fuelled and so at 4.00 a.m. instead of driving across country they moved to Handeni town to fill up. It was 8.00 a.m. before the last truck moved out of the area and already the schedule had gone well awry.

The trucks had been due to arrive at the rendezvous point south of Bukoba early on 14 September but as a result of continuous delays, including petrol stops at towns across Tanzania, they did not arrive until that night and the last truck, which had broken down and got lost, did not get there until 2.00 p.m. on 16 September—some eight hours after they were supposed to be in Kampala. Had the DC-9 operation not failed the guerrillas who were to be flown in would have inevitably been there many hours ahead of the main force and it seems likely that they would have been wiped out.

At the assembly area they were told to pitch tents and were given blankets and food. A few weapons were distributed that day 'but these were very old weapons—older than the ones we had had in training,' one of the men said later. He said there were practically no support weapons and certainly nothing of the type they had trained on at Kingolwira thirteen months earlier. Late that evening a number of other guns, still caked in grease, were also handed over.

On 16 September more weapons and ammunition were distributed including grenades and some belt-action submachineguns. At 6.00 p.m. that evening, Colonel Okello, the elderly commander of the force, briefed 1,000 men. They would be attacking in two groups, he said. One would cross at Mutukula and head due north through Masaka to Kampala. The other would head westwards from the Tanzanian frontier to take the barracks of the Simba Battalion at Mbarara and then would swing back towards the north-east to link up with the main group for the attack on the capital. The Kigwa group were to go to Mbarara and the Sudan group, north through Masaka to spearhead the attack on Kampala. They were instructed to kill any armed soldiers but not to touch civilians unless they behaved suspiciously, in which case they were to be arrested. The Obote force wore Tanzanian National Service uniforms similar to those worn by Ugandan troops, and to identify themselves to each other, a three-inch-wide strip of red cloth through their shoulder epaulets which was tied under the arm pit. Then to the irritation of some of the younger men, the briefing ended with an Acholi traditional war ceremony of songs to give courage.

In fact the plan was more complex than Okello's briefing. Originally, before the DC-9 operation went wrong, it would have been a two-pronged attack in the hope of confusing Amin so he would not know where to concentrate his counter offensive. But with one prong drawn, the intention was now to take Mbarara and Masaka. But thereafter two options had been laid out. From Masaka the main force was to advance towards Kampala swinging around the northern shore of Lake Victoria. This is a very marshy area with the River Katonga running into the lake a few miles north of Masaka. If the Obote force found their way blocked by Amin's advancing armour, they were to take up a defensive position in the marsh area. The armour would not be able to leave the single road without getting bogged down and it was believed that a comparatively small force could hold the road. The remainder of the force would then head north-west through Sembabule, Ntusi and Nabingora to take the battalion at Mubende, where considerable support was expected, then push on northwards through Masindi to Gulu into the Acholi and Langi homelands. The Mbarara group were to take the barracks and in particular the armoury. Then, after distributing the arms and ammunition to the local civilian population, they would head north to link up with the main group. Minor roads had been carefully surveyed in advance and it was thought most likely that Amin would panic and commit his armour and heavy troop concentration down the Masaka road. If they could be held there the remainder of Obote's force could move swiftly over back roads and create a second threat from the north. And the longer they stayed inside Uganda the greater the chances of sizable defections from Amin's army to support the attackers.

Little of the plan ever got off the drawing board. The convoy of twenty-seven trucks, with the Tanzanian drivers who had brought them to the area now replaced by Ugandans, headed out of the rendezvous area at 10.00 p.m. on 16 September with the headlights off which caused further delays. They by-passed Bukoba forking north-west just south of the town at a village called Kanazi and twice they stopped to rest during the night as they moved to the frontier. 'Our mood was very enthusiastic especially as we were going to be back home the next day,' one of them told me later. 'We thought we could not be defeated because we had a cause. But we forgot Amin's soldiers had to defend their lives.'

The Mbarara attacking force were due to cross the frontier at 5.00 a.m.—although there are indications they had originally planned to cross six hours earlier—which would have meant they would have reached the barracks in the garrison town before dawn after a thirty-five-mile drive. But this group, with seven truck-loads of men, did not reach a point three miles from the frontier until 6.00 a.m. An eighth truck-load of guerrillas which should have been with them had taken the wrong turning at

Kakindu, and by mistake had headed north with the Masaka group, further increasing the odds they faced at Mbarara.

While the main body of the Mbarara attacking force waited near the frontier, two platoons were sent ahead on foot to clear a four-man border-post of Amin's soldiers on the frontier at Nsongezi. The four soldiers were killed and the post burned, but it was 7.15 a.m. before the force moved across the frontier and one of them recalled later: 'We were already becoming very unhappy about the time factor.'

Further time was lost on the road to Mbarara. At one point a zone defence was set up while the trucks crossed a road junction wasting another thirty minutes. Then they met a priest driving south who assured them there was no opposition ahead. Next they met a civilian car and waved it through not realising until it accelerated off at high speed that one of the occupants was Colonel Waris Ali, the Mbarara commander. Then on a sharp right-hand bend, eight miles from Mbarara, the convoy met a Land-Rover with eight soldiers in it and a truck with two more, heading south. There was a brief gun battle in which eight of Amin's men were killed.

The way in which Obote's force had dealt with the border post and two army vehicles killing twelve men without any of them being wounded in return was psychologically disastrous. Just before Mbarara town there is a narrow bridge with a girls' school on the southern side and the convoy pulled up here to assess the situation. 'At this point there was a complete lack of control. We were lounging around like schoolboys and had no idea of the danger we were in. One man jumping from a truck, fell on his head and split his face open and he refused to pick up his gun again.' Amin's soldiers on a road-block at the bridge were routed and one who had been captured earlier said the attack was not expected.

There was a near carnival atmosphere as they moved into Mbarara. The convoy, with guns poking out from the trucks in case of trouble, moved through the town and flags of Obote's UPC began to appear.

All the delays had meant they had arrived near the barracks at

11.00 a.m., about four and a half hours late. The plan to seize the barracks was based on a two-pronged attack which meant splitting the force with part moving in from the north and the remainder from the south. But as the guerrillas milled around waiting to move an argument broke out between the commander, Captain Oyile, and his deputy, Lieutenant Okot. The Lieutenant maintained that as they still had the element of surprise they should burst through the main gates of the barracks in their vehicles shooting as they went and thereby prevent the soldiers inside getting to the armoury. Oyile insisted they must stick to the original plan and as they argued two armed jeeps appeared on the road from the barracks and opened fire. The element of surprise had now been totally lost.

A miniature battle followed in which one jeep was captured. But the other jeep with a 106 mm recoilless gun mounted in the rear opened fire hitting the leading truck in the convoy. The shell bounded off the empty first vehicle exploding in another one further back blowing the leg off one man. The double-edged reality of war had at last been brought home to the attackers. The jeep with the 106 mm reversed and made off, but by now there was total chaos among the attacking force. They had scattered over a wide area under fire and there was no sign of either Captain Oyile or Lieutenant Okot.

A staunch UPC supporter and former soldier rallied about 100 of the guerrillas to carry out the original two-pronged attack on both sides of the barracks. But by now the defenders were well armed and the Obote force by way of support weapons had only five mortars and twenty-seven mortar shells. The ground between the force attacking from the south and the barracks offered precious little cover and they had no contact between them and the group moving in from the north.

One of the guerrillas fighting in the northern group says that none of the people on his side got inside Mbarara. But both Amin and Obote's commanders were later to claim that a large group did get into the barracks and assuming this is true they must have been in the assault group on the south, but even this is disputed.

On the northern side the situation was chaotic. A Langi was

killed as he made a desperate run for the barbed wire surrounding Mbarara. The attackers had to cross seventy yards of open ground to reach the perimeter and even then they had no wire-cutters and had to try to hack their way through with pangas. The defenders were shooting from behind the protection of the barrack buildings. None of those who reached the fence returned. An Alur from Amin's own West Nile area named Olega, who had been a prominent UPC member in his home area and a Sergeant-Major in training, crawled under the barbed-wire. But he was riddled by a machine-gun burst.

The fighting had started around noon and continued until 3.00 p.m. The attackers were making little or no progress. Whatever command structure that had existed had broken down and, as men ran out of ammunition, they had to run back to the trucks to get more. After their drive to the frontier, the crossing and the the prolonged fight with the psychological side-effects, most of the Obote force were by now utterly exhausted. Ageta tried to rally them and drove the wounded in one of the captured jeeps to hospital in Mbarara but by mid-afternoon it was a thoroughly dejected force.

The group on the north began to pull out soon after 3.00 p.m. Only one driver could be found and they decided to try to organise another attack. If that failed they would withdraw completely. 'Many of our group still believed we could win. But personally I wanted to withdraw. I thought it was futile and foolish to go on,' one of the Mbarara force said. Finally soon after 5.00 p.m. they decided to pull out. About 200 of them were still in the area and they had six trucks. But when they pulled out some of them were too exhausted to even climb into the truck, one guerrilla told me, and they were simply abandoned.

Panic had set in and the confident force which had crossed into Uganda only ten hours earlier was now a disorganised and disheartened group of men. Five trucks set out through Mbarara with only forty-two of the survivors aboard, one of them said. Another gave the figure as forty-six, while one platoon commander said it was sixty-one, of whom two died. One truck ran out of petrol and another broke down eight miles from the town.

The other three reached Tanzania at 7.00 a.m. on Monday, almost twenty-four hours after the crossing. Another eight made their way back on foot later and seven more subsequently made contact that they were still alive inside Uganda.

One of the survivors of the Mbarara force said later he believed there were five reasons for the failure of the attack. There was the fact that they had spent thirteen months without any training; inadequate arms including that there were no support weapons and eleven of the group had no guns at all when they crossed into Uganda; that the force was too small to attack a full battalion; poor planning which meant that they arrived at their target late; and finally lack of control and bad leadership.

Meanwhile the main force heading for Masaka had apparently initially crossed the frontier closer to their time schedule. They reached a point near the frontier at 4.00 a.m. and again a platoon was sent ahead to deal with Amin's troops at the border post. The sun was just beginning to rise as the twenty trucks carrying the main group crossed over at 5.30 a.m.: 'F' Company with four trucks was in the lead. Its task was to push through fast to Masaka, take and hold the town while the rest of the force would head straight through it in the hope of getting to Kampala.

One of the members of this company subsequently described to me what happened: 'As we drove through Mutukula people were already saying we were crossing too late. But we did not worry about it because we were sure that it was going to be easy.'

The first thirty miles of the journey to Kyotera were uneventful for 'F' Company. Then while the commander was trying to sort out the confusion when one of his trucks took a wrong turning, shots were heard. The company took cover and a soldier was seen up a tree apparently acting as an observer. The company commander, Captain Arach, had been killed with the first shots, but the small group of Ugandan soldiers fled and the attacking force captured their three-ton truck. The company regrouped and waited and then a jeep with a 106 mm mounted on it, which had been captured by the group behind them, was brought up. But it only had three rounds left.

'Our collective decision at this point was just to sit and wait,' the guerrilla said. Another company with the force commander, Colonel Okello, caught up with them and he ordered them to push on. Three trucks had been hit and seven moved forward with most of the men preferring to walk in the bush off the road where they felt safer. 'Most of us were very tired having travelled over 700 miles across the country and then through the night into Uganda. We were just pushing on because we had been told to.' The first experience under fire and the deaths had swiftly dampened enthusiasm.

About 2.00 p.m. when they had walked two miles from the initial battle, ground-fire started again. This time it was a much more formidable force and a plane swept low overhead on a reconnaissance flight. Then tanks and armoured personnel carriers appeared on a hill ahead and the Obote force had no counter as they had already exhausted the ammunition they had for the recoilless rifle. They had crossed with only 100 rounds each for their personal guns, with no ammunition pouches, they had had to stuff it in their pockets and their random fire in the first fighting meant they were now running low.

Just to the south of the village of Kalisizo the other companies piled up behind them and at this point Okello withdrew with some of the men. Why he had gone back is unclear, but it had a bad effect on morale. Lieutenant-Colonel Oyite Ojok detailed four men with a bazooka to move out on to the left flank and try to knock out the tanks which were concentrating their fire from only a quarter of a mile away on the trucks.

'At this point I and quite a lot of other soldiers decided to withdraw to the vehicles. It was a unilateral decision. We were running out of ammunition, had no heavy weapons and there was no point in getting killed.' Under cover of dark they re-treated into Tanzania recrossing the border in the early hours of 18 September, less than twenty-four hours after they had gone into Uganda. A member of 'F' Company estimated that as many as 200 people from the Masaka force did not get back, although Obote's commanders put the figure considerably lower.

As the force had headed north, civilians along the route cheered them. But, as if sensing what the future held, they were eerily silent as the retreating force straggled back to Tanzania, mainly on foot. The Masaka force had had only two 75 mm recoilless rifles, mortars and light machine-guns, rifles, bazookas and grenades. They had no equipment packs and no shovels with which to dig-in when they came under fire. The assumption had been that it would be easy and the planners had lulled themselves into a false sense of security.

In retrospect one thing that is clear is that Amin knew about the attack on Masaka, although he seems to have been caught unaware by the one at Mbarara which was decided at the last moment, and his initial estimate on Radio Uganda of 1,000 guerrillas was remarkably accurate. Lieutenant-Colonel Ojok said that the main body of the Masaka force ran into a series of ambushes before being halted south of Kalisizo. The first was only six miles from the frontier. 'The ambush was very badly placed. Most of the others we encountered were also. If they had been well placed I don't think any of us would have got back.'

Either the defenders at this first ambush were asleep or they were deliberately trying to split the column as two companies had moved past them before they opened fire. The ambushers were located behind a rise running alongside the road firing mortars over the top and unable to see what effect they were having. A company was left behind to wipe this group out and the rest moved northwards. But six miles further on near Sanje village they ran into a second company-strength ambush. This one was better located in a banana plantation with a 106 mm gun firing down the road. Again a company was left to deal with the ambush and the remainder of the convoy moved around it. Several other small ambushes were dealt with as they moved northwards until finally they caught up with 'F' Company halted by the armour of the Malire Mechanised Battalion, just south of Kalisizo.

A further development at this point indicates that Amin was expecting the attack. Reconnaissance by Obote supporters in advance had given details of Amin's troop strength in the area. The series of ambushes meant the attackers were now running five hours behind schedule with no possibility of reaching Kampala. So at this point Oyite Ojok tried a modified version of the second plan with part of his force holding the armour south of Kalisizo and the rest dropping back to Kyotera and then heading north west over a dirt road to Lyantonde on the main road from Mbarara to Masaka. But they ran headlong into Amin's armour which he had moved up unbeknown to them from Malire into this triangle and it took some of this element of Obote's forces a week to fight their way out after heavy casualties.

Briefly on Monday 18 September there was a ray of hope that the attackers had not been completely routed. Fresh supplies and reinforcements were being moved in from Tanzania. But the reinforcements were less than 100 men of 'G' Company hurriedly moved across the country from Kilimanjaro after the DC-9 fiasco.

Nyerere, who had always had major reservations about the conventional military approach of Obote's commanders, preferring guerrilla warfare, is said to have remarked when he learned the attackers had been routed: 'I hope they have learned their lesson.' Now he had to face the political consequences of his rash decision and the people in Uganda the wrath of Amin. Obote's two former Ministers who had gone in with the Masaka force as his representatives were both killed. Wakholi was wounded and it is not clear whether he died from his wounds or was murdered. But there is no doubt that Ojera was murdered. In a bizarre scene he was dragged handcuffed and stripped to the waist into a cocktail party for OAU Secretary-General Ekangaki and unprotesting African diplomats in Kampala where Amin, grinning widely, publicly interrogated him. A few days later it was announced that he and a number of other prisoners, including Captain Oyile, the missing commander of Obote's Mbarara force, had killed their guards in a mass breakout from a prison in a military camp in north-west Uganda. The next day a Government spokesman corrected this and said the breakout had been from a prison in south-west Uganda. But in fact, Ojera and Oyile never left Kampala. They were murdered there and many people are convinced that Amin personally killed them.

———— ◆◆◆◆ ————

Tanzania's Foreign Minister, John Malecela, had had a lucky escape, for shortly before the exile force attacked Uganda he had been sitting at Entebbe Airport in transit on his way to the United Nations General Assembly.

Now, amidst a flurry of peace initiatives, with the two countries poised dangerously close to the brink of war, President Nyerere summoned him back to salvage what he could from the débâcle. Tanzania was to escape remarkably unscathed although there can be no doubt that in Africa the reputations of President Nyerere and his country suffered considerably.

Little more than twenty-four hours after the invasion, with the Obote supporters defeated and streaming back towards Tanzania, a Ugandan air force plane rocketed and strafed the north-western town of Bukoba on the shores of Lake Victoria. Several people were killed and injured. On the following day, 19 September, Bukoba was again attacked but the bombs fell harmlessly into the lake, and two people died at Mwanza on the south-eastern shore of the lake when that town was bombed.

Urgently President Nyerere cabled the current chairman of the Organisation of African Unity, King Hassan II of Morocco and the OAU Secretary-General, Mr. Nzo Ekangaki, drawing their attention to the 'danger to peace which now exists in East Africa'. The cable read:

'On the morning of Sunday, 17 September, fighting broke out in south-west Uganda between supporters and opponents of General Amin. The latter immediately announced that Tanzania had invaded Uganda. Tanzania responded the same day with a denial that any of its troops had crossed the border into Uganda.

'We believe the truth of Tanzania's statement is now clear

to all but if any African state has doubts we would be willing for the OAU to take the steps necessary to verify what we have said. For although the lies of General Amin could be left to time for exposure he is using them to justify bombing Tanzanian towns. On Monday, 18 September, a Ugandan plane bombed the town of Bukoba in north-west Tanzania killing nine and wounding eleven civilians. Today, Tuesday, a further attack was attempted but driven off by anti-aircraft fire and the bombs dropped into Lake Victoria.

'Murderous attacks of this nature cannot be without consequences. They constitute a real and urgent danger to peace in this part of Africa. African unity cannot demand of any nation that it acquiesces in the bombing of its cities by another African state.'

Despite general acceptance of the Tanzanian statement that their troops had not been involved in fighting inside Uganda, there was no denying that Tanzania had aided and abetted to the full the exile force. Captured Tanzanian National Service trucks, with their markings painted out, and boxes of food with items like service biscuits marked 'Specially made for the TPDF' (Tanzania People's Defence Forces) made any denial futile. As such President Nyerere was on weak ground in his complaints as the injured party.

Yet he could not sit by and mutely accept the bombing. A large percentage of the population of Bukoba and Mwanza had fled, with taxi drivers charging exorbitant rates to drive families and their possessions out of the towns. Senior army officers told me plainly during those few tense days: 'We cannot sit on the frontier and talk of protecting the country while civilians are being bombed and killed behind us.' The inference was clear, and had there been further bombing President Nyerere might have had trouble holding his army back. In Dar es Salaam there was a mood of total depression. The folly of the invasion, coupled with the bombings, brought an air of national defeat.

The British press, which eighteen months earlier had welcomed the overthrow of Dr. Obote, had little more to condemn

President Nyerere for than that the invasion failed. In Africa the Nigerian press, still remembering the Tanzanian recognition of secessionist Biafra and the military support for Colonel Ojukwu were predictably hostile. The *New Nigeria* said: 'The attack was nothing but indefensible aggression. Tanzania could not convincingly disclaim connivance. It is no secret that President Nyerere supports ex-President Obote.' It went on after recalling Tanzania's support for Biafra by adding: 'It is foolish for Nyerere to support Obote to the extent of allowing him to raise and train an army on Tanzanian soil. This is indeed against the provisions of the charter of the Organisation of African Unity which Nyerere took part in drawing up. While Nyerere need not support President Idi Amin, it is equally wrong for him to act as if only Obote can represent Uganda. We urge President Nyerere to abandon his policy of personal vendetta.'

But it was mainly the attitude of President Sekou Touré of Guinea which was to shock the Tanzanians. They had long tended to close their eyes to the realities of Guinea, identifying that country as holding common progressive views on African matters. On the evening of 17 September Radio Uganda broadcast a message from President Sekou Touré which read: 'We give you our support in the strong pursuit of the total political independence and destruction of external elements. We support you in your struggle for achieving total liberation of the people of Uganda from any alienation and for all the profound democratisation of the Ugandan society.'

In fact, although this message had been sent before the invasion, in response to one from General Amin, it was used to indicate support. Guinea's Ambassador to Tanzania, Mr. Sakho Damau, in a statement to the government newspaper, the *Daily News*, in Dar es Salaam, was quoted as saying: 'Although I do not have official information from Conakry, I can swear here and now that the Republic of Guinea cannot and will never support Idi Amin. We do not support his allegations that Tanzanian forces have invaded Uganda. One can never expect to support Amin. I must repeat, I swear we will not.' Unfortunately for Mr. Damau, who was recalled soon after, those in West Africa were unaware of the realities of Uganda and he in turn of what Conakry believed. Although the first message was sent before the invasion, and therefore deliberately misused, President Sekou Touré, no doubt remembering the 1970 invasion of his own country, was later to describe it as the work of Zionists and Imperialists. Libya's support for General Amin was to be expected but again the Tanzanians were clearly displeased by the guarded criticism from Cairo.

Egypt's President Anwar Sadat cabled Amin saying:

'Dear brother, we have been following with great concern and sorrow the barbaric aggression against the brotherly Uganda nation, which was moved by the imperialist and Zionist elements to destroy the national benefits achieved by the Ugandan nation under your command and leadership. Your Excellency, we in Egypt put ourselves and efforts at your disposal to stop the imperialist aggression against the Uganda nation.'

That twenty months earlier Cairo had seen the overthrow of Obote as inspired by the Imperialists and Zionists was long forgotten, while the continuing slaughter of Ugandans by Amin was ignored.

A number of peace initiatives had already begun and President Nyerere again cabled Mr. Ekangaki on 21 September, just after Sudan had stopped five Libyan transport Hercules loaded with men and munitions overflying *en route* for Uganda. In this cable he said:

'The government of Tanzania welcomes the work for peace in East Africa which is now being undertaken by the OAU and a number of East and Central African heads of state. We shall co-operate with these efforts which we believe show the genuine concern of Africa for unity and solidarity in the struggle against imperialism and racialism. We welcome also the action of President Nimeri in preventing troops and arms being sent across Sudan to Uganda. Their arrival in Uganda at this time would have greatly worsened an already explosive situation and the President has thus provided valuable time in which action for peace can be taken. But Tanzania believes that the dispatch of these men and weapons resulted from false information and a subsequent misunderstanding of the situation in East Africa on the part of the Libyan leaders. We appeal to all African states to refrain from any action which could possibly escalate the conflict or otherwise increase the dangers inherent in the present circumstances.'

Despite General Nimeri's efforts, the Libyans reached Uganda, and Tanzania intelligence received information to this effect on 21 September soon after they arrived and two full days before it was announced in Kampala.

The Libyan force, consisting of twenty-two officers and 377 other ranks, had been flown in five transporters which also carried weapons, ammunition and one Mig jet-fighter. Nimeri had received an assurance from Nyerere that Tanzanian troops were not involved in the fighting when he sent up fighters to intercept the Libyan transporters and order them to land at Khartoum. The Sudanese ordered the Libyans to fly home realising how dangerously their presence in Uganda would widen what was a conflict between Ugandans. But the planes took off from Khartoum and out of radar range once more headed south to Uganda.

Nimeri's intervention infuriated Colonel Qadhafi, and in May 1973, he, Amin and the Palestinians worked out a plan to overthrow the Sudanese leader. While Nimeri was to be absent at the OAU conference in Addis Ababa it was planned to fly several hundred Palestinian guerrillas into Khartoum to seize the city. Simultaneously a force of over 1,000 Anyanya guerrillas would cross by land from Uganda and seize the southern capital, Juba. Parachute drops were carried out near Mbale in Uganda by the Palestinians during training. But fortunately one of the final meetings was infiltrated by an agent and information was conveyed to Nimeri of the impending attack. He moved his armour into Khartoum and mounted an alert, and through diplomatic channels it was made clear in Kampala that the plan had been discovered. Although the exact date of the planned attack was not known, what was known was that Qadhafi had secretly flown to Uganda during the final planning phase for a meeting with Amin.

On 28 September 1972, three days after arriving back from New York, Malecela flew to the Somalia capital, Mogadishu, for talks centring on a five-point peace plan which had been put to President Nyerere and General Amin by Somalia's Secretary of State for External Affairs, Mr. Omar Arteh Ghalib. The Uganda Foreign Minister, Wanume Kibedi, kept the five-man Tanzanian delegation cooling their heels in Mogadishu for almost a week but despite the obvious humiliation of this for the Tanzanian Foreign Minister it was to give him two distinct advantages. In the first place the delegation devoted many hours to breaking up into two sides—one representing Tanzania and the other Uganda. They argued along the lines of the Somalia peace plan, which was to provide the guidelines for the Mogadishu Agreement, working out concessions and preparing themselves for various eventualities. Secondly, whereas Tanzania, by supporting the invasion, was clearly in part the aggressor, psychologically the roles had been altered. Realising the invasion had been disastrous they publicly and swiftly accepted peace initiatives and Malecela's week-long wait demonstrated their desire, at this point at least, to avoid war.

By allowing himself to be seen increasingly as the belligerent, Amin was to miss the opportunity to score a larger propaganda victory over Nyerere. There was first of all the bombings of Tanzanian towns and then the arrival of Libyan forces which included Palestinian guerrillas.

Finally, while Malecela cooled his heels in Mogadishu, Amin claimed that another invasion had been beaten back with heavy casualties and then added that Tanzania, Zambia and India (whose President Giri was in the area on a series of state visits) were planning a joint attack. In those few days Amin looked increasingly as if he wanted war and not peace, and five questions which

he demanded Kibedi must obtain written replies to, lent weight
to this view. These questions were:

  1. Why Nyerere with Obote decided to train guerrillas
in Tanzania to kill people in Uganda.
  2. Why Nyerere decided to send Tanzanian troops, guerrillas and mercenaries to invade Uganda and kill civilians and
members of the security forces.
  3. Why Nyerere decided to give the guerrillas arms,
ammunition, bombs, rockets, mines and anti-personnel
arms.
  4. Why Nyerere made propaganda against Uganda
especially concerning the decision on the non-citizen Asians.
  5. Whether the four Ugandan soldiers who were kidnapped by Tanzanian troops the previous year were dead
or alive.

The peace talks in Mogadishu's People's Hall overlooking the
Indian Ocean lasted little more than ten hours and the simplicity
of the agreement belied the difficulties in reaching it. The agreement reads:

  'Adhering to the Charter of the OAU and in particular to
  the principle of respect for the territorial integrity of member
  states and non-interference in their internal affairs;
  Mindful of the fact that any hostilities between independent African states are detrimental to the achievement
  of the aims and objectives of the OAU in the face of imperialist designs to disturb the stability of Africa and retard
  her progress;
  Considering further the close relationship that exists within
  the East African Community;
  Aware that misunderstanding and differences can definitely
  be resolved peacefully and in a spirit of brotherhood;
  The government of the Republic of Uganda and the
  government of the United Republic of Tanzania have agreed
  to end all hostilities between them and restore peace and
  cement the fraternal ties that have always existed among
  their peoples. To this end the two governments pledge:

Article 1

To cease forthwith all military operations of any kind against each other's territory and to withdraw not later than 19 October 1972 all their military forces to a distance not less than ten kilometres from the common border. Such withdrawal shall be witnessed by observers sent from Somalia by Major-General Muhammad Siad Barre, in consultation with both Presidents, General Idi Amin Dada of Uganda and Mwalimu Julius Nyerere of Tanzania.

Article 2

To effect an immediate cessation of hostile propaganda directed against each other through the radio, TV and press.

Article 3

To refrain from harbouring or allowing subversive forces to operate in the territory of one state against the other.

Article 4

To release nationals or property, if any, of the other state held by either side.

Article 5

This pledge shall become effective at 8.00 p.m. on Saturday 7 October 1972. It shall be simultaneously announced in Dar es Salaam, Kampala and Mogadishu at the same time.'

The agreement, dated 5 October 1972 was signed by Kibedi, Malecela and Ghalib, as chairman, at the ceremony in the People's Hall, attended by President Barre and Ekangaki.

The preamble was agreed in closed session with little discussion and only minor changes. But there were prolonged discussions on the Articles and at one point Malecela and the Tanzanian delegation walked out. Kibedi had demanded that Obote and other named exiles should be handed over as a part of the terms of the peace agreement. The Tanzanian Foreign Minister, through the chair, asked his counterpart to repeat the demand three times. When he did so the Tanzanians gathered their papers and walked out. A phone call was made to Dar es Salaam during which Malecela spoke in his vernacular, Kigogo, to a friend. The conversation ended in English with the Minister saying that they were likely to be back soon and that a plane should be ready to be sent to them.

The Somali's took this to mean, as was probably intended, that the Tanzanians would not budge on the question of Obote and if the issue was pressed they would break off the peace talks. President Barre immediately intervened and persuaded Kibedi to drop the demand. Prophetically, as only four months later Kibedi himself was to flee into exile, Malecela had warned him not to press too hard the demand for Obote's return, as he might find himself in the same position one day.

With the Tanzanian and Ugandan armies facing each other along their common 100-mile frontier, this was the first major area to reduce the potential conflict. Just before the invasion the Tanzanians had moved up the 4th Battalion from Tabora and the 1st Heavy Mortar Company from Musoma, along with various other support units. The Ugandan army across the frontier had been on a state of alert for some time and its numbers in the area appear to have been about 50 per cent larger than the Tanzanian forces. The Tanzanians were equipped with Chinese artillery up to 122 mm and in the brief skirmishes a year earlier they had displayed they could use it with telling effect. Both Bukoba and Mwanza had limited anti-aircraft cover and the jerry-rigged DC-3 which had bombed Mwanza had been hit by ground fire. In contrast the Ugandans had total air supremacy with Russian built Mig 15s and 17s as well as French Fougas although how many were serviceable is in doubt. They had also moved up a mechanised regiment containing tanks and armoured personnel carriers, but the Tanzanians also had light and medium Chinese tanks in the area from their training ground near Bukoba.

An important point dictating how far the Tanzanians were prepared to withdraw was that on a number of occasions Amin had threatened to seize the northern triangle of the country bounded by the Uganda border in the north, Lake Victoria to the east and the Kagera river to the south. This was in fact the real reason why the troops had been moved up before the invasion, for General Amin's threat a few days before the invasion on the same theme had been taken very seriously, and anyway the senior officers of the Tanzanian army, who had vetoed earlier invasion plans in 1971, appear to have known nothing about the impending attack. The Kagera river is spanned by only one bridge at Kyaka and the bulk of the Tanzanian forces were concentrated here and to the north of Bukoba. When I'd visited the area fifteen months earlier wires could be seen running along the bridge indicating that it was mined and a small unit of troops were located at a disused mission on a hill overlooking the crossing point and armed with light artillery and mortars which would have been adequate to stop any Ugandan advance.

Thus the Tanzanians were determined to retain defensive positions between the border and Kagera and the ten-kilometre withdrawal line was very much to their advantage for this meant a very short move from the positions the forward troops were already holding and in addition their heavy artillery could still adequately cover the potential border crossing points. The ending of all military operations was defined as covering land, air and sea operations within ten kilometres on either side of the frontier, although Uganda was subsequently to hold a military exercise in December 1972 in the no-man's-land area.

On Article 1 Uganda reserved the right to undertake 'mopping up' operations in the specified zone, which the Tanzanians accepted in principle, while insisting that they must be informed through the Somali observers of the timing of these operations and where they would take place. President Barre was given the task of appointing the observer force while finally it was agreed that civilian police could be stationed at the frontier to carry out routine control work.

Article 2 caused considerable problems, for the Tanzanians were reluctant to gag the press in such a broadly defined manner. Although it was not specifically spelt out, they interpreted the Article to mean only government-controlled media, for they argued they had no right to attempt to control foreign or independent media and correspondents. It was a view that Uganda did not share and a Somali diplomat in Dar es Salaam subsequently suggested to at least one Tanzanian government official to my knowledge, that it would be easier if they expelled me, as my reports, particularly on the murders inside Uganda, were angering Amin. On this Article the Tanzanians lodged a reservation to the effect that it was only accepting it in the clear understanding that genuine comments on government policies 'shall not be construed as hostile propaganda'. To this Uganda objected.

Article 3 is the most ambiguous and the most critical. Kibedi made it clear that his delegation did not believe that a lasting peace could be achieved as long as Obote and his supporters—defined as 'subversive' and not 'refugees'—remained in Tanzania. He argued they should therefore be handed over, but Malecela made it clear his government as a matter of principle would never do this.

After Malecela's walk-out and Barre's intervention, the Ugandans said they would be willing to accept a position whereby Obote and his supporters were transferred to another country out of the area where they could not pose a threat. But again the Tanzanians would not accept this, for they argued the exiles were entitled to be treated as refugees under the United Nations Refugee Convention and the OAU Convention on Refugees and they were willing to satisfy the OAU and Somalia that these conditions were being met. If any of the exiles voluntarily elected to move to another country, that was up to them.

Finally the original wording of the Article was accepted subject to the following four provisos:

a. Distinction would be made between the main leaders of the exiled Obote group and the remainder.

b. Uganda lodged a list of those it regarded as the main leaders which included Obote; Sam Odaka, former Foreign Minister; Akena Adoko, formerly head of the General Service Department and Obote's cousin; Colonel Tito Okello, commander of the September invasion; Lieutenant-Colonel David Oyite Ojok, second-in-command of the September invasion; and Adoko Nekyon, another relative of Obote and a former Minister. The future of this group would be a matter for direct discussions between Presidents Nyerere and Barre.

c. As far as the remainder of the exiles were concerned, Somalia as mediator and the OAU Secretary-General would make arrangements to transfer them to another country not bordering on Uganda. However, a critical proviso here was 'If they voluntarily agree'.

d. Here it was agreed that none of the exiles would be forced to leave Tanzania and like the latter part of the third proviso this had the effect of totally blocking Uganda's attempt to have them removed from the area.

Article 4 caused little controversy, for apart from lodging the names of nationals held and property seized there was little point in making a major issue here. Tanzania put in a list of eighteen of her nationals believed to have been arrested in the frontier area in the previous fifteen months, but Uganda denied any knowledge of them and it was presumed they had been killed. The Ugandans named four soldiers captured by Tanzania who were later released, but the Tanzanian delegation denied any knowledge of an arms shipment, which had in fact been ordered by the Obote government before the *coup* and was seized in transit through Tanzania soon after it.

It was finally agreed that there would be a further tripartite meeting in six months to review the implementation of the Agreement and the Tanzanians suggested that any alleged breach should in the meantime be reported to the mediator before any unilateral action was taken. This was a position that the Tanzanians stuck to but there were frequent breaches by Uganda, either directly by Amin or by a 'military spokesman' as they kept up a barrage of charges against Tanzania. So scrupulously did the Tanzanians observe this that in December when seven young students were arrested in Kampala by military police after they had been called to the Ugandan capital for interviews at the headquarters of the East African Posts and Telecommunications Corporation, the Tanzanians said nothing publicly and asked Somalia to look into the matter. The seven Tanzanians were presumed to be dead and many people in the country felt the government should say something publicly and bluntly about the disappearances, as Amin had denied any knowledge of them and Somalia for her own political image was clearly more concerned with maintaining the agreement than vigorously pursuing her task as mediator.

In the final analysis the Tanzanians had escaped remarkably lightly and the Agreement was more than could have been hoped for. The preparatory work done by Malecela and his delegation paid off, while the cumbersome eighteen-man Ugandan delegation, which clearly came with fixed positions and therefore ill-prepared to negotiate, was to some extent placed on the defensive. Yet at Mogadishu it achieved one very important concession from the Tanzanians, for Article 2 effectively gagged not only the official media, but the Tanzanian government, Obote and his exiles and with the remainder of Africa mute and indifferent to the slaughter going on in Uganda there was no voice in the black African states left to condemn.

12 The Second Repression

The price of failure of the September invasion was predictable. Once he had chased Obote's forces back into Tanzania Amin moved swiftly and ruthlessly. On 21 September armed troops burst into the chambers of the Chief Justice, Benedicto Kiwanuka, in the High Court and dragged him away at gunpoint. He was handcuffed and his shoe-laces and tie were taken away and court officials saw him being slapped.

Kiwanuka was expecting to be killed. At a cocktail party on the previous evening for visiting judges of the East African Court of Appeal, he had told one of them: 'I am expecting them to come and take me soon. There is nothing to do but wait.'

The disappearance of a man of Kiwanuka's repute was something Amin could not cover up. The men who took him had been identified and their car number—UUU 171, registered as belonging to the Uganda army—taken. None the less Amin claimed it was the work of Obote guerrillas and eight months later he was to announce that police were investigating the disappearance of the Chief Justice. These investigations were of course both fruitless and pointless.

Kiwanuka had been Uganda's first Prime Minister for eight months until early 1962. He was a Catholic Muganda who had studied in London and had been called to the bar at Gray's Inn in 1956. At the time of the *coup* he was one of the leading political figures detained by Obote and in a flurry of publicity he was released by Amin and made Chief Justice on 27 June 1971.

Three reasons can be advanced for Kiwanuka's death. The first is that he had purchased a shop from a departing Asian in Kampala which Amin wanted for himself. The second was the critical position he had taken on the bench a few days earlier over the illegal detention by soldiers of a Briton whose release the

Chief Justice ordered. These may have contributed, but the third reason, which has not been published before, is that Kiwanuka had agreed to join hands with Obote to overthrow Amin.

The full irony of this liaison can be seen against the background of recent Ugandan political history. In 1962 Obote's UPC had formed a marriage of convenience with the Baganda Kabaka Yekka to oust Kiwanuka, hated by the Baganda Protestant court as a Catholic commoner and seen by Obote as a major threat to attaining independence under his command. After the *coup*, from Sudan, Obote twice sent emissaries with messages to Kiwanuka trying to enlist his co-operation in ousting Amin. Both of these and a third from Dar es Salaam in July 1972 were ignored. Obote tried a fourth time, and on this occasion Kiwanuka responded, agreeing to joint action and in principle to the terms Obote had outlined for the constitutional formation of Uganda after Amin. The message replying to Obote was sent just before the September invasion and ironically the courier carrying it arrived in Dar es Salaam on the morning after Kiwanuka was dragged from his court to his death.

There have been various accounts of how Kiwanuka died, including that a method popular at that time of smashing victims' heads in with hammers was employed. But the method used was far grimmer than any of the stories hitherto published. Reliable sources around Amin say the General ordered his death with the dreaded phrase, 'Finish him.' Kiwanuka had been taken to Amin after his arrest and he was killed by Amin's Nubians. There are eye-witnesses to his death who can one day openly testify. But at present their names must be kept secret to protect their lives. This is the account of a former expatriate judge of the High Court of Uganda who described his source as reliable. The judge said that he understood that Amin ordered Kiwanuka's death. 'I was given to understand that his ears, nose, lips and arms were cut and severed from his body. I also understand that he was disembowelled and his private parts cut and pushed into his mouth and he was finally burnt.' This story tallies very closely with the account of an Asian eye-witness in detention at Makindye Military Prison when Kiwanuka was killed, who also says the Chief

Justice was dismembered alive. The Asian said it took almost two hours for Kiwanuka to die.

His murder was the first of a series of killings which decimated the leadership of the Ankole tribe in the Mbarara area and the Baganda on the western and northern shores of Lake Victoria in the wake of the September invasion.

A number of journalists who had flown into Uganda were detained at Makindye and were eye-witnesses to the brutality. Associated Press correspondent, Andrew Torchia, wrote when he was released after three days in detention:

> 'Uganda soldiers pinned a man to the ground while a woman beat him with a rawhide whip—ten, twenty, fifty times until he screamed and writhed and the blood ran.
>
> 'Thirty other soldiers—officers and men—shouldered around to watch. They laughed, enjoying the spectacle, and no one intervened. The beating went on for minutes, forever it seemed, before the crowd dispersed and the screaming stopped.'

Christopher Munnion, a correspondent of the *Daily Telegraph* was also detained at Makindye and this is part of his account of what happened when he and others arrived at the prison: 'We were clubbed to the ground. Rifle butts hit the backs of our necks, clubs were rammed into backs and swagger sticks chopped at the shoulders.'

But Munnion was comparatively lucky:

> 'Two weeks ago thirty senior police officers including the Commissioner were dismissed for alleged corruption. Their dishonourable discharge took the form of incarceration at the notorious Makindye Military Prison. I was present at the grisly sequel as four of the policemen were taken from a cell we were sharing and led out to be pounded to death with sledgehammers.
>
> 'As other journalists and I were being led from Makindye Prison to be deported, another sixteen senior police officers were being marched into the prison. There was no reason to hope that their fate would be any less horrible.'

A British freelance journalist, Simon Dring, writing in the American magazine *Newsweek* indicated just how easy it was to get into trouble. He had arrived at Entebbe Airport and was driving into town when he was stopped at a road block.

'I was immediately branded a British mercenary. My radio was declared to be a "special transmitter", my tape recorder a "secret message machine", my notes "invasion plans", and my bush hat a "British commando helmet".'

Another horrific killing to which there are many eye-witnesses was the death of the former mayor of Uganda's fourth biggest town, Masaka. Minutes after 10.00 a.m. on 22 September an army Land-Rover and a white Peugeot 504 saloon car pulled up outside the Tropic Inn at Masaka. Major Isaac Maliyamungu, one of the most dreaded of all Amin's killers—who today boasts he has killed so many people that it is now easier than killing a chicken—and four soldiers got out of the Land-Rover. Two wailing women and more soldiers got out of the saloon car.

The victim this time was to be Francis Walugembe, a leading Baganda Catholic and a respected local figure. He was dragged from the back of the Land-Rover and marched at gunpoint into the hotel. The soldiers called for drinks and as the hotel staff gathered around, the Major said: 'Come and see this big confusing agent.'

Dozens of eye-witnesses saw what followed. Walugembe asked for permission to call the President, meaning Amin. Maliyamungu replied: 'There is no other President but me.' The former mayor tried to resist as he was dragged outside and stripped naked. His hands had been tied behind his back and a rope around his ankles and he could barely hobble.

Then the Major gave an order to one of the soldiers which the crowd could not hear. But the meaning was immediately obvious. The soldier took out a knife and slashed Walugembe's penis off. The severed organ was held in front of his face and the Major told the victim who was screaming in agony: 'If you want to speak to the President speak to him through this.' Then Walugembe was thrown into the back of the Land-Rover while the stunned crowd watched too afraid to intervene. Blandly the Uganda press announced on the following day that his body had been found near Masaka. A full investigation was promised.

Although in this second phase of repression, following the invasion, there were no massacres on the scale of 1971 the methods of killing became increasingly bestial. The case of Basil Bataringaya is another example. He had been warned of the impending attack, and Obote, through an envoy, had urged him to leave Uganda and come to Tanzania. But Bataringaya, with a ninety-six-year-old father and nine children under sixteen to maintain, declined. When the attack came he fled from Mbarara to Fort Portal. Ten days later he decided it was safe to return but he was arrested by troops a few days later. A relative who was at Mbarara at the time told me that he was dismembered alive outside the town and finally his severed head was put on display on the end of a pole.

The slaughter around Mbarara in the days after the abortive attack was particularly vicious. The Secretary-General for Uganda Nkemia Bananuka, and most of his family were killed at their home. He, too, was dismembered alive. Over a dozen local saza chiefs were killed as were many prominent members of the UPC local administration.

The slaughter continued unabated throughout the remainder of the year as Amin's henchmen weeded out anyone who might pose any opposition. Ben Otim, the elected leader of the Lango Administration, was ordered to go to Kampala to see Amin. But before he left he was shot by soldiers and his body dismembered. Simayo Oryem, Administrative Secretary of Acholi, was killed with an axe by soldiers and dismembered. James Buwembo, a brother of Obote's wife and a pharmacist, was dragged from his car in Kampala's main street and never seen again. A number of senior prison officers disappeared, and Joseph Mubiru, Governor of the Bank of Uganda, who Amin had threatened would be detained 'under cold water' (a form of torture) was killed by soldiers at Makindye. Frank Kalimuzo, Vice-Chancellor of Makerere University was arrested by the Public Safety Unit early in October and never seen again. Amin said the disappearances were the work of Obote guerrillas but nobody any longer believed this charge.

In all 128 chiefs are believed to have been killed in this phase. Amin replaced them with his soldiers. The gun had been taken nearer the peasants' head and the killing went on. Brothers who went to inquire about missing relatives were killed. Soldiers refused to release bodies for burial. And weeping widows and children tried with little hope to find out what had happened to their husbands and fathers.

Divers employed to clear the intake ducts on the Owen Falls Dam were reported to have removed thirty bodies from them following a purge around Jinja in late September. The same month Jackson Ssentongo, a former Permanent Secretary in the Ministry of Finance and then a leading African businessman disappeared. No more news was heard of him and he joined the growing list of those marked 'missing, presumed dead'. In October the bullet-riddled body of former politician and businessman, Augustine Kamya, was found on the roadside and a government spokesman blithely said he had been shot for trying to rob an Asian. On Christmas Eve, a fifty-year-old British national, Sotos Kargarotos, was gunned down in front of his wife in a Kampala main street by four men with submachine-guns who drove off in the dead man's car.

At 2.00 p.m. on 28 December military police burst into the Kampala offices of a law firm owned by John Kazzora who had already fled into exile in Nairobi. Eye-witnesses say the squad was led by Major Baker Tretre, another of Amin's notorious killers. They dragged out Patrick Ruhinda, son of the former Omugabe (king) of Ankole, Sir Charles Gasyongan, and another senior executive of the firm, Charles Karuku. Neither were ever seen again.

Early in December after publishing another list of names of people 'missing, presumed dead' in the Observer, I received a letter from London from the Jamaican-born wife of Ben Ocan, arrested a fortnight earlier in Kampala by Amin's troops. After reading the story she had rung the Uganda High Commission in London for news of her husband. They had none and she spent the rest of that day and the next on the phone to Kampala. All she could find out was that her husband had missed lectures for some days at a course he was attending. Dorothy Ocan's letter ended: 'I cannot look at the faces of my children. To see our only son aged nine years; to wake and find my sensitive gentle twelve-year-old daughter sobbing in the night. I have not been strong enough to tell the oldest, Angom, our fourteen-year-old who is away at school, or our little Donge . . . Ben held her the moment after her birth and laughed and danced with her. Please send us any scrap of news you can get, I have reached a dead end in my inquiries. I beg you, please, to let me know however terrible the news. These are violent times, I understand.' There was of course no news ever again of Ben Ocan.

That particular story once more made me the target of Amin's wrath. I had listed ten people 'missing, presumed dead'. One was a Kampala businessman named Walusimbi and although a man by that name had been killed, I had been given the wrong Christian name. Two of the other men I named were brought from detention and the story probably provided them with a temporary stay of death and one, a lieutenant-colonel, was killed later. But of the other six there was no mention. John Kakonge, Minister of Agriculture in Obote's government, had been arrested by military police a month earlier at a Kampala wine shop he owned. James Ochola, Obote's Minister of Regional Administration had been arrested about the same time. So too had Ali Kiseka, Obote's Junior Minister to the EAC, been arrested by military police as he drove to his young son's funeral. Another Minister, Shaban Nkutu, Minister of Works, Communications and Housing in Obote's government was to be killed a month later. That meant that of the twenty Cabinet Ministers eight had been murdered, and four had fled into exile within two years of the *coup*.

The reaction to this story came in the form of an announcement on Radio Uganda quoting a military spokesman—which means Amin—stating that arrangements had been made to arrest me 'from any corner of the world' and that I was not to be kept in police custody but taken to the barracks of the Malire Mechanised Regiment to answer for 'crimes' I had committed against Uganda since 1971. The crimes were reporting murders and massacres and I was—and still am—under no illusions what would happen if I fell into Amin's hands. Earlier that year a message had been sent to me from Kampala through diplomatic channels warning me that Amin had ordered I was to be killed. Soon after that I declined an invitation to visit Uganda which Amin sent me through the British High Commission—all expenses paid and safety guaranteed. Then in September, while I was reporting the fighting in Uganda from Dar es Salaam, Amin accused me of 'spearheading' the attack.

The beginning of January 1973 brought a fresh attack from Amin in which he called me 'a liar' for reporting that seven young Tanzanian students, who had been called to Kampala for interviews at the headquarters of the East African Posts and Tele-communications Corporation, had been arrested at their hotels by military police and it was feared they were dead. Amin denied all knowledge of the missing men adding he would like to entertain me in Kampala for lunch. I had a fair idea what the menu would be. Then four months later Amin blandly signed an agreement in Addis Ababa with President Nyerere admitting responsibility for the deaths of the seven and eighteen other Tanzanians arrested in the frontier area, and agreeing to pay compensation. The seven students, it was learned, had had their heads crushed with sledgehammers.

Any credibility that remained was shattered by a spate of resignations early in 1973 and by three of Amin's Ministers fleeing into exile in fear of their lives, including Kibedi. It is believed that while Kibedi was on a visit to Kenya, apparently under orders from Amin to try to have some of the exiles living there handed over, he received a message from a relative that he was also to be killed. For some time it was pretended that he was sick in hospital until he finally fled into exile in London. Kenya was not exactly a healthy place for prominent exiles. In October security officers had arrested a squad of eight Ugandans sent in to kill three exiles living in Nairobi, including a lawyer, John Kazzora. He also swiftly moved out of Kenya to London.

The case of Obote's wife, Miria, illustrates the risks for the exiles in Kenya. Soon after the *coup* Amin forced Miria to ring the deposed President in Dar es Salaam to tell him that a plane would be made available to bring him back and to assure him he had nothing to fear. Miria was to be allowed to fly to Dar es Salaam on the plane but their three sons had to remain in Uganda. Obote refused and later Amin agreed that one child could go as well as Obote's elderly parents. Again Obote refused, knowing that he would be killed, and on 22 February 1971, Amin agreed to allow Miria to leave. She flew to Kenya on a charter flight but the next day Kenya security officers physically put her aboard an East African Airways plane back to Entebbe.

Back in Uganda she was placed under twenty-four-hour guard. With her bank account frozen, she began selling furniture to feed the family. For this she was arrested by guards and she, her sister and children tied up and taken to Malire. After they were released unharmed Amin rang Miria and said: 'We hear you are raising an army.' He warned Miria he could shoot her, that he knew all her brothers and sisters and they would suffer. In April 1972 she smuggled her three children out of Uganda. She drove across the border, passing through the post near Tororo, using a driving licence in her maiden name, and reached Nairobi. Amin contacted Kenya Vice-President, Arap Moi, and sent Jonathan Ekochu to Kenya with a note accusing Miria of leaving the country using a false name. Kenya immigration officers arrived at the house in Nairobi where she was staying, gave her five minutes to pack and with her children she was driven back across the border and handed over to the Uganda police.

She was taken to the headquarters of the Public Safety Unit at Naguru and then she was put on television. The children were asked if they wanted to go to their father and said 'Yes'. Then her house was ransacked by troops who stole all their property including the children's primary school books. Immediately she began planning to escape again, and on 20 June 1972 she finally reached Dar es Salaam.

One day, when it is no longer necessary to protect their identities, the story can be written about a courageous group of people who for nearly three years have been running a 'freedom ferry' from Uganda smuggling out people who were to be killed and the wives and children of exiles.

The wife of former Foreign Minister, Sam Odaka, was smuggled out with her children. They were all disguised as peasants and Margaret Odaka had money braided into her hair.

Before the army lieutenant who had witnessed the death of the two Americans—Stroh and Siedle—would give me the details, I had to get a message into Uganda and seventy-two hours later his wife, children and two brothers had been brought out into Tanzania. Many people living in exile owe their lives to this courageous group of people, and many more, including Bataringaya, could have been saved if they had believed warnings that were sent to them.

On 14 December 1972, an attempt was made to assassinate Amin. An ambush had been laid on the road between Mutukula and Masaka. Amin was in the frontier area where a military exercise was taking place. Gunmen armed with automatic weapons lay in wait as his car headed back to Kampala. There was an army driver in front and a soldier in the rear. The gunmen opened fire killing both men. But the man in the back was an NCO. Amin, as had become his habit, had changed cars some miles back. A number of other assassination attempts have been reported but the only one that can be substantiated was on 14 December and its failure touched off more killing.

Edward Rugumayo, Amin's Minister of Education and a close friend of Kibedi, sent his children out to Kenya before going to attend a meeting there. Then he resigned on 'personal and moral' grounds and fled to Zambia. Professor W. B. Banage, Minister of Animal Industry, Game and Fisheries, also escaped to Kenya and then on to Zambia with his wife. With Kibedi obviously not planning to return, Amin responded by packing his whole Cabinet off on two months leave, which finally extended to nine months. Their departure mattered little for they had been powerless. Amin was bored with the technicalities of government and when he turned up at Cabinet meetings at all he treated his Ministers to lengthy harangues. The barely literate General had no time for his educated Ministers, most of whom had been senior civil servants at the time of the *coup*, and the 'inspiration' for his decisions came mainly from the NCOs and other ranks in the army, with whom Amin was definitely on a more equal intellectual wavelength.

The killings next spilled over into the East African Community and scores of Kenyans and Tanzanians working in Community offices in Uganda fled and refused to return. In January 1973 troops had gone to the offices in Kampala of the East African Railways Corporation, which is one of the Community's common services. The railways' resident Director in Uganda, Henry Berunga; the Regional Personnel Officer, Aliwar Owuor; the Regional Supplies Officer, John Okech-Omara—a Kenyan arrested the day after resuming duty following a four-month course in Britain—and the Regional Industrial Relations Officer, Tomusange, were all dragged from their offices and never seen again. Again the people who had arrested them were recognised and their car numbers were taken. But there was no investigation, and Dan Nabudere, the Ugandan Chairman of the Corporation, resigned in protest from Kenya and then moved to Tanzania.

Even more damaging four days later was the resignation of Amin's Ambassador in Bonn, John Barigye. In his letter of resignation Barigye, the son of the former Omugabe of Ankole and whose brother Patrick a few weeks earlier had been taken from his Kampala law firm—made the most searing public denunciation of Amin to date:

> 'The reign of terror that has been established in our beloved country has shocked the conscience of all men of good will throughout the world. While innocent people continue to be brutally and savagely eliminated your regime has failed to bring to justice the perpetrators of these crimes. Indeed, eyewitness reports and circumstantial evidence tend to implicate you and your henchmen in these barbarous acts which show complete disregard and contempt for human life.
>
> 'In these circumstances, therefore, I have no alternative but to hereby tender my resignation for this I believe is the

only way I can conform to the dictates of my conscience and to universally held principles of civilised conduct.'

Predictably Amin berated him by saying he had become confused by the 'Imperialists and Zionists'.

Perhaps the most damning condemnation of Amin came in a memorandum marked 'Top Secret' which was drawn up by one of the General's own Ministers and sent to a number of African heads of state. The 5,000-word document gives details of the killings and killers, an analysis of Amin the man and in an appeal for action to African leaders notes:

'Too many nations regard what is happening in Uganda as an internal matter. Is systematic genocide an internal matter or a matter for all mankind? The Sharpeville massacres were condemned by the entire civilised world, but nobody has yet condemned the wholesale killings and disappearances of innocent people in Uganda. It is high time the OAU, the Commonwealth and the United Nations condemned the murders being perpetrated by Amin in Uganda.'

This memorandum is worth giving in considerable detail, for although the Minister wants his name still to be kept secret, it provides an insight by a man who had accepted a position as a member of the General's Cabinet and worked for him for some two years.

It begins by stressing the importance of understanding Amin so that what has occurred, and what will occur, can be understood. Here the Minister lists nine points about Amin:

1. That he is an illiterate soldier who became president of a modern state.

2. That he comes from the minority Nubian/Kakwa tribe.

3. That he is a member of a minority religion, Islam, which accounts for less than 6 per cent of Ugandans.

4. That he is of very low intelligence.

5. That he is medically unfit and suffering from a hormonal defect.

6. That he is a racist, tribalist and dictator.

7. That he has no principles, moral standards or scruples.

8. That he will kill, or cause to kill, anyone without hesitation as long as it serves his interests, such as prolonging his stay in power, or getting what he wants such as a woman or money.

9. That he is an incorrigible liar, with no moral or political standards, whose word cannot be relied upon and of whom the only prediction which can safely be made is that he is unpredictable.

The Minister's memorandum goes on to say:

'Amin finds it well-nigh impossible to sit in an office for a day. He cannot concentrate on any serious topic for half a morning. He does not read. He cannot write. The sum total of all these disabilities makes it impossible for him either to sit in the regular Cabinet, to follow up the Cabinet minutes, or to comprehend the briefs written to him by his Ministers. In short he is out of touch with the daily running of the country, not because he likes it but because of illiteracy. He rarely attends Cabinet, and even then it is only when he is giving directions about problems concerning defence or "security" of the country or when he is sacking more civil servants. So the only means of getting information about the country which he rules is by ear from various sources.'

These sources, the Minister says, are mainly fellow illiterates in the security forces. Information is rarely checked and statements are contradictory either through genuine lapses in memory or deliberately. He cites an example when Amin expelled two professors and a senior consultant physician from the Medical Faculty at Makerere University accusing them of spreading 'political gonorrhoea' after one of his sources said they were spying for Britain. A fortnight later he was infuriated when he could not contact two of his doctors to come and give him a medical check. He had forgotten he had expelled them.

Amin, the memorandum states, had bankrupted the country through excessive military spending. The Minister claims that Amin keeps a huge sum of American dollars in his house, has deposited much more in Libya and has three villas in Tripoli as a bolt hole in case he is overthrown. 'His abysmal ignorance has made him hate education, educated people and education institutions.' Senior civil servants who are well educated are removed from their jobs in his office and replaced by less literate people so that Amin can communicate with them.

The most important problems the Minister cites are tribal and religious. Amin's forefathers were Nubians noted for their brutality and the General frequently remarks that the 'gun is their mother, father and brother'. The Nubian/Kakwa tribe have integrated little in the past seventy years and have attached little importance to education. They are largely Muslims and although the followers of Islam make up only 5·6 per cent of Uganda's population, Amin told both the Libyan and Saudi Arabian leaders when he was seeking their moral and material support that 80 per cent of the people were Muslims who had been subjugated by the Christian minority. As a result the Minister says the two Arab states made contributions from their Jihad (Holy War) Fund to Uganda. The leader of a Libyan goodwill delegation handing over a contribution to the Uganda Muslim Supreme Council observed that the money would be used to 'eliminate the few remaining Christians and turn Uganda into a Muslim state'. In the wake of this, a terror campaign was launched against leading Catholics and Protestants from late 1972.

This memorandum was written in early 1973 and the Minister claimed that he knew of a list of 2,000 people including intellectuals, businessmen, church leaders and leading figures in all walks of life who were earmarked for elimination. Ten assassination squads were roaming the country hunting down victims and these were directly under Amin's supervision and drawn from the Public Safety Unit, police and army. All the members were Nubians.

The Minister heavily blames Israel for the initial slaughter in the army. 'Immediately after the *coup* the Israelis advised Amin to liquidate all those in the army who would pose a threat to him. He accomplished this with devilish efficiency. The Israelis also advised him that in order to survive he must keep the army perpetually busy.' This the memorandum says is why Amin has created a series of diversionary activities such as threats from Rwanda, Sudan and Tanzania, the Chinese, then the Asian expulsion, business allocations, the threat of guerrilla attacks and sending the army to the villages. He preached continuously against politicians and had killed seven of Obote's former Cabinet Ministers and had frequently talked of invading Tanzania to seize the north of the country. Amin, the Minister says, is extremely superstitious surrounding himself with witchdoctors, soothsayers and fortunetellers.

His plans, the memorandum says, are to be made President for life by the army; to liquidate anyone who poses a threat, real or imagined; to continue building up the army and to turn Uganda into an Islamic state. A number of prominent army officers who want to overthrow Amin are listed and the Minister claims that on 6 February 1973, three colonels in the Defence Council demanded Amin's resignation to his face. It is said he agreed and said he would give it in a broadcast to the nation two days later. Considerable publicity was given to the broadcast and all Ugandans were told to listen to it but in fact, Amin said nothing of consequence. The three colonels, named as Toko, Mondo and Ozo, are all now listed for elimination and it is noteworthy that since the memorandum was written they have all been removed from command posts.

The Minister says that opposition to Amin is growing inside Uganda as more tribes and families are hit by the killings. Then comes the most horrific part of the memorandum, where he gives details of the methods of killing and disposal of bodies. At first he says people were shot or beaten to death and buried in mass graves in prisons. But too many details of this got out so they were thrown in rivers and lakes for the crocodiles. But this proved unsatisfactory as the crocodiles could not eat all the bodies and the bloated carcases attracted vultures. Next they were dumped in the bush to be eaten by predators or burned with petrol. Police and prison officers tried to investigate the killings, but they all led back to the army and a number were sacked and the Minister responsible moved to another post.

Eight of the more popular methods of killing are listed:

1. The victims would line up, and the first would be ordered to lie down while the prisoner next to him would be ordered to smash his head with a huge hammer. And he would be told to smash the head into pieces. The next man to be ordered to lie down would be the one who had just smashed the dead man's skull. Then the third person would be ordered to demolish his brains . . . and so on until the last man was either shot or killed in the same brutal manner by a police officer.

2. The victim's head would be smashed beyond recognition by one of the appointed executioners.

3. Slow killing is a common practice. A man would be shot in the arms, chest or legs and left to bleed to death.

4. There is a technique of cutting a victim's flesh and forcing him to feed on it raw until he bleeds to death.

5. The other despicable method is to cut a man's flesh, have it roasted and let him feed on it until he dies.

6. There are in Makindye Prison very deep and dark holes in which certain prisoners are kept. These holes are filled with ice cold water in which the prisoners are kept and fed once a day on some form of diet and are at the same time tortured until they die.

7 and 8. There are other horrible methods of torture which are too terrible to describe such as sticking bayonets through prisoners anuses or genitals, or women being raped and afterwards having their reproductive organs set on fire while they are alive.

'The instruments of murder, torture and human degradation have been perfected by Amin. Most of the bodies of important people are put in incinerators, and those who cannot be burnt are buried while wrapped in cloth by prisoners who would not live to tell the tale. In some towns, the army after their killing sprees, carry the dead bodies into the nearest town or hospital mortuary. Nobody can venture to ask any questions. The following day the town or city cemetery workers are told to bury the dead without asking any questions.

'In the period of twenty-five months of Amin's rule it is estimated that as many as between 80,000 and 90,000 people have lost their lives. This might be a conservative figure.'

These charges in the Minister's memorandum sound incredible but it must be stressed that they come from a man who was one of Amin's Ministers until early 1973 and who, in that position, had access to considerable information. There is no way to check his statistic of the death toll but many Ugandans will verify the truth of his charges. His objective was to try to mobilise African and international opinion to publicly condemn Amin to try to stop the killing. Predictably his plea fell on deaf ears.

Mbale town was the first to be hit hard by the guerrilla scare. In February Amin's troops moved in, sealing it off for several days and 300 men, women and children were estimated to have been slaughtered. In the Western region—thugs from Superintendent Ali Towilli's Public Safety Unit, who like the dreaded Ton-Ton Macoutes of the late Haitian dictator, 'Papa Doc' Duvalier, wear coloured sports shirts and heavy dark glasses—buried nine people alive. In Obote's home area, Lango, Captain Henry Agech, warned that whole villages would be wiped out if there was even a hint of guerrillas in the area and Obote's brother-in-law and cousins were killed as well as three of Akena Adoko's brothers. Francis Sembeguya, a Member of the disbanded Parliament and doctor of medicine was dragged from his clinic five miles from Kampala with a noose around his neck by Lieutenant-Colonel Marella's military police and never seen again.

The killings swept the length and breadth of the country throughout the year. A number of prominent people were killed in Busoga, Kibedi's home area, before and after the Minister fled into exile.

The emergence at the beginning of February 1973 of a new guerrilla organisation calling itself 'The Front for National Salvation' (Fronasa) touched off another upsurge of killings. Fronasa's manifesto was entitled 'An Indictment of a Primitive Fascist' and in part read:

> 'People have been choked with their genitals, their heads bashed in with sledgehammers and gun butts, hacked to pieces with *pangas*, disembowelled, blown up with explosives, suffocated in car boots, burned alive in cars and houses after being tied up, drowned, dragged along roads tied to Land-Rovers, starved to death, whipped to death, gradually dismembered. The luckier ones have simply been shot—and what luck is that? Even they are mutilated afterwards.'

Fronasa claimed they had guerrilla camps inside Uganda where people had been training for many months. It was true that some members of the militant front had taken part in the attack on Mbarara during the September invasion, including Yoweri Museveni, a twenty-seven-year-old graduate. But there was little indication that they had any real strength of organisation to compare to Obote's. None the less Fronasa's public announcement touched off another frenzy of killing. One Fronasa camp was discovered inside Uganda and a military spokesman warned on Radio Uganda:

> 'Villages in whose district guerrillas are found will be burned down. Taxi drivers who give guerrillas lifts will be blown up in their cars and house owners hiding them will be blown up in their homes. People hiding guerrillas will lose children and never see them again. Any parent whose son is convicted of hiding or feeding guerrillas will not see that son anymore because that son will be dead.'

In the wake of Fronasa's announcement on 10 February 1973, the first public executions in seventy-five years were carried out. Amin had carefully chosen a Lugbara, the obese 240 lb Lieutenant-Colonel Ozo, to chair the military tribunal which sentenced the twelve guerrillas to death. The twelve were executed in seven separate towns and villages and their weeping relatives were forced to watch them being shot. They were stripped naked and then dressed in a white apron so that the television cameras would be able to show the blood pumping from their chests, and then tied to trees.

Amin found a new excuse for killing in April announcing that a non-existent force of 3,500 men comprising Ugandan exiles, Tanzanian soldiers and expelled Asians, was about to invade. Solemnly Radio Uganda announced that the invasion was expected within hours adding that Ugandan soldiers must be prepared 'To die in the defence of the motherland'. The next day it was announced the invaders had reached Masaka eighty miles from Kampala and it said that they were being driven back. After that no more was said and no bodies, captured trucks or arms displayed as they had been the previous September. It was another figment of Amin's lively imagination and another excuse for a spate of killing.

His next scare came in October during the Middle East war, when he claimed that a joint force of British, Israeli and American commandos were assembling in the Kenya capital to invade Uganda. Again nothing happened, but he kept the army busy looking for mythical enemies and hunting down the civilian populace who might abet foreign invaders or domestic dissidents. And so the killings continued.

All of 1973 was another bloodbath. One of the first prominent men to go that year was David Ocaya, Acting Secretary of Uganda's Lint Marketing Board who was seized at midday by five soldiers in civilian clothes at Wampewo petrol station. Ocaya was thrown in the boot of a BMW car, registration UUV 520, and never seen again.

On the same day Amin issued a bizarre statement listing the names of eighty-five missing Ugandans. In the case of Bataringaya it said that he had been 'reported missing, but investigations have not revealed where he might be'. In the cases of Kalema, Kakonge, Achola and Kiseka it said of each: 'Investigations have revealed that he is not in the country and nobody knows where he went.' No mention was made of the thousands of other missing Ugandans but Amin was desperately trying to avoid the rash of bad publicity in 1972 as more and more details of massacres and murders filtered out. None the less five days later the body of

Father Clement Kigundu, Editor of the Ugandan Roman Catholic daily newspaper *Munno* ('Friend') was found dead in his burnt-out car on the Jinja road ten miles from Kampala on the edge of a forest. His paper had been quietly critical and a post mortem revealed he had been shot and strangled before the car was set on fire.

A series of killings took place in December 1973. A woman who had gone to Mulago morgue to identify the body of a cousin shot by soldiers on 24 December found the bodies of about 50 people, all of whom had been shot. When she asked the morgue attendant what had occurred, she was told she was lucky she had come on a quiet day. A few days earlier a Baganda lawyer was briefed to defend a man in custody charged with embezzlement. He went to court with his client and applied for bail which was granted. Then as they walked out of the court the client was shot dead by men of the Public Safety Unit and the lawyer beaten unconscious. He was detained and flogged for four days before escaping to Kenya. The magistrate who had granted bail only escaped by jumping from a court room window.

Also in December, Kenya handed over three prominent exiles who had fled to Nairobi to save their lives. The men were Joseph 'Jolly Joe' Kiwanuka, a founder of the Uganda National Congress; Captain Kenneth Onzima, who had fled after being involved in the July 1972 Lugbara officers' plot to overthrow Amin; and Captain Wilfred Aswa, the man who in January 1971, then a sergeant, had read the 19 points on Radio Uganda justifying the *coup*. Amin had wanted all three of them for some time and in November had seen President Kenyatta at Mombasa when he had extracted an undertaking that Kenya would return to Uganda people wanted on criminal charges. They were handed over just before Christmas and killed almost immediately in Makindye Prison where the three of them were seen chained together. Relatives in Nairobi were told by Kenya security officers that the men were being taken into custody for their own safety while Amin was on a visit to the Kenya capital and would be released when he left, but the three were never seen again.

13   The Future

———◆◆◆◆———

A Ugandan exile interviewed in the magazine *Africa* late in 1973 summed up the feelings of many of his countrymen: 'People who consider Amin a hero of Africa do not look at the bloodshed in the country. There is no area in Uganda where people have not been killed. There's no clan in Uganda where blood has not been shed. To live with Amin is not to love him. He is feared but not a hero in Uganda.'

Tragically to many in black Africa and to a number of Afro-Americans the General is a hero. If he has reinforced the irrational fears of the white racialist then equally he has activated the reverse racialism of the black man. His expulsion of the Asians, seizure of foreign companies and the baiting of Mr. Heath and President Nixon have all acted as a release for the black man's pent-up humiliation at the hands of white and brown minorities in Africa.

To Afro-Americans such as Roy Innis, National Director of the Congress of Racial Equality (CORE), Amin was a hero, who through the expulsion of the Asians struck 'a significant blow for the economic independence of the African people wherever they are'. Amin was not a racialist, Innis protested at a London press conference on his way back to the United States to recruit Afro-Americans to replace Asians and Europeans in Uganda. A year earlier President Nyerere had told Innis bluntly—as he had told Stokely Carmichael before—that his country condemned all forms of racialism, be they expounded by black or white.

But in Uganda Innis found a kindred spirit in the erratic General. He was taken as a member of the Ugandan delegation to the Organisation of African Unity summit by Amin, and as Innis's recruiting programme got underway in America, everything was apparently set for a migration back to the motherland. That was not to be. Two months later Amin cabled Innis to tell him he was cancelling the recruitment of Afro-Americans. No reason was given but what had occurred was that the army had challenged Amin arguing that the Afro-Americans were as much expatriates as the Asians and Britons. The identity of a common skin colour, despite sympathy for what has happened to the black man in the United States, is not enough. To the African generally, the Afro remains first and foremost an American.

The expulsion of the Asians—and it is said that this occurred only after the widow of an Asian millionaire, refused to marry Amin—gave the General breathing space at a time when he was in deep trouble.

Many in eastern Africa would have liked to see Presidents Kenyatta, Nyerere and Kaunda also summarily dispatch their 'brown Britons' as well as those Asians who had taken citizenship, and the racial tensions checked only just below the surface in the region bubbled over. A Kenyan Junior Minister hailed the General's decision in Parliament and escaped without a public rebuke from his government. In 1973 Tanzania's first Vice-President, Mr. Aboud Jumbe, who is also President of Zanzibar— which has a dismal enough record in dealing with racial minorities in the past decade—described Amin as a 'revolutionary' during an official visit to Uganda. That unnecessary and inaccurate accolade can hardly have pleased Nyerere.

Amin's blatant racialism and anti-Semitism deeply affected African credibility. The most important cornerstone of the OAU is the commitment to the liberation of southern Africa from white minority domination, apartheid and racialism. Continuously Africa vocalises about white oppression south of the Zambezi, but in the case of Uganda, and the ethnic slaughter in Burundi, African leaders and the OAU with few exceptions, have remained silent.

Condemnation here must not however be limited to Africa. During 1971, when both Britain and Israel had considerable influence in Uganda, they remained silent. Public censure by the government and press generally in these two countries came only when relations turned sour. Today the Arabs and Russians are Amin's silent accomplices. Tomorrow it may well be someone else.

A second aspect of the Asian expulsion is economic. A cynical saying throughout 1973 in Uganda was: 'The economic war is on and the war is winning.' But by the end of the year the joke was no longer amusing. Neighbouring Tanzania is far from a cheap country for the African consumer but a comparison on a range of essential African goods reveals what has happened in Uganda since the 'black Patels' took over from the Asians.

A Chinese-made white cup and saucer costing shs 2·50 in Tanzania was retailing at shs 10 in Kampala. Meat eaten by most Africans was shs 3·85 per kg in Dar es Salaam against shs 8 in the Ugandan capital and the price of a dressed chicken was shs 10–12 against shs 20–40 in Uganda. Khanga—a colourful print worn by African women, was shs 30 in Tanzania for a pair against shs 130–150 in Uganda. The same pattern was repeated through the range of African consumer items in the two capitals and in Uganda's rural areas little was available at all. Salt, sugar, flour and other essentials were generally out of stock and even when available they were being sold at exorbitant black-market prices.

Progressively since Amin came to power, Uganda's economy has been drained. At the beginning of 1971 the country's foreign reserves stood at over £20,000,000. By the end of that year they had been reduced to little more than £3,000,000. Massive military expenditure, as Amin sought to consolidate his power base by keeping the troops happy, has swallowed up much of the reserve which by late 1973 stood at a little over £10,000,000.

On 2 May 1971, Amin accused Obote of 'duplicity and lack of economic policy' and announced he intended to undo Obote's plan to take a majority shareholding in eighty foreign companies and instead the government's share would be restricted to a maximum of 49 per cent.

But more revealing were the Ugandan budget estimates published on 28 July 1971. The estimates showed that expenditure on defence was up from £7,300,000 in Obote's last year to £15,200,000 in Amin's first. Over £8,000,000 of the development budget or 28 per cent of the total was to be spent on defence. And at the same time the health development budget was cut back 60 per cent to £950,000 and education by 40 per cent to £2,150,000. Added to this, a deficit was allowed on the development account of £6,500,000 which was in fact earmarked for defence. Thus while health expenditure was more than cut in half, the military allocation was tripled.

These statistics, taken on face value, are bad enough. But it has to be remembered that one of the factors behind the final Obote–Amin showdown was the way in which the military had exceeded its budget and monies had disappeared. Not surprisingly, no statistics are available but all the indications are that military over-expenditure and accountability—to the point where the Auditor General was ordered by Amin not to make public his annual report because it only aided enemies of the country—has become even more excessive since the coup.

Several military airports were built in 1971 and by August the situation had become so serious that financial restraints were imposed on all Ministries—except Defence. At the same time, Amin was ordering £4,000,000 worth of armoured cars from Britain.

Mounting restrictions through 1972 cut back on imports with the trade surplus in Amin's first year of £4,000,000 against £40,000,000 in Obote's last. But there was little or nothing Amin's Ministers and senior civil servants could do to check the financial wastage. The Asian expulsion brought some respite, for with the few people, nearly all ejected, with the skill to run businesses and order from overseas, imports fell. Stocks were not replaced, with the result that the demand on foreign reserves lessened.

The spoils of the economic war went to the soldiers. The chief army medical officer, Lieutenant-Colonel Bogere, was awarded Kampala's £45,000 Speke Hotel by Amin. Initially the 'Business Allocation Committee' was run by civil servants but this was taken over by the army when it was realised many of the firms were going to civilians. At least five African civilians in Kampala awarded shops by the civilian committee are known to have been killed by soldiers who seized the properties and today over half the capital's businesses are in the hands of soldiers, almost all

Muslim Nubians. Many others found their way into the hands of soldiers' relatives and at least three Kampala businesses were allocated to two of Amin's wives.

The tourist industry, which in 1972 had drawn 100,000 visitors, was closed down and despite an advertising campaign late in 1973, few foreigners were willing to risk their lives at the hands of the unpredictable soldiers. The Asian population dropped from 50,000 to around 500 and the European population from 10,000 to under 2,000 and over 50,000 Africans were estimated to have been made jobless. Burglaries and crimes of violence increased as a result of the unemployment in the urban centres and the general breakdown in law and order with police morale destroyed.

One after another foreign-aid donors closed down their programmes. Britain suspended and then finally withdrew aid in the pipeline; Israel's was terminated; Canada and Sweden withdrew their aid personnel; and America initially stopped its aid programme because of the General's anti-Semitism and then finally closed its Embassy altogether after Amin expelled the Marine security guards and threatened to detain American diplomats because of Washington's support for Israel. To this Amin responded by saying he would appoint a private as Ambassador to the United States until Nixon's term in the White House ended.

In less than three years Amin's achievement was to dispose of the country's foreign reserves on the military, by building twelve new airports, increasing pay, improving conditions and purchasing new equipment. Prices spiralled, trade balances were reduced to a tenth of their former level, increased shortages occurred and with few spare parts imported the marketing system was under considerable strain with little transport to get the produce to export points. Major aid donors withdrew and his new-found friends in the Arab world and Soviet Union came across with far less than he hoped for.

Against this background a word of warning for the future is needed. Whoever takes over from Amin will not only be faced with salvaging the economy but also with the external pressures for compensation for seized property. Just how much the seized Asian properties are worth is in doubt but estimates put the figure between £100,000,000 and £200,000,000. There is little chance that compensation can ever be paid on this. Stocks that were taken over with the businesses were sold by the new owners and the money pocketed and spent. The Asians' cars were sold at two auctions, the first where the army had their pick at nominal prices and it is doubtful whether even these were paid for. Thus Amin's successor will be faced with the task of trying to bring order from the economic chaos. The last thing he will need at that point is foreign governments pressuring him for compensation. He will not be able to pay and this will only increase his internal difficulties.

How Amin has stayed in power so long is a mystery to many people. Part of the explanation lies in his highly developed instinct for survival. That is why many people who posed a threat, or were merely suspected of doing so, have been killed. He seized power in January 1971 to survive. He has killed ever since for the same reason.

One of the greatest dangers in assessing Amin is to under-estimate him. The London tabloid which in September 1972 devoted its whole front page to the two words: 'HE'S NUTS' fell into that trap. So too did Obote, Nyerere and many Ugandans who have lost their lives as a result.

The September 1972 bid to oust Amin by direct confrontation was undoubtedly a major blunder. Inside Uganda there were many people, including certain army elements, who would have supported him. But on 17 September when Radio Uganda first announced the invasion, some soldiers who would have moved, thought it was simply another piece of bluster by the General. By the time they realised that it was true, it was too late to influence events. And the degree of support Obote received from the Tanzanians was far less than was necessary to give the attack a reasonable chance of success.

It is a consistent and valid criticism of Obote that he tends to be too secretive trusting too few people. At the time of the *coup* his circle of confidants had narrowed. Yet in many ways he was a unique African leader. Regularly he was to be found at the Uganda Club in the evenings arguing with anyone who wanted to put a contrary view or complaint. No similar institution existed anywhere on a continent where often for security reasons Africa's leaders have become cocooned from the realities of the daily problems their people face and hear only what those around them want them to know. Obote was not of that type, yet none the less he remained a secretive man.

In the eyes of some Ugandans the massive repression which followed the abortive September invasion is blamed on Obote. Yet in many ways this is an unfair view given the background as to why the attack occurred at all. Nyerere in the first place apparently had been misled into believing that Fronasa's strength in Uganda was considerably more than it really was and in addition at this juncture it was Nyerere as much as Obote who wanted to remove Amin for he believed the security of his own country and that of the region was at stake and he feared intervention by the British in Uganda.

Yet despite this view the fact remains that Obote is the only civilian politician of national repute left—Amin has insured that by killing men like Kiwanuka, Bataringaya and many others. It is unlikely that Obote can now remove Amin. He had the opportunity in September 1972 and failed. But he can still count on a substantial following inside Uganda and, although underground, part of the structure of the UPC still exists.

However, initially at least, there seems little likelihood that anyone but a soldier can take over. Thus today the content of his army is important. After the *coup* the Acholi and Langi were wiped out and Amin recruited heavily from West Nile and from among southern Sudanese. Just how many southern Sudanese are in the army today is not known but the figure is variously put at between 1,500 and 3,000. This sizable force, which controls most of the armouries is one danger point for Amin. Those who fought in the southern Sudan were generally anti-Arab and often anti-Muslim. Amin's friendship with the Arabs and determination to turn Uganda into an Islamic state could therefore rebound.

But if this group were to seize power the position in Uganda would become even worse for much of the killing has been done by the Nubians on whom Amin relies heavily.

His recruitment through 1971 from the West Nile area brought its own problems and it is by no means certain that these have been resolved. Of the five West Nile tribes, the Kakwa are the smallest, numbering only about 50,000. The Lugbara is the largest and it is from there that greatest element among the new recruits came. The first indication of Amin's difficulties with the Lugbara came in May 1972 when he was forced to fly home hurriedly from the OAU summit in Rabat. A group of junior Lugbara officers had been involved in a plot to overthrow him and one of them, Captain Avudria, was killed by Amin's Nubians. Another fled to Nairobi and tensions ran high in the army for several days.

An intriguing incident occurred soon after at Entebbe Airport on 14 June, again while Amin was away overseas. A BOAC VC-10 carrying a two-ton shipment of mortar barrels from Britain to Zambia was impounded in transit.

The armaments transit at Entebbe had been cleared by the local BOAC manager, who had informed the air force commander, Major Wilson Toko, that armaments for Zambia would be passing through and no objection had been raised. Minutes after it landed the plane was impounded and it was not finally released until 2 July by which time it had cost BOAC over £200,000 through the plane standing idle. The whole incident seemed inexplicable but one theory was that the Lugbara planned to use the armaments on the plane in another plot.

Toko, who is reputed to have little time for Amin, is said by Amin's Ministers to have been one of a group of three senior officers who, in the Defence Council in February 1973, demanded Amin's resignation because of the economic plight of the country. Amin, it is said, finally agreed and the whole country, including the army, were ordered to listen to a broadcast he would make to the nation three days later on 8 February. The broadcast was so important that the advance publicity said that it would be made in Swahili so that people in neighbouring countries could understand it. But when the broadcast was finally made, Amin said nothing of consequence.

At least three more Lugbara plots were timed for the middle of 1973. The first was for 28 May while Amin was away at the OAU summit in Addis Ababa but apparently the plotters fell out among themselves as to who would be the new leader. The second was timed for the latter half of June but news of this reached Amin after the army commander, Major-General Francis Nyangweso and the air force deputy commander, Captain Smarts Guweddeko, were approached to support the *coup*. They were rewarded on 26 June when Amin announced he was setting up a Supreme Council which would also be the executive committee of the Defence Council. Amin said he would chair the Supreme Council whose members would be Nyangweso, Guweddeko and the armed forces chief of staff, Brigadier Charles Arube.

A few days earlier he had removed Toko as air force commander and sent him on leave pending a new appointment. Weeks later he was named as Director-General of East African Airways based at the airline's headquarters in Nairobi. Another senior Lugbara, Lieutenant-Colonel Musa, commander of the Malire Mechanised Battalion, who was said to be one of the group who demanded Amin's resignation, was removed from his command and a third Lugbara, Major Baker Tretre, the army chief signals officer and referred to as Amin's 'Lord High Executioner' was dismissed. Two more, Lieutenant-Colonel Ozo from the Moroto Battalion and Brigadier Barnabas Kili from Magamaga Ordnance Depot, were also removed from command posts.

The third of the series of Lugbara plots was scheduled for early July when it was planned to seize the British-made Saladin armoured cars at Jinja. But once more the plot misfired. Now every Lugbara senior officer has been removed from command posts and Lieutenant-Colonel Obitre Gama, the most influential of them, who was a Minister for over two years, has been dropped and sent home. That Amin has dared to move against this group indicates his confidence, yet among the Lugbara, including the many still in the army, bitterness runs deep. The accusation, although they were cleared by Amin, made publicly in late August that Lieutenant-Colonel Musa and Major Tretre had been involved in a plot can only have added to the feeling of insecurity. In November, troops went to Obitre Gama's home in West Nile demanding that he hand in a gun he had drawn while still in the army. The fact that he had no gun left a feeling that they had actually gone to kill him but had been deterred by the number of former soldiers around the area.

It has been incorrectly reported on many occasions that Amin has put the army command structure totally in the hands of Muslims. In reality a number of the leading officers are professed Christians including the army commander, Major-General Nyangweso; the commander of the 2nd Infantry Brigade, Lieutenant-Colonel Isaac Maliyamungu, and until his dismissal, the air force commander, Toko.

But what Amin has done is appoint only people from West Nile, or in the case of the head of Military Police, Lieutenant-Colonel Hussein Marella, who is from the southern Sudan's Baka tribe, people from outside the country to command posts. Of the twenty-four top military posts late in 1973 only three were held by non-West Nilers. There was Nyangweso from Bukedi; the commander of the Paratroop School, Lieutenant-Colonel Bunyenyezi; a Rwandan refugee who had settled in Uganda and Lieutenant-Colonel Omaria, commander of the Mubende Battalion who comes from Teso. Omaria was in fact dismissed late in 1973 and the British tea estate he had been allocated, seized, leaving the Iteso, who have a substantial contingent in the army, without an officer in a command post.

Thus apart from recruiting almost entirely from West Nile and southern Sudan some 16,000 men since the *coup* Amin has also ensured that the command posts are firmly in West Nile hands. The *coup* itself was very much an other ranks affair and his junta is largely made up of former senior non-commissioned officers. Probably the most powerful and influential man around Amin is Lieutenant-Colonel Waris Faduli Ali, the Commander of the 'Simba' Battalion at Mbarara who as a Sergeant-Major at Malire on the eve of the *coup* led the first fighting in the barracks.

Nyangweso has little power and is a weak man used largely as a showpiece by Amin as a Christian non-West Nile officer. It is one of Amin's habits to avoid, wherever possible, Kakwa being seen to be publicly involved in killings. That was why he appointed a Lugbara, Lieutenant-Colonel Ozo, to head the tribunal which sentenced twelve 'guerrillas' to be publicly executed and why Major Ozi, another non-Kakwa, headed the dreaded State Research Department, which was simply another description for murder squad, until Amin fired him also late in 1973.

The religious harassment of late 1972 and early 1973, with forced conversions to Islam in the army, slowed down after that but if Amin presses ahead with his plans to turn Uganda into a Muslim state this could be another area of backlash. Like the early Baganda Kabakas, Amin has tried to use religion as a political weapon. He has met some success in the Arab Muslim world but when he claimed that the churches supported his expulsion of the Asians the Roman Catholic Archbishop of Kampala, Emmanuel Nsubuga, made it publicly clear that they did not. The Archbishop was rumoured to be under house arrest for several days and some members of his family disappeared. A Dutch Roman Catholic Bishop, Joseph Willegers, was reported to have been stripped naked at Makindye Prison and kept for twenty-four hours without food or water. Amin announced he would 'Africanise' all religions and appointed a Kakwa, Ahmed Sulaiman, who had trained as an army intelligence officer, to be chairman of the Muslim Supreme Council of Uganda. Many missionaries have been expelled and scores of others have left. A census of white missionaries Amin ordered in 1972 showed there were 1,455 in the country of whom 1,300 were Catholics. He ordered troops to physically search missionaries they came across referring to 'the so-called missionaries who are actually military generals and majors here to plan subversive activities'. A few weeks later when he expelled fifty-eight he said they were 'majors, colonels and commandoes in disguise'.

These are all potential seats of major opposition but there appears no alternative to a soldier taking over initially from Amin. Yet in Uganda today the man with the gun has become synonymous with terror and murder and once Amin is finally removed there remains the problem of weeding out his Nubian killers and managing the expanded army.

One thing that is now apparent is that Ugandans can count on precious little outside help to end their misery. Here in a sense Nyerere's refusal to recognise Amin and his condemnation of the General created a false promise. There was never any possibility that the Tanzanian was going to change things for Ugandans. Largely he was motivated by concern about his own country's security and that of the region and in this he was completely justified as Amin's approach to both Britain and Israel for arms to invade Tanzania, demonstrates.

But from very early on he was realistic about UPC. On 20 July 1971, Nyerere told a press conference: 'Nobody claims that the UPC government was a popular one—certainly not in Buganda. But now there is a problem of greater realisation throughout Uganda—including Buganda—that if they thought they were in the frying pan before January they are rapidly getting into the fire.'

Nyerere's refusal to recognise him clearly haunted Amin during his first two years in power. The Somalis tried to manipulate a meeting soon after the Mogadishu peace talks but Nyerere was having none of it. When the Tanzanian was finally forced to meet Amin in Addis Ababa during the tenth anniversary celebrations of the OAU in May 1973 it was largely because he trapped himself into it. As soon as he arrived in Addis Ababa, Emperor Haile Selassie indicated he wanted to mediate between the two men. There was nothing to discuss, Nyerere insisted, but the Emperor pressed Nyerere to give his conditions for a *rapprochement*.

Not expecting that Amin would meet them, Nyerere spelled out that the Ugandan would have to drop his continuous demand that Obote should leave Tanzania and would have to admit the murders of twenty-four Tanzanians in Uganda.

In part the pressure on Nyerere in Addis Ababa was accidental. Amin, in an extraordinary performance reduced African leaders to incredulous laughter in his OAU speech, insisting that Obote was a great man who had done much for Uganda and Africa. 'Even Obote knows that I am his best friend,' he declared. He strode from the rostrum up to Nyerere and put out his hand. The Tanzanian's first reaction was to ignore it. But in the circumstances he felt he could not, but with calculated rudeness he stayed seated as he shook the hand.

The next day when a list of former leaders who would receive special medals to mark the anniversary was under discussion Amin shouted that the list was incomplete. Had he not told them on the previous day what a great man Obote was.

However, part of the cause of the first meeting and the Addis Ababa Agreement, which Amin and Nyerere signed, was carefully orchestrated. A number of other African leaders went to see the Tanzanian to bring pressure on him to end his differences with Amin. Then the Emperor returned to say Amin was willing to admit to the murders of seven Tanzanians and drop his demand about Obote. Nyerere was trapped. He insisted all twenty-four deaths must be admitted and compensation paid and Amin swiftly agreed. At this point again Nyerere tried to avoid the meeting telling Malecela to sign the agreement but the Emperor blocked this.

Even at this point the security of Tanzania and the region were factors which influenced Nyerere. He had backed Obote largely because of the threat from Uganda and this had failed. However the security threat in 1971 and 1972 was of a restricted nature because Amin could not get the weapons he wanted. By early 1973 the position had begun to change considerably.

First of all it was learned that France had agreed to sell Amin a substantial quantity of armaments. The French government had licensed the sale of 120 armoured vehicles, eighty of them to be fitted with surface-to-surface missiles; they were to be supplied by a firm called Savien, and Uganda made the first payment with Libya to meet the remainder. The vehicles were to be sent to Tripoli and then flown to Uganda as it was feared if they went through the Kenya port of Mombasa they would be seized.

On learning about this sale the Tanzanians called in the French Ambassador in Dar es Salaam to point out in no uncertain terms what this would mean to the military balance in the area. Possibly embarrassed by the amount of publicity the sale received, or because of payment problems, the vehicles were not delivered.

However the Russians were prepared to help Amin and military reports from Kampala indicated that they had offered an un-limited supply of light and medium tanks. In November 1973 the first shipment arrived in Mombasa and there appears to have been difficulty in clearing it as before the tanks and armoured vehicles were moved out on a special train to Uganda, Amin had to personally fly to see Kenyatta.

Nyerere's relations with the Russians had always been poor since they and the East Germans tried to disrupt the union with Zanzibar after it was implemented in April 1964. There are indications that when Amin and Nyerere met for the first time in Addis Ababa that one of the thoughts in the Tanzanian's mind at that time was to try to neutralise the increasing Soviet push into Uganda.

Nyerere met Amin twice more in 1973. Once in Algiers during the non-aligned summit and again late in the year at Mwanza. Amin's visit to Mwanza was typical of his impetuous behaviour. Nyerere was in the town for one of his regular quarterly informal sessions with Kaunda and Zaïre President, General Mobutu Sese Seko. Amin was not invited but was determined to be there, so on the eve of the Mwanza meeting he flew to Cairo for a briefing on the Middle East war from President Sadat. As soon as he returned to Kampala, less than twenty-four hours later, he cabled Nyerere claiming, which was not true, that he had to come to Mwanza to deliver a message from Sadat. The Tanzanians, who had received a message from Sadat on the previous day through his Ambassador in Dar es Salaam, cabled back that it would not be convenient. But Amin was not to be deterred. He cabled back that he was coming anyway and despite a very blunt reply from the Tanzanian

Foreign Ministry's protocol section, telling him he could not stay in the country the night, he flew into the town his air force had bombed fourteen months earlier. Tanzanian security officers were horrified as he strutted around among the three Presidents with a loaded pistol on his belt.

It is still quite clear that Nyerere has not greatly changed his view of Amin. On 9 December 1973, the Tanzanian's third book of collected speeches was published. It contained a photograph of him with Obote and one of his speeches attacking Amin. The final proofs had only been finally passed two months earlier, long after the initial signs of a degree of *rapprochement*.

Yet the timing of Nyerere's first meeting with Amin and the Addis Ababa Agreement could not have been more unfortunate for Obote. He was working to unite all the exile groups into a common front to oppose Amin and the first exploratory meeting was to take place shortly in Dar es Salaam.

In addition Obote had just sent a letter to all of Africa's heads of state breaking his twenty-six-month silence. It had been intended originally that the letter would be distributed in Addis Ababa during the tenth anniversary summit, but with so many other disputes in the offing it was felt unwise to further disrupt the celebrations. Instead Obote sent it to the leaders in their capitals and it is quite clear that he could not have done so without first obtaining Nyerere's consent.

The letter listed a series of murders and massacres and ended by saying: 'In conclusion I affirm that I have brought to your attention the grave matter of genocide in Uganda for the sake of Africa. I have no doubt whatsoever that the Assembly would not want Africa to stand condemned by its enemies of double standards and hypocrisy. I therefore plead that even if as Africans you feel you cannot materially and morally support Ugandans in their determination to overthrow Amin, do not materially or morally support him and do not arm him; for to support him and to arm him is to give him an international certificate to massacre the people of Uganda at will.' Obote's appeal was probably doomed from the outset to fall on deaf ears, but Nyerere's agreement with Amin completely pulled the rug out from under the deposed President and the meeting of exiles to form a united front never took place.

Somalia as mediator between the two countries began to try to bring pressure to bear for Obote to leave Tanzania and even offered to let him live in Mogadishu. That two years earlier they had been willing to put troops at his disposal and said they would not recognise Amin was long forgotten. Obote told them that the continued tension in Uganda was not because he was in Tanzania but because of the killings and he added that the two outbreaks of border fighting between Tanzania and Uganda had in fact occurred while he was living in Sudan.

In a letter to the Somalis he said: 'The tension will continue whether I am here, or in Mogadishu, or in Outer Mongolia, or dead.' The Israelis had been the first to cover up the slaughter in Uganda and now the Arabs were doing the same.

The two countries Obote had counted on most to help him remove Amin had now withdrawn and the Sudan had been forced out by the southern settlement. Ironically today Amin no longer considers that his enemies are in the north and south—Sudan and Tanzania. He believes they are in the east and west—Kenya and Zaïre. People close to him say he despises Kenyatta and refers frequently to Mobutu as a 'Zionist'. But the threat to security in the region, because of Amin, remains as great. The only difference is that at the moment the gun is apparently pointed in a different direction.

In Uganda the civil service has been emasculated. Many of those who remain do not know when they will be dismissed or simply disappear. The secretary of Uganda's National Insurance Corporation, Mr. J. B. Tibhamulala, was beaten to death in his office in November 1973 by troops, and several other employees including the Chairman, Mr. C. M. Wakiro, were badly injured and detained. On Radio Uganda they were accused of embezzling £100,000. But in fact their 'crime' was of a very different nature. Since the *coup* lawless troops have been stopping motorists and stealing their cars at gunpoint. The dispossessed owners had made insurance claims and the amount of £100,000 was how much the Insurance Corporation had paid out.

Uganda's once brave and able judiciary has been demoralised and some of its most prominent members murdered although in 1973 they were bold enough to accuse the army of 'widespread interference with the course of justice'. The police force also has been ruined and many senior officers killed.

All of this has been done by a man who sanctimoniously declared on 18 September 1972: 'What we want is peace in the world and we are strongly opposed to killings of any nature.' It is the same man who seized power giving one of his reasons as being that he had done so to avoid bloodshed and who told his first press conference: 'I do not believe in the one-party system. The President cannot be a proper leader if there is no one opposing him.'

Instead of Obote's one-party state, Uganda today has no political parties. Amin and his Nubian killers are absolute for they have the guns and the keys to the armouries. How long he can continue is anyone's guess but it could be years for most of the potential opponents are dead and the possible opposition elements in the army have been dismissed or killed.

The most likely outcome is that Amin will be assassinated. The legacy of hatred he has built up in Uganda means that there are plenty of people willing to pull the trigger. This is a course that Obote has always opposed. He argues that those who condemn Amin cannot answer him with personal violence and that his Nubians are now so deeply entrenched that it serves little purpose killing one man in an isolated act.

Obote talked much of the common man as his political philosophy. And Amin when he came to power with his early charisma, barrack-room *bonhomie* and almost attractive *naïveté*, appeared to many to personify that common man. He pandered to that early euphoric mood by bringing back the Kabaka's body, releasing fifty-five political detainees and disbanding the General Service Department about which there is more myth than reality. The department's role was meant to be counter intelligence and the GSD had no powers of arrest in Uganda nor armaments other than those held by the Presidential bodyguard. It has been claimed that it had a number of armoured personnel carriers but this is not correct. The head of the department, Akena Adoko, during a visit to Czechoslovakia, had been given some by the government but these were handed over to the army after they arrived. The image as Obote's evil alter-ego given to Adoko is an unfair one. Among the eighteen reasons given for the *coup* the General Service was not mentioned so this was clearly not a motivating factor. Adoko was President of Uganda's Law Society and was in fact one of the people in Uganda most opposed to detention.

It was fear that drew out two traits in Amin's character after the *coup*—wilfulness and cunning. He has always been an outsider coming from a minority tribe and having been brought to power in a *coup* supported by a minority of the army. His prætorian guard are his Nubian mercenaries and trusted Kakwa. They have killed so much that they must continue killing for fear of the revenge which will inevitably be unleashed once Amin falls.

Another important part of Amin's character—and nowhere was this better displayed than over the Asian expulsion—is his determination to command those who once commanded him. Britain was his commander when he was a soldier in colonial times, and when he expelled the Asians he wanted to teach Britain who was now in command. One of Amin's present Ministers firmly believes that had Britain takenhim seriously at the outset and flown out a single plane-load of Asians his point would have been made and many of the remainder would have been able to stay. But the British Government and press took the view that he was bluffing and said so, with the result Amin felt obliged to go the whole way. When he threatens to detain American diplomats because of Nixon's support for Israel or to level to the ground Kigali, the Rwanda capital, 'in less than a minute' he is again asserting his command and power.

One medical explanation advanced for Amin's erratic behaviour is that he is a manic-depressive. This form of mental disease certainly goes far to explain the wild variations in his moods—periods of great elation and then followed by violent action. But it is as dangerous to over-simplify Amin's behaviour as it is to underestimate him.

He is deeply superstitious and a Ghanaian evangelist known as Prophet John, who has considerable influence over Amin, has predicted that he will rule for twenty years. Amin himself has said he has been told by God in a dream when he will die—but the information, he adds, is 'top secret'. One can only hope that for Uganda's sake, Prophet John is wrong.

Amin is a man with a big grudge—against all the real and imagined slights he feels he has suffered throughout his life. He has always wanted to please those above him, to have their smiling approval. When it was not forthcoming he would bludgeon it out of them, using deception, pretended innocence, a quick smile and apology, violence or plain bluff and bluster as his weapons.

His survival through his violent life has been astonishing. If he is not in the spotlight, he cannot sit still. There is a restlessness that keeps him constantly on the move, whether fidgeting at a public ceremony or, unannounced and unwanted, just popping off to another country.

But his restlessness is perhaps caused by the knowledge of the thousands of dead Ugandans. And as long as he is a haunted man like Macbeth there will certainly be no security in this part of Africa. But saddest of all is the destruction and desecration of what Winston Churchill described as the 'Pearl of Africa'. Uganda has suffered the most and will continue to suffer until the removal of the man who holds the bloodstained knife at her throat—General Idi Amin Dada.

Index